NOTES ON THE BOOK

OF EXODUS

NOTES ON THE BOOK OF EXODUS

C H MACKINTOSH

CHAPTER TWO
LONDON • ENGLAND

Notes on the Book of Exodus by C. H. Mackintosh
UK ISBN 978 1 85307 221 5
Set of Six Notes on the Pentateuch ISBN 978 1 85307 219 2
This edition © Chapter Two 2007

The first edition of *Notes on the Book of Exodus* was first published in 1857 by co-publishers T H Gregg, 24 Warwick Lane, London and W H Broom, 8 Athol Place, Edinburgh. 1st official American edition 1880, first single volume edition of *Notes on the Pentateuch* by Loizeaux Bros. USA 1972

Translated into Amharic, Arabic, Bulgarian, Chinese, Croatian, Czech, Danish, Dutch, Finnish, French, German, Greek, Hindi, Hungarian, Italian, Japanese, Korean, Norwegian, Polish, Portuguese, Romanian, Russian, Spanish and Swedish.

All rights reserved. No part of this publication may be reproduced or transmitted in any form or by any means, electronic or mechanical, including photocopying, recording, or storage in any information retrieval system, without written permission from Chapter Two.

CHAPTER TWO
Fountain House, Conduit Mews, London SE18 7AP, UK
www.chaptertwobooks.org.uk

Distributors:
- Bible, Book and Tract Depôt, 23 Santarosa Avenue, Ryde, NSW 2112, Australia
- The Bible House, Gateway Mall, 35 Tudor Street, Bridgetown, Barbados, WI
- Believers Bookshelf, 5205 Regional Road 81, Unit 3, Beamsville, ON, L0R 1B3, Canada
- Bible Treasury Bookstore, 46 Queen Street, Dartmouth, Nova Scotia, B2Y 1G1, Canada
- El-Ekhwa Library, 3 Anga Hanem Street, Shoubra, Cairo 11231, Egypt
- Bibles & Publications Chrétiennes, 30 rue Châteauvert, 26000 Valence, France
- CSV, An der Schloßfabrik 30, 42499 Hückeswagen, Germany
- Christian Literature Service, PO Box GP 20872, Accra, Ghana
- Christian Truth Bookroom, Paddisonpet, Tenali 522 201, Andhra Pradesh, India
- Words of Life Trust, 3 Chuim, Khar, Mumbai, 400 052, India
- Words of Truth, 38-P.D.A Lamphelpat, Imphal 795 004, Manipur, India
- Uit het Woord der Waarheid, Postbox 260, 7120AG Aalten, Netherlands
- Bible and Book Depot, Box 25119, Christchurch 5, New Zealand
- Christian Literature Depot, PO Box 436, Ijeshatedo, Surulere, Lagos, Nigeria
- Believers Bookshelf, PO Box 777, Shadewell Heights, Basseterre, St. Kitts, WI
- Grace & Truth Book-room, 87 Chausee Road, Castries, St. Lucia, WI
- Chapter Two S.A., Box 2234, Alberton 1450, South Africa
- Beröa Verlag, Zellerstrasse 61, 8038 Zürich, Switzerland
- Éditions Bibles et Littérature Chrétienne, La Foge C, Case Postale, 1816 Chailly-Montreux, Switzerland
- Chapter Two Bookshop, 199 Plumstead Common Road, London, SE18 2UJ, UK
- HoldFast Bible & Tract Depôt, 41 York Road, Tunbridge Wells, Kent, TN1 1JX, UK
- Words of Truth, PO Box 147, Belfast, BT8 4TT, Northern Ireland, UK
- Believers Bookshelf Inc., Box 261, Sunbury, PA 17801, USA

Printed in The Netherlands by Van der Perk Printers

PREFACE

In manuscript and proof sheets, we have been travelling over a deeply instructive and most interesting portion of the Word of God – THE BOOK OF EXODUS.

Redemption by blood occupies a prominent place therein. It characterizes the book. God's many mercies to His redeemed, in the display of His power, the patience of His love, and the riches of His grace, flow from it. The great question of Israel's relationship to God is settled by the blood of the Lamb. It changes their condition entirely. Israel within the blood-sprinkled door-posts was God's redeemed blood-bought people.

God being holy, and Israel guilty, no happy relationship could exist between them till judgment was accomplished. Sin must be judged. A happy friendship once existed between and man on the ground of innocence; but sin having entered and snapped the link asunder, there can be no reconciliation, but through the full expression of the moral judgment of God against sin. We can only have "life through death." God is the God of holiness, and he must judge sin. In saving the sinner, He condemns his sin. The cross is the full and perfect expression of this.

Typically, this was the great question on "the evening of the fourteenth day of the first month" namely, *how can God exempt from judgment, and receive into His favour, those whom His holiness condemns?* To this most solemn question, there was but one answer that would satisfy the demands of the God of holiness, and that was *the blood of the Lamb of His own providing.* "When I see the blood, I will pass over you." This settled the all-important question. It was one of life or death, of deliverance or judgment. The blood-sprinkled door-post was a perfect answer to all the claims of holiness, and to all the need of the congregation. All was settled now. God was glorified, sin judged and put away, and Israel saved through the blood of the lamb.

Blessed truth! Israel was now at peace with God, a sheltered, saved, and happy people, though still in Egypt, the land of death and judgment. God was now *pledged* to deliver Israel – precious type of the perfect security of all who are trusting to the blood of Christ! They were securely and peacefully feeding on the roasted lamb, when "at midnight, the Lord smote all the firstborn in the land of Egypt, from the firstborn of Pharaoh that sat on his throne, unto the firstborn of the captive that was in the dungeon, and all the firstborn of cattle. And Pharaoh rose up in the night, he and all his servants, and all the Egyptians; and there was a great cry in Egypt; for there was not a house where there was not one dead" (12:29, 30). "But against any of the children of Israel shall not a dog move his tongue, against man or beast; that ye may know how that the Lord doth put a difference between the Egyptians and Israel" (11:7).

But why, some may ask, put this difference? The Israelites were sinners as well as the Egyptians. True, on this ground, there was "no difference." But, in type, the judgment of God against sin had been expressed in the death of the unblemished lamb. The blood "on the lintel and the two side posts" was the proof of this. It proclaimed, with a loud voice, that the lamb was slain, the ransom paid, the captive freed, justice satisfied, and the hour of Israel's deliverance fully come. *It was the blood that made the difference, and nothing else.* "For all have sinned and come short of the glory of God" (Rom. 3:23).

But oh! what a difference! The one divinely shielded from the sword of judgment; the other, defenceless and slain by it. The one, feasting on the rich provisions of grace; the other, compelled to taste the bitterness of the cup of wrath. The destroying angel entered every house, throughout all the land of Egypt, that was not sprinkled with the blood. The firstborn of Pharaoh on the throne, and the firstborn of the captive in the dungeon, fell together.

No rank, age, or character escaped. The day of God's long-suffering was ended, and the hour of His judgment was come. One thing alone guided the angel of death on that dark and dreadful night, and that was, WHERE THERE IS NO BLOOD, THERE IS NO SALVATION.

Dear reader! This is as true now as it was then! Where there is no blood there is no salvation. "Without shedding of blood is no remission." Can any question be of such importance to you as this one, Am I shielded by the blood of Jesus? Oh! have you fled for refuge to the blood that was shed on Calvary? There "Christ our passover was sacrificed for us." His blood is represented as being sprinkled on "the mercy-seat above." There, God's eye ever sees the blood of our true paschal Lamb. Have you faith in that precious blood? Though deeply sensible of your guilt, can you say in truth, This is my only hiding place, "I do depend upon the blood?" Then rest assured that you are perfectly safe; that you are eternally saved. You have God's own word for it – "When I see the blood, I will pass over you." "We have redemption *through his blood*, the forgiveness of sins, according to the riches of his grace." "But now, in Christ Jesus, ye who sometimes were afar off, are made nigh *by the blood of Christ*." "Whom God hath set forth to be a propitiation *through faith in his blood*" (Ephesians 1:7; 2:13; Romans 3:25).

> Happy they who trust in Jesus,
> Sweet their portion is and sure.

But, on the other hand, if the blood of Jesus is neglected, or despised, there can be no security, no peace, and no salvation. "How shall we escape if neglect so great salvation?" (Heb. 2:3). Unless the destroying angel sees the blood, he enters as the judge of sin. Every sin must be punished, either in the person of the sinner, or the sinner's substitute. This is a deeply solemn truth; but how blessed to know that "Christ hath once suffered for sins, the just for the unjust, that he might bring us to God." "For he hath made him to be sin for us, who knew no sin, that we might be made the righteousness of God in him" (1 Peter 3:18; 2 Corinthians 5:18). To neglect this divine Substitute, and the shelter which He has provided, is to expose the soul to the judgment of God. No sin, however, small, can escape judgment, either on the cross of Christ, or in the lake of fire. Oh! the priceless value of that blood which "cleanseth us from ALL sin!" – which makes us clean enough for heaven!

Redemption being now accomplished, and Israel divinely prepared, they commence their journey, But, observe in passing, *how* they start. Before taking one step, every question between the conscience and God is divinely settled. They are forgiven, justified, and accepted, in His sight. Hence, it is written, "When Israel was a child, then I loved him, and called my son out of Egypt" (Hosea 11:1). Blessed type of the real condition in which every true believer begins his Christian course! He may not see this blessed truth, or he may have a very feeble apprehension of it, as Israel had, but that does not alter the fact. God acts according to His own knowledge of the relationship, and the affections which belong to it. We see this, in the glorious deliverance of His people at the Red Sea, in the manna from heaven, the water from the flinty rock, and in the pillar of His presence, which accompanied them in all their wanderings. He ever acts according to the purposes of His love, and the value of the blood of Jesus.

Once more, dear reader, allow me to ask, Are you sure that you are under the safe shelter, the secure refuge, the blessed hiding place of the Redeemer's blood?

But I must now leave my reader, earnestly recommending him to pursue the journey across the wilderness in company with God and His redeemed. He will find the "NOTES" most useful. They convey truth, agreeably and intelligently, to the heart, the conscience, and the understanding. May many find them to be a real oasis in the desert. The journey will prove a most profitable one, if we thereby learn more of the natural unbelief of our own hearts and the abiding faithfulness of

God's. He never changes, blessed be His name; and the blood of the slain Lamb never loses its efficacy.

> Blessed Lamb of God! Thy precious blood
> Shall never lose its power,
> Till every ransomed saint of God
> Be saved to sin no more.

May the Lord graciously own and use the following "Notes" for His own glory and the blessing of many souls.

Andrew Miller
London

PREFACE TO THE THIRD EDITION

The writer cannot suffer a new edition of this volume to issue from the press without a line or two of deep thankfulness to the Lord for His grace, in making use of such a feeble instrumentality in the furtherance of His truth, and the edification of His people. Blessed be His name, when He takes up a book or a tract, He can make it effectual in the accomplishment of His gracious ends. He can clothe, with spiritual power, pages and paragraphs which, to us, might seem pointless and powerless. May He continue to own and bless this service, and His name shall have all the praise.

C. H. M.
Dublin, April, 1862.

Chapter 1

THE WAYS OF GOD TOWARDS ISRAEL

Why was Israel in Egypt?

We now approach, by the mercy of God, the study of the Book of Exodus, of which the great prominent theme is redemption. The first five verses recall to the mind the closing scenes of the preceding book. The favoured objects of God's electing love are brought before us; and we find ourselves, very speedily, conducted, by the inspired penman, into the action of the book.

In our meditations on the Book of Genesis, we were led to see that the conduct of Joseph's brethren toward him was that which led to their being brought down into Egypt. This fact is to be looked at in two ways. In the first place, we can read therein a deeply solemn lesson as taught in Israel's actings toward God; and, secondly, we have, therein unfolded, an encouraging lesson, as taught in God's actings toward Israel.

And, first, as to Israel's actings toward God, what can be more deeply solemn than to follow out the results of their treatment of him who stands before the spiritual mind as the marked type of the Lord Jesus Christ? They, utterly regardless of the anguish of his soul, consigned Joseph into the hands of the uncircumcised. And what was the issue, as regards them? They were carried down into Egypt, there to experience those deep and painful exercises of heart which are so graphically and touchingly presented in the closing chapters of Genesis. Nor was this all. A long and dreary season awaited their offspring in that very land in which Joseph had found a dungeon.

How God accomplishes His purposes

But then God was in all this, as well as man; and it is His prerogative to bring good out of evil. Joseph's brethren might sell him to the Ishmaelites, and the Ishmaelites might sell him to Potiphar, and Potiphar might cast him into prison; but Jehovah was above all, and He was accomplishing His own mighty ends. "The wrath of man shall praise him." The time had not arrived in which the heirs were ready for the inheritance, and the inheritance for the heirs. The brick-kilns of Egypt were to furnish a rigid school for the seed of Abraham, while, as yet, "the iniquity of the Amorites" was rising to a head, amid the "hills and valleys" of the promised land.

All this is deeply interesting and instructive. There are "wheels within wheels" in the government of God. He makes use of an endless variety of agencies, in the accomplishment of His unsearchable designs. Potiphar's wife, Pharaoh's butler, Pharaoh's dreams, Pharaoh himself, the dungeon, the throne, the fetters, the royal signet, the famine – all are at His sovereign disposal, and all are made instrumental in the development of His stupendous counsels. The spiritual mind delights to dwell upon this. It delights to range through the wide domain of creation and providence, and to recognize, in all, the machinery which an All-wise and an Almighty God is using for the purpose of unfolding His counsels of redeeming love. True, we may see many traces of the serpent; many deep and well-defined footprints of the enemy of God and man; many things which we cannot explain nor even comprehend; suffering innocence and successful wickedness may furnish an apparent basis for the infidel-reasoning of the sceptic mind; but the true believer can piously repose in the assurance that "the Judge of all the earth shall do right." He knows right well that,

> "Blind unbelief is sure to err,
> And scan His ways in vain;
> God is His own interpreter,
> And He will make it plain."

Blessed be God for the consolation and encouragement flowing out of such reflections as these. We need them, every hour, while passing through an evil world, in which the enemy has wrought such appalling mischief, in which the lusts and passions of men produce such bitter fruits, and in which the path of the true disciple presents roughnesses which mere nature could never endure. Faith knows, of a surety, that there is One behind the scenes whom the world sees not nor regards; and, in the consciousness of this, it can calmly say, "it is well," and, "it shall be well."

The above train of thought is distinctly suggested by the opening lines of our book. "God's counsel shall stand, and he will do all his pleasure." The enemy may oppose; but God will ever prove Himself to be above him; and all we need is a spirit of simple, child-like confidence and repose in the divine purpose. Unbelief will rather look at the enemy's efforts to countervail, than at God's power to accomplish. It is on the latter that faith fixes its eye. Thus it obtains victory. It has to do with God and His infallible faithfulness. It rests not upon the ever shifting sands of human affairs and earthly influences, but upon the immovable rock of God's eternal Word. That is faith's holy and solid resting-place. Come what may, it abides in that sanctuary of strength. "Joseph died, and all his brethren, and all that generation." What then? Could death affect the counsels of the living God? Surely not. He only waited for the appointed moment, the due time, and then the most hostile influences were made instrumental in the development of His purposes.

The efforts of Pharaoh to crush Israel

"Now there arose up a new king over Egypt, which knew

not Joseph. And he said unto his people, Behold, the people of the children of Israel are more and mightier than we: come on, let us deal *wisely* with them, lest they multiply, and it come to pass that when there falleth out any war they join also unto our enemies, and fight against us, and so get them up out of the land" (vv. 8-10). All this is the reasoning of a heart that had never learnt to take God into its calculations. The unrenewed heart never can do so; and hence, the moment you introduce God, all its reasonings fall to the ground. Apart from, or independent of Him, they may seem very wise; but only bring Him in, and they are proved to be perfect folly.

But why should we allow our minds to be, in any wise, influenced by reasonings and calculations which depend, for their *apparent* truth, upon the total exclusion of God? To do so is, in principle, and according to its measure, practical atheism. In Pharaoh's case, we see that he could accurately recount the various contingencies of human affairs, the multiplying of the people, the falling out of war, their joining with the enemy, their escape out of the land. All these circumstances he could, with uncommon sagacity, put into the scale; but it never once occurred to him that God could have anything whatever to do in the matter. Had he only thought of this, it would have upset his entire reasoning, and have written folly upon all his schemes.

Now it is well to see that it is ever thus with the reasonings of man's sceptic mind. God is entirely shut out; yea, the truth and consistency thereof depend upon His being kept out. The death-blow to all scepticism and infidelity is the introduction of God into the scene. Till He is seen, they may strut up and down upon the stage, with an amazing show of wisdom and cleverness; but the moment the eye catches even the faintest glimpse of that Blessed One, they are stripped of their cloak, and disclosed in all their nakedness and deformity.

In reference to the king of Egypt, it may, assuredly, be said, he did "greatly err," not knowing God, or His changeless counsels. He knew not that, hundreds of years back, before ever he had breathed the breath of mortal life, God's word and oath – "two immutable things" – had infallibly secured the full and glorious deliverance of that very people whom he was going, in his wisdom, to crush. All this was unknown to him; and, therefore, all his thoughts and plans were founded upon ignorance of that grand foundation-truth of all truths, namely, that GOD IS. He vainly imagined that he, by his management, could prevent the increase of those concerning whom God had said, "they shall be as the stars of heaven, and as the sand which is upon the sea-shore." His wise dealing, therefore, was simply madness and folly.

The wildest mistake which a man can possibly fall into is to act without taking God into his account. Sooner or later, the thought of God will force itself upon him, and then comes the awful crash of all his schemes and calculations. At best, everything that is undertaken, independently of God, can last but for the present time. It cannot, by any possibility, stretch itself into eternity. All that is merely human, however solid, however brilliant, or however attractive, must fall into the cold grasp of death, and moulder in the dark, silent tomb. The clod of the valley must cover man's highest excellencies and brightest glories; mortality is engraved upon his brow, and all his schemes are evanescent. On the contrary, that which is connected with, and based upon, God, shall endure for ever. "His name shall endure for ever, and his memorial to all generations."

What a sad mistake, therefore, for a feeble mortal to set himself up against the eternal God, to "rush upon the thick bosses of the shield of the Almighty!" As well might the monarch of Egypt have sought to stem, with his puny hand, the ocean's tide, as to prevent the increase of those who were the subjects of Jehovah's everlasting purpose. Hence, although "they did set over them taskmasters to afflict them with their burdens," yet, "the more they afflicted them, the more they multiplied and grew." Thus it must ever be. "He that sitteth in the heavens shall laugh; the Lord shall have them in derision" (Ps. 2:4). Eternal confusion shall be inscribed upon all the opposition of men and devils. This gives sweet rest to the heart, in the midst of a scene where all is, apparently, so contrary to God and so contrary to faith. Were it not for the settled assurance that "the wrath of man shall praise" the Lord, the spirit would often be cast down, while contemplating the circumstances and influences which surround one in the world. Thank God, "we look not at the things which are seen, but at the things which are not seen: for the things which are seen are temporal; but the things which are not seen are eternal" (2 Cor. 4:18). In the power of this, we may well say, "*rest* in the Lord, and *wait patiently for him:* fret not thyself because of him who prospereth in his way, because of the man who bringeth wicked devices to pass" (Ps. 37:7). How fully might the truth of this be seen in the case of both the oppressed and the oppressor, as set before us in our chapter! Had Israel "looked at the things that are seen," what were they? Pharaoh's wrath, stern taskmasters, afflictive burdens, rigorous service, hard bondage, mortar and brick. But, then, "the things which are not seen," what were they? God's eternal purpose, His unfailing promise, the approaching dawn of a day of salvation, the "burning lamp" of Jehovah's deliverance. Wondrous contrast! Faith alone could enter into it. Nought save that precious principle could enable any poor, oppressed Israelite to look from out the smoking furnace of Egypt, to the green fields and vine-clad mountains of the land of Canaan. Faith alone could recognise in those oppressed slaves, toiling in the brick-kilns of Egypt, the heirs of salvation, and the objects of Heaven's peculiar interest and favour.

Thus it was then, and thus it is now. "We walk by faith, not by sight" (2 Cor. 5:7). "It doth not yet appear what we shall be" (1 John 3:2). We are "here in the body pent," "absent from the Lord." As to fact, we are in Egypt, yet, in spirit, we are in the heavenly Canaan. Faith brings the heart into the power of divine and unseen things, and thus enables it to mount above everything down here, in this place "where death and darkness reign." Oh! for that simple child-like faith that sits beside the pure and eternal fountain of truth, there to drink those deep and refreshing draughts, which lift up the fainting spirit, and impart energy to the new man, in its upward and onward course.

The closing verses of this section of our book present an edifying lesson in the conduct of those God-fearing women, Shiphrah and Puah. They would not carry out the king's cruel scheme, but braved his wrath, and hence, God made them houses. "Them that honour me I will honour, and they that despise me shall be lightly esteemed" (1 Sam. 2:30). May we ever remember this, and act for God, under all circumstances!

Chapter 2

THE BIRTH OF MOSES

The activity of that which had the power of death

This section of our book abounds in the weightiest principles of divine truth – principles, which range themselves under the three following heads, namely, the power of Satan, the power of God, and the power of faith.

In the last verse of the previous chapter, we read, "And Pharaoh charged all his people, saying, Every son that is born ye shall cast into the river." This was Satan's power. The river was the place of death; and, by death, the enemy sought to frustrate the purpose of God. It has ever been thus. The serpent has, at all times, watched, with malignant eye, those instruments which God was about to use for his own gracious ends. Look at the case of Abel, in Genesis 4. What was that but the serpent watching God's vessel and seeking to put it out of the way by death? Look at the case of Joseph, in Gen. 37. There you have the enemy seeking to put the man of God's purpose in the place of death. Look at the case of "the seed royal," in 2 Chron. 22, the act of Herod, in Matt. 2, the death of Christ, in Matt. 27. In all these cases, you find the enemy seeking, by death, to interrupt the current of divine action.

But, blessed be God, there is something beyond death. The entire sphere of divine action, as connected with redemption, lies beyond the limits of death's domain. When Satan has exhausted his power, then God begins to show Himself. The grave is the limit of Satan's activity; but there it is that divine activity begins. This is a glorious truth. Satan has the power of death; but God is the God of the living; and He gives life beyond the reach and power of death – a life which Satan cannot touch. The heart finds sweet relief in such a truth as this, in the midst of a scene where death reigns. Faith can stand and look on at Satan putting forth the plenitude of his power. It can stay itself upon God's mighty instrumentality of resurrection. It can take its stand at the grave which has just closed over a beloved object, and drink in, from the lips of Him who is "the resurrection and the life," the elevating assurance of a glorious immortality. It knows that God is stronger than Satan, and it can, therefore, quietly wait for the full manifestation of that superior strength, and, in thus waiting, find its victory and its settled peace.

Faith triumphant over death

We have a noble example of this power of faith in the opening verses of our chapter.

"And there went a man of the house of Levi, and took to wife a daughter of Levi. And the woman conceived and bare a son; and when she saw him that he was a goodly child, she hid him three months. And when she could no longer hide him, she took for him an ark of bulrushes and daubed it with slime and with pitch, and put the child therein; and she laid it in the flags by the river's brink. And his sister stood afar off, to wit what would be done to him" (chap 2:1-4). Here we have a scene of touching interest, in whatever way we contemplate it. In point of fact, it was simply faith triumphing over the influences of nature and death, and leaving room for the God of resurrection to act in His own proper sphere and character. True, the enemy's power is apparent, in the circumstance that the child had to be placed in such position – a position of death, in principle. And, moreover, a sword was piercing through the mother's heart, in thus beholding her precious offspring laid, as it were, in death. Satan might act, and nature might weep; but the Quickener of the dead was behind the dark cloud, and faith beheld Him there, gilding heaven's side of that cloud with His bright and life-giving beams. "By faith Moses when he was born was hid three months of his parents, because they saw he was a proper child; and they were not afraid of the king's commandment" (Heb. 11:23).

Thus, this honoured daughter of Levi teaches us a holy lesson. Her "*ark* of bulrushes, daubed with slime and *pitch*," declares her confidence in the truth that there was a something which could keep out the waters of death, in the case of this "proper child," as well as in the case of Noah, "the preacher of righteousness." Are we to suppose, for a moment, that this "ark" was the invention of mere nature? Was it nature's forethought that devised it, or nature's ingenuity that constructed it? Was the babe placed in the ark at the suggestion of a mother's heart, cherishing the fond but visionary hope of thereby saving her treasure from the ruthless hand of death? Were we to reply to the above inquiries in the affirmative, we should, I believe, lose the beauteous teaching of this entire scene. How could we ever suppose that the "*ark*" was devised by one who saw no other portion or destiny for her child but death by *drowning?* Impossible. We can only look upon that significant structure, as faith's draft handed in at the treasury of the God of resurrection. It was devised by the hand of faith, as a vessel of mercy, to carry "a proper child" safely over death's dark waters, into the place assigned him by the immutable purpose of the living God. When we behold this daughter of Levi bending over that "ark of bulrushes," which her faith had constructed, and depositing therein her babe, we see her "walking in the steps of that faith of her father Abraham, which he had," when "he rose up from before his dead," and purchased the cave of Macpelah from the sons of Heth (Gen. 23). We do not recognise in her the energy of mere nature, hanging over the object of its affections, about to fall into the iron grasp of the king of terrors. No; but we trace in her the energy of a faith which enabled her to stand, as a conqueror, at the margin of death's cold flood, and behold the chosen servant of Jehovah in safety at the other side.

Yes, my reader, faith can take those bold and lofty flights into regions far removed from this land of death and widespread desolation. Its eagle eye can pierce the gloomy clouds which gather around the tomb, and behold the God of resurrection displaying the results of His everlasting counsels, in the midst of a sphere which no arrow of death can reach. It can take its stand upon the top of the Rock of Ages, and listen, in holy triumph, while the surges of death are lashing its base.

And what, let me ask, was "the king's commandment" to one who was in possession of this heaven-born principle? What weight had that commandment with one who could calmly stand beside her "ark of bulrushes" and look death straight in the face? The Holy Ghost replies, "they were not afraid of the king's commandment." The spirit that knows anything of communion with Him who quickens the dead, is not afraid of anything. Such an one can take up the triumphant language of 1 Cor. 15 and say, "O death, where is thy sting? O grave, where is thy victory? The sting of death is sin, and the strength of sin is the law. But thanks be to God which giveth us the victory, through our Lord Jesus Christ." He can give forth these words of triumph over a martyred Abel; over Joseph in the pit; over Moses in his ark of bulrushes; in the midst of "the seed royal," slain by the hand of Athaliah; and in the babes of Bethlehem, murdered by the mandate of the cruel Herod; and far above all, he can utter them at the tomb of the Captain of our salvation.

Now, it may be, there are some who cannot trace the activities of faith, in the matter of the ark of bulrushes. Many may not be able to travel beyond the measure of Moses' sister, when "she stood afar off, to wit what would be done to him." It is very evident that "his sister" was not up to "the measure of faith" possessed by "his mother." No doubt, she possessed deep interest and true affection, such as we may trace in "Mary Magdalene and the other Mary sitting over against the sepulchre" (Matt. 27:61). But there was something far beyond either interest or affection in the maker of the "ark." True, she did not "stand afar off to wit what would be done to" her child, and hence, what frequently happens, the dignity of faith might seem like indifference, on her part. It was not, however, indifference, but true elevation – the elevation of faith. If natural affection did not cause her to linger near the scene of death, it was only because the power of faith was furnishing her with nobler work, in the presence of the God of resurrection. Her faith had cleared the stage for Him, and most gloriously did He show Himself thereon.

God's providential intervention

"And the daughter of Pharaoh came down to wash herself at the river; and her maidens walked along by the river's side; and when she saw the ark among the flags she sent her maid to fetch it. And when she had opened it she saw the child; and, behold, the babe wept. And she had compassion on him, and said, This is one of the Hebrews' children." Here, then, the divine response begins to break, in sweetest accents, on the ear of faith. God was in all this. Rationalism, or scepticism, or infidelity, or atheism, may laugh at such an idea. And faith can laugh also; but the two kinds of laughter are very different. The former laughs, in cold contempt, at the thought of divine interference in the trifling affair of a royal maiden's walk by the river's side. The latter laughs, with real heart-felt gladness, at the thought that God is in everything. And, assuredly, if ever God was in anything, He was in this walk of Pharaoh's daughter, though she knew it not.

The renewed mind enjoys one of its sweetest exercises, while tracing the divine footsteps in circumstances and events in which a thoughtless spirit sees only blind chance or rigid fate. The most trifling matter may, at times, turn out to be a most important link in a chain of events by which the Almighty God is helping forward the development of His grand designs. Look, for instance, at Esther 6:1, and what do you see? A heathen monarch, spending a restless night. No uncommon circumstance, we may suppose; and, yet, this very circumstance was a link in a great chain of providence at the end of which you find the marvellous deliverance of the oppressed seed of Israel.

Thus was it with the daughter of Pharaoh, in her walk by the river's side. Little did she think that she was helping forward the purpose of "the Lord God of the Hebrews!" How little idea had she that the weeping babe, in that ark of bulrushes, was yet to be Jehovah's instrument in shaking the land of Egypt to its very centre! Yet so it was. The Lord can make the wrath of man to praise Him, and restrain the remainder. How plainly the truth of this appears in the following passage!

"Then said his sister to Pharaoh's daughter, Shall I go and call to thee a nurse of the Hebrew women, that she may nurse the child for thee? And Pharaoh's daughter said unto her, Go. And the maid went and called the child's mother. And Pharaoh's daughter said unto her, Take this child away, and nurse it for me, and I will give thee thy wages. And the woman took the child and nursed it. And the child grew and she brought him unto Pharaoh's daughter, and he became her son. And she called his name Moses: and she said, Because I drew him out of the water" (chap. 2:7-10). The beautiful faith of Moses' mother here meets its full reward; Satan is confounded; and the marvellous wisdom of God is displayed. Who would have thought that the one who had said, "If it be a son, then ye shall kill him," and, again, "every son that is born ye shall cast into the river," should have in his court one of those very sons, and *such* "a son." The devil was foiled by his own weapon, inasmuch as Pharaoh, whom he was using to frustrate the purpose of God, is used of God to nourish and bring up Moses, who was to be His instrument in confounding the power of Satan. Remarkable providence! Admirable wisdom! Truly, Jehovah is "wonderful in counsel and excellent in working." May we learn to trust Him with more artless simplicity, and thus our path shall be more brilliant, and our testimony more effective.

MOSES WHEN FORTY

Preparation for service

In considering the history of Moses, we must look at him in two ways, namely, personally and typically.

First, in his personal character, there is much, very much, for us to learn. God had not only to raise him up, but also to train him, in one way or another, for the lengthened period of eighty years – first in the house of Pharaoh's daughter; and then at "the backside of the desert." This, to our shallow thoughts, would seem an immense space of time to devote to the education of a minister of God. But then God's thoughts are not as our thoughts. He knew the need of those forty years, twice told, in the preparation of His chosen vessel. When God educates, He educates in a manner worthy of Himself and His most holy service. He will not have a novice to do His work. The servant of Christ has to learn many a lesson, to undergo many an exercise, to pass through many a conflict, in secret, ere he is really qualified to act in public. Nature does not like this. It would rather figure in public than learn in private. It would rather be gazed upon and admired by the eye of man than be disciplined by the hand of God. But it will not do. We must take God's way. Nature may rush into the scene of operation; but God does not want it there. It must be withered, crushed, set aside. The place of death is the place for nature. If it *will* be active, God will so order matters, in His infallible faithfulness and perfect wisdom, that the results of its activity will prove its utter defeat and confusion. He knows what to do with nature, where to put it, and where to keep it. Oh! that we may all be in deeper communion with the mind of God, in reference to self and all that pertains thereto. Then shall we make fewer mistakes. Then shall our path be steady and elevated, our spirit tranquil, and our service effective.

"And it came to pass in those days, when Moses was grown, that he went out unto his brethren, and looked on their burdens; and he spied an Egyptian smiting an Hebrew, one of his brethren. And he looked this way and that way, and when he saw there was no man, he slew the Egyptian, and hid him in the sand." This was zeal for his brethren; but it was "not according to knowledge." God's time was not yet come for judging Egypt and delivering Israel; and the intelligent servant will ever wait for God's time. "Moses was grown;" and "he was learned in all the wisdom of the Egyptians;" and, moreover, "he supposed his brethren would have understood how that God by his hand would deliver them." All this was true; yet he evidently ran before the time, and when one does this failure must be the issue.[1]

And not only is there failure in the end, but also manifest uncertainty, and lack of calm elevation and holy independence in the progress of a work begun before God's time. Moses *looked this way and that way.*" There is no need of this when a man is acting with and for God, and in the full intelligence of His mind, as to the details of his work. If God's time had really come, and if Moses was conscious of being divinely commissioned to execute judgment upon the Egyptian, and if he felt assured of the divine presence with him, he would not have "looked this way and that way."

The fear of man

This action teaches a deep practical lesson to all the servants of God. There are two things by which it is superinduced: namely, the fear of man's wrath, and the hope of man's favour. The servant of the living God should neither regard the one nor the other. What avails the wrath or favour of a poor mortal, to one who holds the divine commission, and enjoys the divine presence? It is, in the judgment of such an one, less than the small dust of the balance. "*Have not I commanded thee?* Be strong and of a good courage; be not afraid, neither be thou dismayed: for *the Lord thy God is with thee,* whithersoever thou goest" (Joshua 1:9). "Thou, therefore, gird up thy loins, and arise, and speak unto them *all that I command thee:* be not dismayed at their faces, lest I confound thee before them. For, behold, I have made thee this day a defened city, and an iron pillar, and brazen walls against the whole land, against the kings of Judah, against the princes thereof, against the priests thereof, and against the people of the land. And they shall fight against thee, but they shall not prevail against thee; for *I am with thee*, saith the Lord, to deliver thee" (Jer 1:17-19).

When the servant of Christ stands upon the elevated ground set forth in the above quotations, he will not "look this way and that way;" he will act on wisdom's heavenly counsel, "let thine eyes look straight on, and thine eyelids look straight before thee." Divine intelligence will ever lead us to look upward and onward. Whenever we look around to shun a mortal's frown or catch his smile, we may rest assured there is something wrong; we are off the proper ground of divine service. We lack the assurance of holding the divine commission, and of enjoying the divine presence, both of which are absolutely essential.

True, there are many who, through profound ignorance, or excessive self-confidence, stand forward in a sphere of service for which God never intended them, and for which He, therefore, never qualified them. And not only do they thus stand forward, but they exhibit an amount of coolness and self-possession perfectly amazing to those who are capable of forming an impartial judgment about their gifts and merits. But all this will very speedily find its level; nor does it in the least interfere with the integrity of the principle that nothing can effectually deliver a man from the tendency to "look this way and that way," save the consciousness of the divine commission and the divine presence. When these are possessed, there is entire deliverance from human influence, and consequent independence. No man is in a position to serve others who is not wholly independent of them; but a man who knows his proper place can stoop and wash his brethren's feet.

When we turn away our eyes from man, and fix them

upon the only true and perfect Servant, we do not find him looking this way and that way, for this simple reason, that He never had His eye upon men, but always upon God. He feared not the wrath of man nor sought his favour. He never opened His lips to elicit human applause, nor kept them closed to avoid human censure. This gave holy stability and elevation to all He said and did. Of Him alone could it be truly said, "His leaf shall not wither, and *whatsoever* he doeth shall prosper." Everything He did turned to profitable account, because everything was done to God. Every action, every word, every movement, every look, every thought, was like a beauteous cluster of fruit, sent up to refresh the heart of God. He was never afraid of the results of His work, because He always acted with and for God, and in the full intelligence of His mind. His own will, though divinely perfect, never once mingled itself in anything that He did, as a man, on the earth. He could say, "I came down from heaven, not to do mine own will, but the will of him that sent me." Hence, He brought forth fruit, "*in its season*" He did "*always* those things which pleased the Father," and, therefore, never had any occasion to "fear," to "repent," or to "look this way and that way."

Now in this, as in everything else, the blessed Master stands in marked contrast with His most honoured and eminent servants. Even a Moses "feared," and a Paul "repented;" but the Lord Jesus never did either. He never had to retrace a step, to recall a word, or correct a thought. All was absolutely perfect. All was "fruit in season." The current of His holy and heavenly life flowed onward without a ripple and without a curve. His will was divinely subject. The best and most devoted men make mistakes; but it is perfectly certain that the more we are enabled, through grace, to mortify our own will, the fewer our mistakes will be. Truly happy it is when, in the main, our path is really a path of faith and single-eyed devotedness to Christ.

The way of faith

Thus it was with Moses. He was a man of faith – a man who drank deeply into the spirit of his Master, and walked with marvellous steadiness in His footsteps. True, he anticipated, as has been remarked, by forty years, the Lord's time of judgment on Egypt and deliverance for Israel; yet, when we turn to the inspired commentary, in Hebrews 11, we find nothing about this. We there find only the divine principle upon which, in the main, his course was founded. "By faith Moses, *when he was come to years*, refused to be called the son of Pharaoh's daughter, choosing rather to suffer affliction with the people of God than to enjoy the pleasures of sin for a season; esteeming the reproach of Christ greater riches than the treasures in Egypt; for he had respect unto the recompense of the reward. By faith he forsook Egypt, not fearing the wrath of the king; for he endured as seeing him who is invisible" (ver. 24-27).

This quotation furnishes a most gracious view of the actings of Moses. It is ever thus the Holy Ghost deals with the history of Old Testament saints. When He *writes* a man's history, He presents him to us as he is, and faithfully sets forth all his failures and imperfections. But when, in the New Testament, he *comments* upon such history, He merely gives the real principle and main result of a man's life. Hence, though we read, in Exodus, that "Moses looked this way and that way" – that "he feared and said, surely this thing is known" – and, finally, "Moses fled from the face of Pharaoh;" yet, we are taught, in Hebrews, that what he did, he did "by faith" – that he did not fear "the wrath of the king" – that "he endured as seeing him who is invisible."

Thus will it be, by and by, when "the Lord comes, who both will bring to light the hidden things of darkness, and will make manifest *the counsels of the hearts:* and then shall every man have praise of God" (1 Cor. 4:5). This is a precious and consolatory truth for every upright mind and every loyal heart. Many a "counsel" the "*heart*" may form, which, from various causes, the *hand* may not be able to execute. All such "counsels" will be made "manifest" when "the Lord comes." Blessed be the grace that has told us so! The affectionate counsels of the heart are far more precious to Christ than the most elaborate works of the hand. The latter may shine before the eye of man; the former are designed only for the heart of Jesus. The latter may be spoken of amongst men; the former will be made manifest before God and His holy angels. May all the servants of Christ have their hearts undividedly occupied with His person, and their eyes steadily fixed upon His advent.

In contemplating the path of Moses, we observe how that faith led him entirely athwart the ordinary course of nature. It led him to despise all the pleasures, the attractions, and the honours of Pharaoh's court. And not only that, but also to relinquish an apparently wide sphere of usefulness. Human expediency would have conducted him along quite an opposite path. It would have led him to use his influence on behalf of the people of God – to act *for* them instead of suffering *with* them. According to man's judgment, Providence would seem to have opened for Moses a wide and most important sphere of labour; and surely if ever the hand of God was manifest in placing a man in a distinct position, it was in his case. By a most marvellous interposition – by a most unaccountable chain of circumstances, every link of which displayed the finger of the Almighty – by an order of events which no human foresight could have arranged, had the daughter of Pharaoh been made the instrument of drawing Moses out of the water, and of nourishing and educating him until he was "full forty years old." With all these circumstances in his view, to abandon his high, honourable, and influential position, could only be regarded as the result of a misguided zeal which no sound judgment could approve.

Thus might poor blind nature reason. But faith thought differently; for nature and faith are always at issue. They cannot agree upon a single point. Nor is there anything, perhaps, in reference to which they differ so widely as what are commonly called "openings of Providence." Nature will constantly regard such openings as warrants for self-indulgence; whereas faith will find in them opportunities for self-denial. Jonah might have deemed it a very remarkable opening of Providence to find a ship going to Tarshish; but in truth it was an opening through which he slipped off the path of obedience.

No doubt, it is the Christian's privilege to see his Father's hand, and hear His voice, in everything; but he is not to be guided by circumstances. A Christian so guided is like a vessel at sea without rudder or compass; she is at the mercy of the waves and the winds. God's promise to His child is, "I will guide thee with mine eye" (Ps. 32:8). His warning is, "Be not as the horse or as the mule, which have no understanding; whose mouth must be held in with bit and bridle, lest they come near unto thee." It is much better to be guided by our Father's eye, than by the bit and bridle of circumstances; and we know that in the ordinary acceptation of the term, "Providence" is only another word for the impulse of circumstances.

Now, the power of faith may constantly be seen in refusing and forsaking the apparent openings of Providence. It was so in the case of Moses. "By faith he refused to be called the son of Pharaoh's daughter;" and "by faith he forsook Egypt." Had he judged according to the sight of his eyes, he would have grasped at the proffered dignity, as the manifest gift of a kind Providence, and he would have remained in the court of Pharaoh as in a sphere of usefulness plainly thrown open to him by the hand of God. But, then, he walked by faith, and not by the sight of his eyes; and, hence, he forsook all. Noble example! May we have grace to follow it!

And observe what it was that Moses "esteemed greater riches than the treasures in Egypt;" it was the "reproach of Christ." It was not merely reproach *for* Christ. "The reproaches of them that reproached thee have fallen upon me." The Lord Jesus, in perfect grace, identified Himself with His people. He came down from heaven, leaving His Father's bosom, and laying aside all His glory, He took His people's place, confessed their sins, and bore their judgment on the cursed tree. Such was His voluntary devotedness, He not merely acted *for* us, but made Himself one *with* us, thus perfectly delivering us from all that was or could be against us.

Hence, we see how much in sympathy Moses was with the spirit and mind of Christ, in reference to the people of God. He was in the midst of all the ease, the pomp and dignity of Pharaoh's house, where "the pleasures of sin," and "the treasures of Egypt," lay scattered around him, in richest profusion. All these things he might have enjoyed if he would. He could have lived and died in the midst of wealth and splendour. His entire path, from first to last, might, if he had chosen, have been enlightened by the sunshine of royal favour: but that would not have been "faith;" it would not have been Christ-like. From his elevated position, he saw his brethren bowed down beneath their heavy burden, and faith led him to see that his place was to be *with* them. Yes; with them, in all their reproach, their bondage, their degradation, and their sorrow. Had he been actuated by mere benevolence, philanthropy, or patriotism, he might have used his personal influence on behalf of his brethren. He might have succeeded in inducing Pharaoh to lighten their burden, and render their path somewhat smoother, by royal grants in their favour; but this would never do, never satisfy a heart that had a single pulsation in common with the heart of Christ. Such a heart Moses, by the grace of God, carried in his bosom; and, therefore, with all the energies and all the affections of that heart, he threw himself, body, soul, and spirit, into the very midst of his oppressed brethren. He "chose rather to suffer affliction *with* the people of God." And, moreover, he did this "by faith."

Let my reader ponder this deeply. We must not be satisfied with wishing well to, doing service for, or speaking kindly on behalf of, the people of God. We ought to be fully identified *with* them, no matter how despised or reproached they may be. It is, in a measure, an agreeable thing to a benevolent and generous spirit, to patronise Christianity; but it is a wholly different thing to be identified with Christians, or to suffer with Christ. A *patron* is one thing, a *martyr* is quite another. This distinction is apparent throughout the entire book of God. Obadiah took care of God's witnesses, but Elijah was a witness for God. Darius was so attached to Daniel that he lost a night's rest on his account, but Daniel spent that selfsame night in the lion's den, as a witness for the truth of God. Nicodemus ventured to speak a word *for* Christ, but a more matured discipleship would have led him to identify himself *with* Christ.

These considerations are eminently practical. The Lord Jesus does not want patronage; He wants fellowship. The truth concerning Him is declared to us, not that we might patronise His cause on earth, but have fellowship with His Person in heaven. He identified Himself with us, at the heavy cost of all that love could give. He might have avoided this. He might have continued to enjoy His eternal place "in the bosom of the Father." But how, then, could that mighty tide of love, which was pent up in His heart, flow down to us guilty and hell-deserving sinners? Between Him and us there could be no oneness, save on conditions which involved the surrender of everything on His part. But, blessed, throughout the everlasting ages, be His adorable Name, that surrender was voluntarily made. "He gave himself for us, that he might redeem us from all iniquity, and purify *unto himself* a peculiar people, zealous of good works" (Titus 2:14). He would not enjoy His glory alone. His loving heart would gratify itself by associating "many sons" with Him in that glory. "Father," He says, "I will that they also whom thou hast given me be *with me* where I am, that they may behold my glory, which thou hast given me; for thou lovedst me before the foundation of the world" (John 17:24). Such were the thoughts of Christ in reference to His people; and we can easily see how much in sympathy with these precious thoughts was the heart of Moses. He, unquestionably, partook largely of his Master's spirit; and he manifested that excellent spirit in freely sacrificing every personal consideration, and associating himself, unreservedly, with the people of God.

The typical character of Moses

The personal character and actings of this honoured servant of God will come before us again in the next section of our book. We shall here briefly consider him as a type of the Lord Jesus Christ. That he was a type of Him is evident from the following passage, "The Lord thy God will raise up unto thee a Prophet from the midst of thee, of thy brethren, like unto me; unto him ye shall hearken" (Deut. 18:15). We are not, therefore, trafficking in human imagination in viewing Moses as a type; it is the plain teaching of scripture, and, in the closing verses of Exodus 2 we see this type in a double way: first, in the matter of his rejection by Israel; and, secondly, in his union with a stranger in the land of Midian.

These points have already been, in some measure, developed in the history of Joseph, who, being cast out by his brethren, according to the flesh, forms an alliance with an Egyptian bride. Here, as in the case of Moses, we see shadowed forth Christ's rejection by Israel, and His union with the Church, but in a different phase. In Joseph's case, we have the exhibition of positive enmity against his *person*. In Moses it is the rejection of his *mission*. In Joseph's case we read, "they hated *him*, and could not speak peaceably unto *him*" (Gen. 37:4). In the case of Moses, the word is, "*Who made thee a prince and a judge over us?*" In short, the former was personally hated; the latter, officially refused.

So also in the mode in which the great mystery of the Church is exemplified, in the history of those two Old Testament saints. "Asenath" presents quite a different phase of the Church from that which we have in the person of "Zipporah." The former was united to Joseph in the time of his exaltation; the latter was the companion of Moses, in the obscurity of his desert life (comp. Gen. 41:41-45 with Exod.

2:15; 3:1). True, both Joseph and Moses were, at the time of their union with a stranger, rejected by their brethren; yet the former was "governor over all the land of Egypt;" whereas the latter tended a few sheep at "the backside of the desert."

Whether, therefore, we contemplate Christ, as manifested in glory, or as hidden from the world's gaze, the Church is intimately associated with Him. And now, inasmuch as the world seeth Him not, neither can it take knowledge of that body which is wholly one with Him. "The world knoweth us not, because it knew him not" (1 John 3:1). By and by, Christ will appear in His glory, and the Church *with* Him. "When Christ our life shall appear, then shall ye also appear with him in glory" (Col. 3:4). And, again, "The glory which thou gavest me I have given them; that they may be one, even as we are one: I in them, and thou in me, that they may be made perfect in one; and that the world may know that thou hast sent me, and hast loved them as thou hast loved Me" (John 17:22, 23).[2]

Such, then, is the Church's high and holy position. She is one with Him who is cast out by this world, but who occupies the throne of the Majesty in the heavens. The Lord Jesus made Himself responsible for her on the cross, in order that she might share with Him His present rejection and His future glory. Would that all who form a part of such a highly privileged body were more impressed with a sense of what becomes them as to course and character down here! Assuredly, there should be a fuller and clearer response on the part of all the children of God, to that love wherewith He has loved them, to that salvation wherewith He has saved them, and to that dignity wherewith He has invested them. The walk of the Christian should ever be the natural result of realised privilege, and not the constrained result of legal vows and resolutions, the proper fruit of a position known and enjoyed by faith, and not the fruit of one's own efforts to reach a position "by works of law." All true believers *are* a part of the bride of Christ. Hence they owe Him those affections which become that relation. The relationship is not obtained because of the affections, but the affections flow out of the relationship.

So let it be, O Lord, with all thy beloved and blood bought people!

---

[1] In Stephen's address to the council, at Jerusalem, there is an allusion to Moses' acting, to which it may be well to advert. "And when he was full forty years old it came into his heart to visit his brethren, the children of Israel. And seeing one of them suffer wrong, he defended him, and avenged him that was oppressed, and smote the Egyptian; for he supposed his brethren would have understood how that God, by his hand, would deliver them; but they understood not" (Acts 7:23-25). It is evident that Stephen's object, in his entire address, was to bring the history of the nation to bear upon the consciences of those whom he had before him; and it would have been quite foreign to this object, and at variance with the Spirit's rule in the New Testament, to raise a question as to whether Moses had not acted before the divinely-appointed time.

Moreover, he merely says, "it came into his heart to visit his brethren." He does not say that God sent him, *at that time*. Nor does this, in the least, touch the question of the moral condition of those who rejected him. "They understood not." This was the fact as to them, whatever Moses might have personally to learn in the matter. The spiritual mind can have no difficulty in apprehending this.

Looking at Moses, typically, we can see the mission of Christ to Israel, and their rejection of Him, and refusal to have Him to reign over them. On the other hand, looking at Moses, personally, we find that he, like others, made mistakes and displayed infirmities; sometimes went too fast, and sometimes too slow. All this is easily understood, and only tends to magnify the infinite grace and exhaustless patience of God.

[2] There are two distinct unities spoken of in John 17:21, 23. The first is that unity which the Church was responsible to have maintained, but in which she has utterly failed. The second is that unity which God will infallibly accomplish, and which He will manifest in glory. If the reader will turn to the passage he will at once see the difference, both as to character and result, of the two.

Chapter 3

THE CALL OF MOSES

The school of God

We shall now resume the personal history of Moses, and contemplate him during that deeply-interesting period of his career which he spent in retirement – a period including, as we should say, forty of his very best years – the prime of life. This is full of meaning. The Lord had graciously, wisely, and faithfully, led His dear servant apart from the eyes and thoughts of men, in order that He might train him under His own immediate hand. Moses needed this. True, he had spent forty years in the house of Pharaoh; and, while his sojourn there was not without its influence and value, yet was it as nothing when compared with his sojourn in the desert. The former might be valuable; but the latter was indispensable.

Nothing can possibly make up for the lack of secret communion with God, or the training and discipline of His school. "All the wisdom of the Egyptians" would not have qualified Moses for his future path. He might have pursued a most brilliant course through the schools and colleges of Egypt. He might have come forth laden with literary honours – his intellect stored with learning, and his heart full of pride and self-sufficiency. He might have taken out his degree in the school of man, and yet have to learn his alphabet in the school of God. Mere human wisdom and learning; how valuable soever in themselves, can never constitute any one a servant of God, nor equip him for any department of divine service. Such things may qualify unrenewed nature to figure before the world; but the man whom God will use must be endowed with widely-different qualifications – such qualifications as can alone be found in the deep and hallowed retirement of the Lord's presence.

All God's servants have been made to know and experience the truth of these statements. Moses at Horeb, Elijah at Cherith, Ezekiel at Chebar, Paul in Arabia, and John at Patmos, are all striking examples of the immense practical importance of being alone with God. And when we look at the Divine Servant, we find that the time He spent in private was nearly ten times as long as that which He spent in public. He, though perfect in understanding and in will, spent nearly thirty years in the obscurity of a carpenter's house at Nazareth, ere He made His appearance in public. And, even when He had entered upon His public career, how oft did He retreat from the gaze of men, to enjoy the sweet and sacred retirement of the divine presence!

Now we may feel disposed to ask, how could the urgent demand for workmen ever be met, if all need such protracted training, in secret, ere they come forth to their work? This is the Master's care – not ours. He can provide the workmen, and He can train them also. This is not man's work. God alone can provide and prepare a true minister. Nor is it a question with Him as to the length of time needful for the education of such an one. We know He could educate him in a moment, if it were His will to do so. One thing is evident, namely, that God has had all His servants very much alone with Himself, both before and after their entrance upon their public work; nor will any one ever get on without this. The absence of secret training and discipline will, necessarily leave us barren, superficial, and theoretic. A man who ventures forth upon a public career ere he has duly weighed himself in the balances of the sanctuary, or measured himself in the presence of God, is like a ship putting out to sea without proper ballast: he will doubtless overset with the first stiff breeze. On the contrary, there is a depth, a solidity, and a steadiness flowing from our having passed from form to form in the school of God, which are essential elements in the formation of the character of a true and effective servant of God.

Hence, therefore, when we find Moses, at the age of forty years, taken apart from all the dignity and splendour of a court, for the purpose of spending forty years in the obscurity of a desert, we are led to expect a remarkable course of service; nor are we disappointed. The man whom God educates, is educated, and none other. It lies not within the range of man to prepare an instrument for the service of God. The hand of man could never mould "a vessel meet for the Master's use." The One who is to use the vessel can alone prepare it; and we have before us a singularly beautiful sample of His mode of preparation.

"Now, Moses kept the flock of Jethro, his father-in law, the priest of Midian: and he led the flock to the backside of the desert, and came to the mountain of God, even to Horeb" (Exod. 3:1). Here, then, we have a marvellous change of circumstances. In Genesis 46:31, we read, "every shepherd is an abomination to the Egyptians;" and yet Moses, who was " learned in all the wisdom of the Egyptians," is transferred from the Egyptian court to the back of a mountain to tend a flock of sheep, and to be educated for the service of God. Assuredly, this is not "the manner of man." This is not nature's line of things. Flesh and blood could not understand this. We should have thought that Moses' education was finished when he had become master of all Egypt's wisdom, and that, moreover, in immediate connexion with the rare advantages which a court life affords. We should have expected to find in one so highly favoured, not only a solid and varied education; but also such an exquisite polish as would fit him for any sphere of action to which he might be called. But then, to find such a man with such attainments, called away from such a position to mind sheep at the back of a mountain, is something entirely beyond the utmost stretch of human thought and feeling. It lays prostrate in the dust all man's pride and glory. It declares plainly that this world's appliances are of little value in the divine estimation; yea, they are as "dung and dross," not only in the eyes of the Lord, but also in the eyes of all those who have been taught in His school.

There is a very wide difference between human and divine education. The former has for its end the refinement and exaltation of nature; the latter begins with withering it up and setting it aside. "The natural man receiveth not the things of the Spirit of God; for they are foolishness unto him; neither can he know them, because they are spiritually discerned" (1 Cor. 2:14). Educate the "natural man" as much as you please, and you cannot make him a "spiritual man." "That which is born of the flesh is flesh; and that which is born of the Spirit is spirit" (John 3:6). If ever an educated "natural man" might look for success in the service of God, Moses might have counted upon it; he was "grown," he was "learned," he was "mighty in word and deed," and yet he had to learn something at "the backside of the desert," which Egypt's schools could never have taught him. Paul learnt more in Arabia than ever he had learnt at the feet of Gamaliel.[3] None can teach like God; and all who will learn *of* Him must be alone *with* Him. "In the desert God will teach thee." There it was that Moses learnt his sweetest, deepest, most influential and enduring lessons. Thither, too, must all repair who mean to be educated for the ministry.

Beloved reader, may you prove, in your own deep experience, the real meaning of "the backside of the desert," that sacred spot where nature is laid in the dust, and God alone exalted. There it is that men and things – the world and self – present circumstances and their influence, are all valued at what they are really worth. There it is, and there alone, that you will find a divinely-adjusted balance in which to weigh all within and all around. There are no false colours, no borrowed plumes, no empty pretensions there. The enemy of your soul cannot gild the sand of that place. All is reality there. The heart that has found itself in the presence of God, at "the backside of the desert," has right thoughts about everything. It is raised far above the exciting influence of this world's schemes. The din and noise, the bustle and confusion of Egypt do not fall upon the ear in that distant place. The crash in the monetary and commercial world is not heard there. The sigh of ambition is not heaved there. This world's fading laurels do not tempt there. The thirst for gold is not felt there. The eye is never dimmed with lust, nor the heart swollen with pride there. Human applause does not elate, nor human censure depress there. In a word, everything is set aside save the stillness and light of the divine presence. God's voice alone is heard – His light enjoyed – His thoughts received. This is the place to which all must go to be educated for the ministry; and there all must remain, if they would succeed in the ministry.

Would that all who come forward to serve in public knew more of what it is to breathe the atmosphere of this place. We should, then, have far less vapid attempts at ministry, but far more effective Christ-honouring service.

The burning bush

Let us now enquire what Moses saw and what he heard at "the backside of the desert." We shall find him learning lessons which lay far beyond the reach of Egypt's most gifted masters. It might appear, in the eyes of human reason, a strange loss of time for a man like Moses to spend forty years doing nothing save to keep a few sheep in the wilderness. But he was there with God, and the time that is thus spent is never lost. It is salutary for us to remember that there is something more than mere *doing* necessary on the part of the true servant. A man who is always doing will be apt to do too much. Such an one would need to ponder over the deeply-practical words of the perfect Servant, "He wakeneth morning by morning, he wakeneth mine ear *to hear* as the learned" (Isa. 50:4). This is an indispensable part of the servant's business. The servant must frequently stand in his master's presence, in order that he may know what he has to do. The "ear" and the "tongue" are intimately connected, in more ways than one; but, in a spiritual or moral point of view, if my ear be closed and my tongue loose, I shall be sure to talk a great deal of folly. "Wherefore, my beloved brethren, let every man be swift *to hear,* slow *to speak"* (James 1:19). This seasonable admonition is based upon two facts, namely, that everything good comes from above, and that the heart is brim full of naughtiness, ready to flow over. Hence, the need of keeping the ear open and the tongue quiet – rare and admirable attainments! – attainments in which Moses made great proficiency at "the backside of the desert," and which all can acquire, if only they are disposed to learn in that school.

"And the angel of the Lord appeared unto him in a flame of fire, out of the midst of a bush: and he looked, and behold the bush burned with fire, and the bush was not consumed. And Moses said, I will now turn aside, and see this great sight, why the bush is not burnt" (chap. 3:2, 3). This was, truly, "a great sight" – a bush burning, yet not burnt. The palace of Pharaoh could never have afforded such a sight. But it was a gracious sight as well as a great sight, for therein was strikingly exhibited the condition of God's elect. They were in the furnace of Egypt; and Jehovah reveals Himself in a burning bush. But as the bush was not consumed, so neither were they, for God was there. "The Lord of hosts is with us, the God of Jacob is our refuge" (Ps. 46). Here is strength and security – victory and peace. God *with* us, God *in* us, and God *for* us. This is ample provision for every exigence.

The holiness of God

Nothing can be more interesting or instructive than the mode in which Jehovah was pleased to reveal Himself to Moses, as presented in the above quotation. He was about to furnish him with his commission to lead forth His people out of Egypt, that they might be His assembly – His dwelling-place, in the wilderness, and in the land of Canaan; and the place from which He speaks is a burning bush. Apt, solemn, and beautiful symbol of Jehovah dwelling in the midst of His elect and redeemed congregation! "Our God is a consuming fire," not to consume *us,* but to consume all in us and about us which is contrary to His holiness, and, as such, subversive of our true and permanent happiness. "Thy testimonies are very sure; holiness becometh thy house, O Lord, for ever."

There are various instances, both in the Old and New Testaments, in which we find God displaying Himself as "a consuming fire." Look, for example, at the case of Nadab and Abihu, in Leviticus 10. This was a deeply solemn occasion. God was dwelling in the midst of His people, and He would keep them in a condition worthy of Himself. He could not do otherwise. It would neither be for His glory nor for their profit, were He to tolerate anything in them inconsistent with the purity of His presence. God's dwelling-place must be holy.

So, also, in Joshua 7 we have another striking proof, in the case of Achan, that Jehovah could not possibly sanction, by His presence, evil, in any shape or form, how covert soever that evil might be. He was "a consuming fire," and, as such, He should act, in reference to any attempt to defile that assembly in the midst of which He dwelt. To seek to connect God's presence with evil unjudged, is the very highest character of wickedness.

Again, in Acts 5 Ananias and Sapphira teach us the same solemn lesson. God the Holy Ghost was dwelling in the midst of the Church, not merely as an influence, but as a divine Person, in such a way as that one could lie to Him. The Church was, and is still, His dwelling place; and He must rule and judge in the midst thereof. Men may walk in company with deceit, covetousness, and hypocrisy; but God cannot. If God is going to walk with us, we must judge our ways, or He will judge them for us (see also 1 Cor. 11:29-32).

In all these cases, and many more which might be adduced, we see the force of that solemn word, "holiness becometh thy house, O Lord, for ever." The moral effect of this will ever be similar to that produced in the case of Moses, as recorded in our chapter. "Draw not nigh hither: put off thy shoes from off thy feet, for *the place whereon thou standest is holy ground*" (verse 5). The place of God's presence is holy, and can only be trodden with unshod feet. God, dwelling in the midst of His people, imparts a character of holiness to their assembly, which is the basis of every holy affection and every holy activity. The character of the dwelling place takes its stamp from the character of the Occupant.

The application of this to the Church, which is now the habitation of God, through the Spirit, is of the very utmost practical importance. While it is blessedly true that God, by His Spirit, inhabits each individual member of the Church, thereby imparting a character of holiness to the individual; it is equally true that He dwells in the assembly; and, hence the assembly must be holy. The centre round which the members are gathered is nothing less than the Person of a living, victorious, and glorified Christ. The energy by which they are gathered is nothing less than God the Holy Ghost; and the Lord God Almighty dwells in them and walks in them (see Matt. 18:20; 1 Cor. 6:19; 1 Cor. 3:16, 17; Eph. 2:21, 22). Such being the holy elevation belonging to God's dwelling-place, it is evident that nothing which is unholy, either in principle or practice, must be tolerated. Each one connected therewith should feel the weight and solemnity of that word, "the place whereon thou standest is holy ground." "If any man defile the temple of God, him will God destroy"(1 Cor. 3:17). Most weighty words these, for every member of God's assembly – for every stone in His holy temple! May we all learn to tread Jehovah's courts, with unshod feet!

The grace of God towards His people

However, the visions of Horeb bear witness to the grace of the God of Israel as well as to His holiness. If God's holiness is infinite, His grace is infinite also; and, while the manner in which He revealed Himself to Moses, declared the former, the very fact of His revealing Himself at all evidenced the latter. He came down, because He was gracious; but when come down, He should reveal Himself as holy. "Moreover he said, I am the God of thy father, the God of Abraham, the God of Isaac, and the God of Jacob. And Moses hid his face; for he was afraid to look upon God" (verse 6). The effect of the divine presence must ever be to make nature hide itself; and, when we stand before God, with unshod feet and covered head, i.e. in the attitude of soul which those acts so aptly and beautifully express, we are prepared to hearken to the sweet accents of grace. When man takes his suited place, God can speak, in the language of unmingled mercy.

"And the Lord said, I have surely seen the affliction of my people which are in Egypt, and have heard their cry by reason of their taskmasters; for I know their sorrows. And I am come down to deliver them out of the hand of the Egyptians, and to bring them up out of that land unto a good land and a large, unto a land flowing with milk and honey . . . Now, therefore, behold, the cry of the children of Israel is come up unto me; and I have also seen the oppression wherewith the Egyptians oppress them" (ver. 7-9). Here the absolute, free, unconditional grace of the God of Abraham, and the God of Abraham's seed, shines forth in all its native brightness, unhindered by the "ifs" and "buts," the vows, resolutions, and conditions of man's legal spirit. God had come down to display Himself, in sovereign grace, to do the whole work of salvation, to accomplish His promise made to Abraham, and repeated to Isaac and Jacob. He had not come down to see if, indeed, the subjects of His promise were in such a condition as to *merit* His salvation. It was sufficient for Him that they *needed* it. Their oppressed state, their sorrows, their tears, their sighs, their heavy bondage, had all come in review before Him; for, blessed be His name, He counts His people's sighs and puts their tears into His bottle. He was not attracted by their excellencies or their virtues. It was not on the ground of anything that was good in them, either seen or foreseen, that he was about to visit them, for He knew what was in them. In one word, we have the true ground of His gracious acting set before us in the words, "I am the God of Abraham," and "I have seen the affliction of my people."

These words reveal a great fundamental principle in the ways of God. It is on the ground of what He is, that He ever acts. "I AM," secures all for "MY PEOPLE." Assuredly He was not going to leave *His* people amid the brick-kilns of Egypt, and under the lash of Pharaoh's taskmasters. They were His people, and He would act toward them in a manner worthy of Himself. To be His people – to be the favoured objects of Jehovah's electing love – the subjects of His unconditional promise, settled everything. Nothing should hinder the public display of His relationship with those for whom His eternal purpose had secured the land of Canaan. He had come down to deliver them; and the combined power of earth and hell could not hold them in captivity one hour beyond His appointed time. He might and did use Egypt as a school, and Pharaoh as a schoolmaster; but when the needed work was accomplished, both the school and the schoolmaster were set aside, and His people were brought forth with a high hand and an outstretched arm.

The secret of effective service

Such, then, was the double character of the revelation made to Moses at Mount Horeb. What he saw and what he heard combined the two elements of holiness and grace – elements which, as we know, enter into, and distinctly characterise, all the ways and all the relationships of the blessed God, and which should also mark the ways of all those who, in any wise, act for, or have fellowship with, Him. Every true servant is sent forth from the immediate presence of God, with all its holiness and all its grace; and he is called to be holy and gracious – he is called to be the reflection of the grace and holiness of the divine character; and, in order that he may be so, he should not only start from the immediate presence of God, at the first, but abide there, in spirit, habitually. This is the true secret of effectual service.

> "Childlike, attend what thou wilt say
> Go forth and do it, while 'tis day,
> Yet never leave my sweet retreat."

The spiritual man alone can understand the meaning of the two things, "go forth and do," and, "yet never leave." In order to act *for* God outside, I should be *with* Him inside. I must be in the secret sanctuary of His presence, else I shall utterly fail.

Very many break down on this point. There is the greatest possible danger of getting out of the solemnity and calmness of the divine presence, amid the bustle of intercourse with men, and the excitement of active service. This is to be carefully guarded against. If we lose that hallowed tone of spirit which is expressed in "the unshod foot," our service will, very speedily, become vapid and unprofitable. If I allow my work to get between my heart and the Master, it will be little worth. We can only effectually serve Christ as we are enjoying Him. It is while the heart dwells upon His powerful attractions that the hands perform the most acceptable service to His name; nor is there any one who can minister Christ with unction, freshness, and power to others, if he be not feeding upon Christ, in the secret of his own soul. True, he may preach a sermon, deliver a lecture, utter prayers, write a book, and go through the entire routine of outward service, and yet not minister Christ. The man who will present Christ to others must be occupied with Christ for himself.

Happy is the man who ministers thus, whatever be the success or reception of his ministry. For should his ministry fail to attract attention, to command influence, or to produce apparent results, he has his sweet retreat and his unfailing portion in Christ, of which nothing can deprive him. Whereas, the man who is merely feeding upon the fruits of his ministry, who delights in the gratification which it affords, or the attention and interest which it commands, is like a mere pipe, conveying water to others, and retaining only rust itself. This is a most deplorable condition to be in; and yet is it the actual condition of every servant who is more occupied with his work and its results, than with the Master and His glory.

This is a matter which calls for the most rigid self-judgment. The heart is deceitful, and the enemy is crafty; and, hence there is great need to hearken to the word of exhortation, "be sober, be vigilant." It is when the soul is awakened to a sense of the varied and manifold dangers which beset the servant's path, that it is, in any measure, able to understand the need there is for being much alone with God: it is there one is secure and happy. It is when we begin, continue, and end our work at the Master's feet, that our service will be of the right kind.

The sending of Moses

From all that has been said, it must be evident to any reader that every servant of Christ will find the air of "the backside of the desert" most salutary. Horeb is really the starting post for all whom God sends forth to act for Him. It was at Horeb that Moses learnt to put off his shoes and hide his face. Forty years before he had gone to work; but his movement was premature. It was amid the flesh-subduing solitudes of the mount of God, and forth from the burning bush, that the divine commission fell on the servant's ear, "Come now, therefore, and I will send thee unto Pharaoh, that thou mayest bring forth my people, the children of Israel, out of Egypt" (ver. 10). Here was real authority. There is a vast difference between God sending a man, and a man running unsent. But it is very manifest that Moses was not ripe for service when first he set about acting. If forty years of secret training were needful for him, how could he have got on without it? Impossible! He had to be divinely educated, and divinely commissioned; and so must all who go forth upon a path of service and testimony for Christ. Oh! that these holy lessons may be deeply graven on all our hearts, that so our every work may wear upon it the stamp of the Master's authority, and the Master's approval.

However, we have something further to learn at the foot of Mount Horeb. The soul finds it seasonable to linger in this place. "It is good to be here." The presence of God is ever a deeply practical place; the heart is sure to be laid open there.

The light that shines in that holy place makes everything manifest; and this is what is so much needed in the midst of the hollow pretension around us, and the pride and self complacency within.

We might be disposed to think that, the very moment the divine commission was given to Moses, his reply would be, "Here am I," or "Lord, what wilt thou have me to do?" But no; he had yet to be brought to this. Doubtless, he was affected by the remembrance of his former failure. If a man acts in anything without God, he is sure to be discouraged, even when God is sending him. "And Moses said unto God, Who am I that I should go unto Pharaoh, and that I should bring forth the children of Israel out of Egypt?" (ver. 11). This is very unlike the man who, forty years before, "supposed that his brethren would have understood how that God, by his hand, would deliver them." Such is man! – at one time too hasty; at another time too slow. Moses had learnt a greet deal since the day in which he smote the Egyptian. He had grown in the knowledge of himself, and this produced diffidence and timidity. But, then, he manifestly lacked confidence in God. If I am merely looking at myself, I shall do "nothing;" but if I am looking at Christ, "I can do all things." Thus, when diffidence and timidity led Moses to say, "Who am I?" God's answer was, "Certainly *I* will be with thee" (ver. 12). This ought to have been sufficient. If God be with me, it makes very little matter who I am, or what I am. When God says, "I will send thee," and "I will be with thee," the servant is amply furnished with divine authority and divine power; and he ought, therefore, to be perfectly satisfied to go forth.

"I AM THAT I AM"

But Moses puts another question; for the human heart is full of questions. "And Moses said unto God, Behold, when I come unto the children of Israel and shall say unto them, The God of your fathers hath sent me unto you; and they shall say to me, What is his name? what shall I say unto them?" It is marvellous to see how the human heart reasons and questions, when unhesitating obedience is that which is due to God; and still more marvellous is the grace that bears with all the reasonings and answers all the questions. Each question seems but to elicit some new feature of divine grace.

"And God said unto Moses, I AM THAT I AM: and he said, Thus shalt thou say unto the children of Israel, I AM hath sent me unto you" (ver 14). The title which God here gives Himself is one of wondrous significancy. In tracing through Scripture the various names which God takes, we find them intimately connected with the varied need of those with whom He was in relation. "Jehovah-jireh" (the Lord will provide), "Jehovah-nissi" (the Lord my banner), "Jehovah-shalom" (the Lord send peace), "Jehovah-tsidkenu" (the Lord our righteousness). All these His gracious titles are unfolded to meet the necessities of His people; and when He calls Himself "I AM," it comprehends them all. Jehovah, in taking this title, was furnishing His people with a blank cheque, to be filled up to any amount. He calls Himself "I AM," and faith has but to write over against that ineffably precious name whatever we want. God is the only significant figure, and human need may add the ciphers. If we want life, Christ says, "I AM the life." If we want righteousness, He is "THE LORD OUR RIGHTEOUSNESS. If we want peace, "He is our peace." If we want "wisdom, sanctification, and redemption," He "is made" all these "unto us." In a word, we may travel through the wide range of human necessity, in order to have a just conception of the amazing depth and fullness of this profound and adorable name, "I AM."

What a mercy to be called to walk in companionship with One who bears such a name as this! We are in the wilderness, and there we have to meet with trial, sorrow, and difficulty; but, so long as we have the happy privilege of betaking ourselves, at all times, and under all circumstances, to One who reveals Himself in His manifold grace, in connexion with our every necessity and weakness, we need not fear the wilderness: God was about to bring His people across the sandy desert, when He disclosed this precious and comprehensive name; and, although the believer now, as being endowed with the Spirit of adoption, can cry, "Abba Father," yet is he not deprived of the privilege of enjoying communion with God in each and every one of those manifestations which He has been pleased to make of Himself. For example, the title "God" reveals Him as acting in the solitariness of His own being, displaying His eternal power and Godhead in the works of creation. "The Lord God" is the title which He takes in connexion with man. Then, as "the Almighty God," He rises before the view of His servant Abraham, in order to assure his heart in reference to the accomplishment of His promise touching the seed. As Jehovah, He made Himself known to Israel, in delivering them out of the land of Egypt, and bringing them into the land of Canaan.

Such were the various measures and various modes in which "God spake in times past unto the fathers, by the prophets" (Heb. 1:1): and the believer, under this dispensation or economy, as possessing the spirit of sonship, can say, "It was my Father who thus revealed himself – thus spoke – thus acted."

Nothing can be more interesting or practically important in its way than to follow out those great dispensational titles of God. These titles are always used in strict moral consistency with the circumstances under which they are disclosed; but there is, in the name "I AM," a height, a depth, a length, a breadth, which truly pass beyond the utmost stretch of human conception.

"When God would teach mankind His name,
He calls Himself the great 'I AM,'
And leaves a blank – believers may
Supply those things for which they pray."

And, be it observed, it is only in connexion with His own people that He takes this name. He did not address Pharaoh in this name. When speaking to him, He calls Himself by that commanding and majestic title, "The Lord God of the Hebrews;" i.e., God, in connexion with the very people whom he was seeking to crush. This ought to have been sufficient to show Pharaoh his awful position with respect to God. "I AM" would have conveyed no intelligible sound to an uncircumcised ear – no divine reality to an unbelieving heart. When God manifest in the flesh declared to the unbelieving Jews of His day those words, "before Abraham was, *I am*," they took up stones to cast at Him. It is only the true believer who can feel, in any measure, the power, or enjoy the sweetness of that ineffable name, "I AM." Such an one can rejoice to hear from the lips of the blessed Lord Jesus such declarations as these:- "*I am* that bread of life," "*I am* the light of the world," "*I am* the good shepherd," "*I am* the resurrection and the life," "*I am* the way, the truth, and the life," "*I am* the true vine," "*I am* Alpha and Omega, "*I am* the bright and morning star." In a word, he can take every name of divine excellence and beauty, and, having placed it after "I AM," find JESUS therein, and admire, adore, and worship.

Thus, there is a sweetness, as well as a comprehensiveness, in the name "I AM," which is beyond all power of expression. Each believer can find therein that which exactly suits his own spiritual need, whatever it be. There is not a single winding in all the Christian's wilderness journey, not a single phase of his soul's experience, not a single point in his condition which is not divinely met by this title, for the simplest of all reasons, that whatever he wants, he has but to place it, by faith, over against "I AM" and find it all in Jesus. To the believer, therefore, however feeble and faltering, there is unmingled blessedness in this name.

But, although it was to the elect of God that Moses was commanded to say, "I AM hath sent me unto you," yet is there deep solemnity and reality in that name, when looked at with reference to the unbeliever. If one who is yet in his sins contemplates, for a moment, this amazing title, he cannot, surely, avoid asking himself the question, "How do I stand as to this Being who calls Himself, "I AM THAT I AM." If, indeed, it be true that HE IS, then what *is* He to *me?* What am *I* to write over against this solemn name, "I AM?" I shall not rob this question of its characteristic weight and power by any words of my own; but I pray that God the Holy Ghost may make it searching to the conscience of any reader who really needs to be searched thereby.

I cannot close this section without calling the attention of the Christian reader to the deeply-interesting declaration contained in the 15th verse: "And God said, moreover, unto Moses, Thus shalt thou say unto the children of Israel, The Lord God of your fathers, the God of Abraham, the God of Isaac, and the God of Jacob, hath sent me unto you: *this is my name for ever, and this is my memorial to all generations.*" This statement contains a very important truth – a truth which many professing Christians seem to forget, namely, that God's relationship with Israel is an eternal one. He is just as much Israel's God now, as when He visited them in the land of Egypt. Moreover, He is just as positively dealing with them now as then, only in a different way. His word is clear and emphatic: "This is my name for ever." He does not say, "This is my name for a time, so long as they continue what they ought to be." No; "this is my name *for ever,* and this is my memorial unto *all generations.*" Let my reader ponder this. "God hath not cast away his people which he foreknew" (Rom. 11:2). They are His people still, whether obedient or disobedient, united together, or scattered abroad; manifested to the nations, or hidden from their view. They are His people, and He is their God. Exodus 3:15 is unanswerable. The professing church has no warrant whatever, for ignoring a relationship which God says is to endure "for ever." Let us beware how we tamper with this weighty word, "for ever." If we say it does not mean for ever, when applied to Israel, what proof have we that it means for ever when applied to us? God means what He says; and He will, ere long, make manifest to all the nations of the earth, that His connexion with Israel is one which shall outlive all the revolutions of time. "The gifts and calling of God are

54 PENTATEUCH - THE BOOK OF EXODUS

without repentance." When He said, "this is my name for ever," He spoke absolutely. "I AM" declared Himself to be Israel's God for ever; and all the Gentiles shall be made to understand and bow to this; and to know, moreover, that all God's providential dealings with them, and all their destinies, are connected, in some way or other, with that favoured and honoured, though now judged and scattered, people. "When the Most High divided to the nations their inheritance, when he separated the sons of Adam, he set the bounds of the people, according to the number of the children of Israel. For the Lord's portion is his people. Jacob is the lot of his inheritance" (Deut. 32:8, 9).

Has this ceased to be true? Has Jehovah given up His "portion," and surrendered "the lot of His inheritance?" Does His eye of tender love no longer rest on Israel's scattered tribes, long lost to man's vision? Are the walls of Jerusalem no longer before Him? or has her dust ceased to be precious in His sight? To reply to these inquiries would be to quote a large portion of the Old Testament, and not a little of the New but this would not be the place to enter elaborately upon such a subject. I would only say, in closing this section, let not Christendom " be ignorant of this mystery, that blindness *in part* is happened to Israel, until the fullness of the Gentiles be come in. And so *all Israel shall be saved*" (Rom. 11:25, 26).

---

[3] Let not my reader suppose for a moment that the design of the above remarks is to detract from the value of really useful information, or the proper culture of the mental powers. By no means. If, for example, he is a parent, let him store his child's mind with useful knowledge; let him teach him everything which may, hereafter, turn to account in the Master's service: let him not burden him with anything which he would have to "lay aside" in running his Christian course, nor conduct him, for educational purposes through a region from which it is well-nigh impossible to come forth with an unsoiled mind. You might just as well shut him up for ten years in a coal mine, in order to qualify him for discussing the properties of light and shade, as cause him to wade through the mire of a heathen mythology, in order to fit him for the interpretation of the oracles of God, or prepare him for leading the flock of Christ.

Chapter 4

MOSES' OBJECTIONS

The first objection: they will not believe me

We are still called to linger at the foot of Mount Horeb, at "the backside of the desert;" and, truly, the air of this place is most healthful for the spiritual constitution. Man's unbelief and God's boundless grace are here made manifest in a striking way.

"And Moses answered and said, But, behold, they will not believe me, nor hearken unto my voice: for they will say, The Lord hath not appeared unto thee." How hard it is to overcome the unbelief of the human heart! How difficult man ever finds it to trust God! How slow he is to venture forth upon the naked promise of Jehovah. Anything, for nature, but that. The most slender reed that the human eye can *see* is counted more substantial, by far, as a basis for nature's confidence, than the unseen "Rock of ages." Nature will rush, with avidity, to any creature stream or broken cistern, rather than abide by the unseen "Fountain of living waters."

We might suppose that Moses had seen and heard enough to set his fears entirely aside. The consuming fire in the unconsumed bush, the condescending grace, the precious, endearing, and comprehensive titles, the divine commission, the assurance of the divine presence, – all these things might have quelled every anxious thought, and imparted a settled assurance to the heart. Still, however, Moses raises questions, and still God answers them; and, as we have remarked, each successive question brings out fresh grace. "And the Lord said unto him, What is that in thine hand? And he said, A rod." The Lord would just take him as he was, and use what he had in his hand. The rod with which he had tended Jethro's sheep was about to be used to deliver the Israel of God, to chastise the land of Egypt, to make a way through the deep, for the ransomed of the Lord to pass over, and to bring forth water from the flinty rock to refresh Israel's thirsty hosts in the desert. God takes up the weakest instruments to accomplish His mightiest ends. "A rod," "a ram's horn," "a cake of barley meal," "an earthen pitcher," "a shepherd's sling," anything, in short, when used of God, will do the appointed work. Men imagine that splendid ends can only be reached by splendid means; but such is not God's way. He can use a crawling worm as well as a scorching sun, a gourd as well as a vehement east wind (see Jonah).

But Moses had to learn a deep lesson, both as to the rod and the hand that was to use it. He had to learn and the people had to be convinced. "And he said, Cast it on the ground. And he cast it on the ground, and it became a serpent; and Moses fled from before it. And the Lord said unto Moses, Put forth thine hand and take it by the tail. And he put forth his hand and caught it, and it became a rod in his hand: that they may believe that the Lord God of their fathers, the God of Abraham, the God of Isaac, and the God of Jacob, hath appeared unto thee." This is a deeply significant sign. The rod became a serpent, so that Moses fled from it; but, being commissioned by Jehovah, he took the serpent by the tail, and it became a rod. Nothing could more aptly express the idea of Satan's power being turned against himself. This is largely exemplified in the ways of God. Moses himself was a striking example. The serpent is entirely under the hand of Christ; and when he has reached the highest point in his mad career, he shall be hurled into the lake of fire, there to reap the fruits of his work throughout eternity's countless ages. "That old serpent, the accuser, and the adversary," shall be eternally crushed beneath the rod of God's Anointed.

> "Then the end – beneath His rod,
> Man's last enemy shall fall;
> Hallelujah! Christ in God,
> God in Christ, is all in all."

"And the Lord said furthermore unto him, Put now thine hand into thy bosom. And he put his hand into his bosom; and when he took it out, behold, his hand was leprous as snow. And he said, Put thine hand into thy bosom again. And he put his hand into his bosom again, and plucked it out of his bosom; and, behold, it was turned again as his other flesh." The leprous hand and the cleansing thereof present to us the moral effect of sin, as also the way in which sin has been met in the perfect work of Christ. The clean hand, placed in the bosom, becomes leprous; and the leprous hand placed there becomes clean. Leprosy is the well-known type of sin; and sin came in by the first man and was put away by the second. "By man came death, by man came also the resurrection of the dead" (1 Cor. 15:21). Man brought in ruin, man brought in redemption; man brought in guilt, man brought in pardon; man brought in sin, man brought in righteousness; man filled the scene with death, man abolished death and filled the scene with life, righteousness, and glory. Thus, not only shall the serpent himself be eternally defeated and confounded, but every trace of his abominable work shall be eradicated and wiped away by the atoning sacrifice of Him who "was manifested that he might destroy the works of the devil."

"And it shall come to pass, if they will not believe also these two signs, neither hearken unto thy voice, that thou shalt take of the water of the river, and pour it upon the dry land; and the water which thou takest out of the river shall become blood upon the dry land." This was a solemn and most expressive figure of the consequence of refusing to bow to the divine testimony. This sign was only to be wrought in the event of their refusing the other two. It was, first, to be a sign to Israel, and afterwards a plague upon Egypt (comp. chap. 7:17).

The second objection: *I am not an eloquent man*

All this, however, fails to satisfy the heart of Moses. "And Moses said unto the Lord, O my Lord, I am not eloquent, neither heretofore, nor since thou hast spoken unto thy servant; but I am slow of speech and of a slow tongue." Terrible backwardness! Nought save Jehovah's infinite patience could have endured it. Surely when God Himself had said, "I will be with thee," it was an infallible security, in reference to everything which could possibly be needed. If an eloquent tongue were necessary, what had Moses to do but to set it over against "I AM?" Eloquence, wisdom, might, energy, everything was contained in that exhaustless treasury. "And the Lord said unto him, Who hath made man's mouth? or who maketh the dumb, or deaf, or the seeing, or the blind? have not I the Lord? Now, therefore, go, and I will be with thy mouth, and teach thee what thou shalt say." Profound, adorable, matchless grace! worthy of God! There is none like unto the Lord our God, whose patient grace surmounts all our difficulties, and proves itself amply sufficient for our manifold need and weakness. "I THE LORD" ought to silence for ever the reasonings of our carnal hearts. But, alas! these reasonings are hard to be put down. Again and again they rise to the surface, to the disturbance of our peace, and the dishonour of that blessed One, who sets Himself before our souls, in all His own essential fullness, to be used according to our need.

It is well to bear in mind that when we have the Lord with us, our very deficiencies and infirmities become an occasion for the display of His all-sufficient grace and perfect patience. Had Moses remembered this, his want of eloquence need not have troubled him. The Apostle Paul learnt to say, "most gladly, therefore, *will I rather glory* in my infirmities, that the power of Christ may rest upon me. Therefore *I take pleasure* in infirmities, in reproaches, in necessities, in persecutions, in distresses, for Christ's sake: for when I am weak then am I strong" (2 Cor. 12:9, 10). This is, assuredly, the utterance of one who had reached an advanced form in the school of Christ. It is the experience of one who would not have been much troubled because of not possessing an eloquent tongue, inasmuch as he had found an answer to every description of need in the precious grace of the Lord Jesus Christ.

The knowledge of this truth ought to have delivered Moses from his diffidence and inordinate timidity. When the Lord had so graciously assured him that He would be with his mouth, it should have set his mind at rest as to the question of eloquence. The Maker of man's mouth could fill that mouth with the most commanding eloquence, if such were needed. This, in the judgment of faith, is most simple; but, alas! the poor doubting heart would place far more confidence in an eloquent tongue than in the One who created it. This would seem most unaccountable, did we not know the materials of which the natural heart is composed. That heart cannot trust God; and hence it is that even the people of God, when they suffer themselves to be, in any measure, governed by nature, exhibit such a humiliating lack of confidence in the living God.

Moses refuses his commission

Thus, in the scene before us, we find Moses still demurring. "And he said, O my Lord, send, I pray thee, by the hand of him whom thou wilt send." This was, in reality, casting from him the high honour of being Jehovah's sole messenger to Egypt and to Israel.

It were needless to say that divinely-wrought humility is an inestimable grace. To "be clothed with humility" is a divine precept; and humility is, unquestionably, the most becoming dress in which a worthless sinner can appear. But, it cannot be called humility to refuse to take the place which God assigns, or to tread the path which His hand marks out for us. That it was not true humility in Moses is obvious from the fact that "the anger of the Lord was kindled against him." So far from its being humility, it had actually passed the limit of mere weakness. So long as it wore the aspect of an excessive timidity, however reprehensible, God's boundless grace bore with it, and met it with renewed assurances; but when it assumed the character of unbelief and slowness of heart, it drew down Jehovah's just displeasure; and Moses, instead of being the sole, is made a joint, instrument in the work of testimony and deliverance.

Nothing is more dishonouring to God or more dangerous for us than a mock humility. When we refuse to occupy a position which the grace of God assigns us, because of our not possessing certain virtues and qualifications, this is not humility, inasmuch as if we could but satisfy our own consciences in reference to such virtues and qualifications, we should then deem ourselves entitled to assume the position. If, for instance, Moses had possessed such a measure of eloquence as he deemed needful, we may suppose he would have been ready to go. Now the question is, how much eloquence would he have needed, to furnish him for his mission? The answer is, without God no amount of human eloquence would have availed; but, with God, the merest stammerer would have proved an efficient minister.

This is a real practical truth. Unbelief is not humility, but thorough pride. It refuses to believe God because it does not find, in *self*, a reason for believing. This is the very height of presumption. If, when God speaks, I refuse to believe, on the ground of something in myself, I make Him a liar (1 John 5:10). When God declares His love, and I refuse to believe because I do not deem myself a sufficiently worthy object, I make Him a liar and exhibit the inherent pride of my heart. The bare supposition that I could ever be worthy of anything save the lowest pit of hell, can only be regarded as the most profound ignorance of my own condition and of God's requirements. And the refusal to take the place which the redeeming love of God assigns me, on the ground of the finished atonement of Christ, is to make God a liar, and cast gross dishonour upon the sacrifice of the cross. God's love flows forth spontaneously. It is not drawn forth by my deserts, but by my misery. Nor is it a question as to the place which I deserve, but which Christ deserves. Christ took the sinner's place, on the cross, that the sinner might take His place in the glory. Christ got what the sinner deserved, that the sinner might get what Christ deserves. Thus, *self* is totally set aside, and this is true humility. No one can be truly humble until he has reached heaven's side of the cross; but there he finds divine life, divine righteousness, and divine favour. He is done with himself for ever, as regards any expectation of goodness or righteousness, and he feeds upon the princely wealth of another. He is morally prepared to join in that cry which shall echo through the spacious vault of heaven, throughout the everlasting ages, "Not unto us, O Lord, not unto us, but unto thy name give glory" (Ps. 115:1).

It would ill become us to dwell upon the mistakes or infirmities of so honoured a Servant as Moses, of whom we read that he "was verily faithful in all his house, as a servant, for a testimony of those things which were to be spoken after" (Heb. 3:5). But, though we should not dwell upon them, in a spirit of self-complacency, as if we would have acted differently, in his circumstances, we should, nevertheless, learn from such things those holy and seasonable lessons which they are manifestly designed to teach. We should learn to judge ourselves and to place more implicit confidence in God – to set self aside, that He might act in us, through us, and for us. This is the true secret of power.

A companion in service

We have remarked that Moses forfeited the dignity of being Jehovah's sole instrument in that glorious work which He was about to accomplish. But this was not all. "The anger of the Lord was kindled against Moses; and he said, Is not Aaron the Levite thy brother? I know that he can speak well: and, also, behold, he cometh forth to meet thee; and when he seeth thee, he will be glad in his heart. And *thou shalt speak unto him, and put words in his mouth:* and I will be with thy mouth, and with his mouth, and will teach you what ye shall do. And he shall be thy spokesman unto the people: and he shall be, even he shall be to thee instead of a mouth, and thou shalt be to him instead of God. And thou shalt take this rod in thine hand, wherewith thou shalt do signs" (chap. 4:14-17). This passage contains a mine of most precious practical instruction. We have noted the timidity and hesitation of Moses, notwithstanding the varied promises and assurances with which divine grace had furnished him. And, now, although there was nothing gained in the way of real power, although there was no more virtue or efficacy in one mouth than in another, although it was Moses after all who was to speak unto Aaron; yet was Moses quite ready to go when assured of the presence and co-operation of a poor feeble mortal like himself; whereas he could not go when assured, again and again, that Jehovah would be with him.

Oh! my reader, does not all this hold up before us a faithful mirror in which you and I can see our hearts reflected? Truly it does. We are more ready to trust anything than the living God. We move along, with bold decision, when we possess the countenance and support of a poor frail mortal like ourselves; but we falter, hesitate, and demur, when we have the light of the Master's countenance to cheer us, and the strength of His omnipotent arm to support us. This should humble us deeply before the Lord, and lead us to seek a fuller acquaintance with Him, so that we might trust Him with a more unmixed confidence, and walk on with a firmer step, as having Him *alone* for our resource and portion.

No doubt, the fellowship of a brother is most valuable – "Two are better than one" – whether in labour, rest, or conflict. The Lord Jesus, in sending forth His disciples, "sent them two by two," – for unity is ever better than isolation – still, if our personal acquaintance with God, and our experience of His presence, be not such as to enable us, if needful, to walk alone, we shall find the presence of a brother of very little use. It is not a little remarkable, that Aaron, whose companionship seemed to satisfy Moses, was the man who afterwards made the golden calf (Exod. 32:21). Thus it frequently happens, that the very person whose presence we deem essential to our progress and success, afterwards proves a source of deepest sorrow to our hearts. May we ever remember this!

MOSES' RETURN TO EGYPT

Circumcision

However, Moses, at length, consents to go; but ere he is fully equipped for his work, he must pass through another deep exercise; yea, he must have the sentence of death inscribed by the hand of God upon his very nature. He had learnt deep lessons at "the backside of the desert;" he is called to learn something deeper still, "by the way in the inn." It is no light matter to be the Lord's servant. No ordinary education will qualify a man for such a position. Nature must be put in the place of death and kept there. "We had the sentence of death in ourselves, that we should not trust in ourselves, but in God which raiseth the dead (2 Cor. 1:9). Every successful servant will need to know something of this. Moses was called to enter into it, in his own experience, ere he was morally qualified. He was about to sound in the ears of Pharaoh the following deeply-solemn message, "Thus saith the Lord, Israel is my son, even my first-born: and I say unto thee, Let my son go, that he may serve me: and if thou refuse to let him go, behold I will slay thy son, even thy firstborn." Such was to be his message to Pharaoh; a message of death, a message of judgment; and, at the same time, his message to Israel was a message of life and salvation. But, be it remembered, that the man who will speak, on God's behalf, of death and judgment, life and salvation, must, ere he does so, enter into the practical power of these things in his own soul. Thus it was with Moses. We have seen him, at the very outset, in the place of death, typically; but this was a different thing from entering into the experience of death in his own person. Hence we read, "And it came to pass, by the way in the inn, that the Lord met him, and sought to kill him. Then Zipporah took a sharp stone, and cut off the foreskin of her son, and cast it at his feet, and said, Surely a bloody husband art thou to me. So he let him go: then she said, A bloody husband thou art, because of the circumcision." This passage lets us into a deep secret, in the personal and domestic history of Moses. It is very evident that Zipporah's heart had, up to this point, shrunk from the application of *the knife* to that around which the affections of nature were entwined. She had avoided that mark which had to be set in the flesh of every member of the Israel of God. She was not aware that her relationship with Moses was one involving death to nature. She recoiled from the cross. This was natural. But Moses had yielded to her in the matter; and this explains to us the mysterious scene "in the inn." If Zipporah refuses to circumcise her *son*, Jehovah will lay His hand upon her *husband*; and if Moses spares the feelings of his wife, Jehovah will "seek to kill him." The sentence of death must be written on nature; and if we seek to avoid it in one way, we shall have to encounter it in another.

It has been already remarked, that Zipporah furnishes an instructive and interesting type of the Church. She was united to Moses, during the period of his rejection; and from the passage just quoted, we learn that the Church is called to know Christ, as the One related to her "by blood." It is her privilege to drink of His cup, and be baptised with His baptism.

The Christian position

Being crucified with Him, she is to be conformed to His death; to mortify her members which are on the earth; to take up the cross daily, and follow Him. Her relationship with Christ is founded upon blood, and the manifestation of the power of that relationship will, necessarily, involve death to nature. "And ye are complete in him, which is the head of all principality and power; in whom also ye are circumcised with the circumcision made without hands, in putting off the body of the sins of the flesh by the circumcision of Christ; buried with him in baptism, wherein also ye are risen with him through the faith of the operation of God, who hath raised him from the dead" (Col. 2:10-12).

Such is the doctrine as to the Church's place with Christ – a doctrine replete with the richest privileges for the Church, and each member thereof. Everything, in short, is involved: the perfect remission of sin, divine righteousness, complete acceptance, everlasting security, full fellowship with Christ in all His glory. "Ye are *complete* in him." This, surely, comprehends everything. What could be added to one who is "complete?" Could "philosophy," "the tradition of men," "the rudiments of the world," "meats, drinks, holy days, new moons, or sabbaths?" "Touch not" this, "taste not" that, "handle not" the other, "the commandments and doctrines of men," "days and months, and times, and years," could any of these things, or all of them put together, add a single jot or tittle to one whom God has pronounced "complete?" We might just as well enquire, if man could have gone forth upon the fair creation of God, at the close of the six days' work, to give the finishing touch to that which God had pronounced "very good?"

Nor is this completeness to be, by any means, viewed as a matter of attainment, some point which we have not yet reached, but after which we must diligently strive, and of the possession of which we cannot be sure until we lie upon a bed of death, or stand before a throne of judgment. It is the portion of the feeblest, the most inexperienced, the most unlettered child of God. The very weakest saint is included in the apostolic "*ye.*" All the people of God "*are* complete in Christ." The apostle does not say, "ye *will* be," "ye *may* be," "*hope* that ye may be," "*pray* that ye may be:" no; he, by the Holy Ghost, states, in the most absolute and unqualified manner, that "ye *are* complete." This is the true Christian starting-post: and for man to make a goal of what God makes a starting-post, is to upset everything.

But, then, some will say, "have we no sin, no failure, no imperfection?" Assuredly we have. "If we say that we have no sin, we deceive ourselves, and the truth is not in us" (1 John 1:8). We have sin *in* us, but no sin *on* us. Moreover, our standing is not in *self*, but in Christ. It is "*in him*" we "are complete." God sees the believer in Christ, with Christ, and as Christ. This is his changeless condition, his everlasting standing. "The body of the sins of the flesh" is "put off by the circumcision of Christ." The believer is not in the flesh, though the flesh is in him. He is united to Christ in the power of a new and an endless life, and that life is inseparably connected with divine righteousness in which the believer stands before God. The Lord Jesus has put away everything that was against the believer, and He has brought him nigh to God, in the self-same favour as that which He Himself enjoys. In a word, Christ is his righteousness. This settles every question, answers every objection, silences every doubt. "Both he that sanctifieth and they who are sanctified, are all of one" (Heb. 2:11).

Moses and Aaron

The foregoing line of truth has flowed out of the deeply-interesting type presented to us in the relationship between Moses and Zipporah. We must, now, hasten to close this section, and take our leave, for the present, of "the backside of the desert," though not of its deep lessons and holy impressions, so essential to every servant of Christ, and every messenger of the living God. All who would serve effectually, either in the important work of evangelization, or in the varied ministries of the house of God – which is the Church – will need to imbibe the precious instructions which Moses received at the foot of Mount Horeb, and "by the way in the inn."

Were these things properly attended to, we should not have so many running unsent – so many rushing into spheres of ministry for which they were never designed. Let each one who stands up to preach, or teach, or exhort, or serve in any way, seriously enquire if, indeed, he be fitted, and taught, and sent of God. If not, his work will neither be owned of God nor blessed to men, and the sooner he ceases, the better for himself and for those upon whom he has been imposing the heavy burden of hearkening to him. Neither a humanly-appointed, nor a self-appointed ministry, will ever suit within the hallowed precincts of the Church of God. All must be divinely gifted, divinely taught, and divinely sent.

"And the Lord said to Aaron, Go into the wilderness to meet Moses. And he went and met him in the mount of God, and kissed him. And Moses told Aaron all the words of the Lord who had sent him, and all the signs which he had commanded him." This was a fair and beauteous scene – a scene of sweet brotherly love and union – a scene which stands in marked contrast with many of those scenes which were afterwards enacted in the wilderness-career of these two men. Forty years of wilderness life are sure to make great changes in men and things. Yet it is sweet to dwell upon those early days of one's Christian course, before the stern realities of desert life had, in any measure, checked the gush of warm and generous affections – before deceit, and corruption, and hypocrisy had well-nigh dried up the springs of the heart's confidence, and placed the whole moral being beneath the chilling influences of a suspicious disposition.

That such results have been produced, in many cases, by years of experience, is, alas! too true. Happy is he who, though his eyes have been opened to see nature in a clearer light than that which this world supplies, can, nevertheless, serve his generation by the energy of that grace which flows forth from the bosom of God. Who ever knew the depths and windings of the human heart as Jesus knew them? "He knew *all*, and needed not that any should testify of man: for he knew what was in man" (John 2:24, 25). So well did He know man that He could not commit Himself unto him. He could not accredit man's professions, or endorse his pretensions. And yet, who so gracious as He? Who so loving, so tender, so compassionate, so sympathising? With a heart that understood all, He could feel for all. He did not suffer His perfect knowledge of human worthlessness to keep Him aloof from human need. "He went about doing good." Why? Was it because He imagined that all those who flocked around Him were real? No; but "because God was with him" (Acts 10:38). This is our example. Let us follow it, though, in doing so, we shall have to trample on *self* and all its interests, at every step of the way.

Who would desire that wisdom, that knowledge of nature, that experience, which only lead men to ensconce themselves within the enclosures of a hard-hearted selfishness, from which they look forth with an eye of dark suspicion upon everybody? Surely such a result could never follow from anything of a heavenly or excellent nature. God gives wisdom; but it is not a wisdom which locks the heart against all the appeals of human need and misery. He gives a knowledge of nature; but it is not a knowledge which causes us to grasp with a selfish eagerness that which we, falsely, call "our own." He gives experience; but it is not an experience which results in suspecting everybody except myself. If I am walking in the footprints of Jesus, if I am imbibing, and therefore manifesting, His excellent spirit, if, in short, I can say, "to me to live is Christ;" then, while I walk through the world, with a knowledge of what the world is; while I come in contact with man, with a knowledge of what I am to expect from him; I am able, through grace, to manifest Christ in the midst of it all. The springs which move me, and the objects which animate me, are all *above*, where He is, who is "the same yesterday, and today, and for ever" (Heb. 13:8). It was this which sustained the heart of that beloved and honoured servant, whose history, even so far, has furnished us with such deep and solid instruction. It was this which carried him through the trying and varied scenes of his wilderness course. And we may safely assert that, at the close of all, notwithstanding the trial and exercise of forty years, Moses could embrace his brother, when he stood on Mount Hor, with the same warmth as he had when first he met him, "in the mount of God." True, the two occasions were very different. At "the mount of God" they met, and embraced, and started together on their divinely-appointed mission. Upon "Mount Hor" they met by the commandment of Jehovah, in order that Moses might strip his brother of his priestly robes, and see him gathered to his fathers, because of an error in which he himself had participated. (How solemn! How touching!) Circumstances vary: men may turn away from one; but with God "is no variableness, neither shadow of turning" (James 1:17).

"And Moses and Aaron went and gathered together all the elders of the children of Israel; and Aaron spake all the words which the Lord had spoken unto Moses, and did the signs in the sight of the people. And the people believed; and when they heard that the Lord had visited the children of Israel and that he had looked upon their affliction, then they bowed their heads and worshipped" (ver. 29-31). When God works, every barrier must give way. Moses had said, "the people will not believe me." But the question was not, as to whether they would believe him, but whether they would believe God. When a man is enabled to view himself simply as the messenger of God, he may feel quite at ease as to the reception of his message. It does not detract, in the smallest degree, from his tender and affectionate solicitude, in reference to those whom he addresses. Quite the contrary; but it preserves him from that inordinate anxiety of spirit which can only tend to unfit him for calm, elevated, steady testimony. The messenger of God should ever remember whose message he bears. When Zacharias said to the angel, "Whereby shall I know this?" was the latter perturbed by the question? Not in the least. His calm, dignified reply was, "I am Gabriel, that stand in the presence of God; and am sent to speak unto thee, and to show thee these glad tidings" (Luke 1:18, 19). The angel rises before the doubting mortal, with a keen and exquisite sense of the dignity of his message. It is as if he would say, "How can you doubt, when a messenger has actually been dispatched from the very presence-chamber of the Majesty of heaven?" Thus should every messenger of God, in his measure, go forth, and, in this spirit, deliver his message.

Chapters 5 & 6

ISRAEL'S SLAVERY BECOMES EVEN HARDER

Moses' and Aaron's first visit to Pharaoh
The effect of the first appeal to Pharaoh seemed anything but encouraging. The thought of losing Israel made him clutch them with greater eagerness and watch them with greater vigilance. Whenever Satan's power becomes narrowed to a point, his rage increases. Thus it is here. The furnace is about to be quenched by the hand of redeeming love; but, ere it is, it blazes forth with greater fierceness and intensity. The devil does not like to let go any one whom he has had in his terrible grasp. He is "a strong man armed," and while he "keepeth his palace, his goods are in peace." But, blessed be God, there is "a stronger than he," who has taken from him "his armour wherein he trusted," and divided the spoils among the favoured objects of His everlasting love.

"And afterward, Moses and Aaron went in, and told Pharaoh, Thus saith the Lord God of Israel, let my people go, that they may hold a feast unto me in the wilderness" (chap. 5:1). Such was Jehovah's message to Pharaoh. He claimed full deliverance for the people, on the ground of their being His; and, in order that they might hold a feast to Him in the wilderness. Nothing can ever satisfy God in reference to His elect, but their entire emancipation from the yoke of bondage. "Loose him, and let him go" is, really, the grand motto in God's gracious dealings with those who, though held in bondage by Satan, are, nevertheless, the objects of His eternal love.

The sinner delivered from Satan's slavery

When we contemplate Israel amid the brick-kilns of Egypt, we behold a graphic figure of the condition of every child of Adam by nature. There they were, crushed beneath the enemy's galling yoke, and having no power to deliver themselves. The mere mention of the word *liberty* only caused the oppressor to bind his captives with a stronger fetter, and to lade them with a still more grievous burden. It was absolutely necessary that deliverance should come from without. But from whence was it to come? Where were the resources to pay their ransom? or where was the power to break their chains? And, even were there both the one and the other, where was the *will?* Who would take the trouble of delivering them? Alas! there was no hope, either within or around. They had only to look up. Their refuge was in God. He had both the power and the will. He could accomplish a redemption both by price and by power. In Jehovah, and in Him alone, was there salvation for ruined and oppressed Israel.

Thus is it in every case. "Neither is there salvation in any other: for there is none other name under heaven given among men, whereby we must be saved" (Acts 4:12). The sinner is in the hands of one who rules him with despotic power. He is "sold under sin" – "led captive by Satan at his will" – fast bound in the fetters of lust, passion, and temper, "without strength" – "without hope" – "without God." Such is the sinner's condition. How, then, can he help himself? What can he do? He is the slave of another, and everything he does is done in the capacity of a slave. His thoughts, his words, his acts, are the thoughts, words, and acts of a slave. Yea, though he should weep and sigh for emancipation, his very tears and sighs are the melancholy proofs of his slavery. He may struggle for freedom; but his very struggle, though it evinces a desire for liberty, is the positive declaration of his bondage.

Nor is it merely a question of the sinner's *condition*; his very *nature* is radically corrupt – wholly under the power of Satan. Hence, he not only needs to be introduced into a new condition, but also to be endowed with a new nature. The nature and the condition go together. If it were possible for the sinner to better his condition, what would it avail so long as his nature was irrecoverably bad? A nobleman might take a beggar off the streets and adopt him; he might endow him with a noble's wealth and set him in a noble's position; but he could not impart to him nobility of nature; and thus the nature of a beggarman would never be at home in the condition of a nobleman. There must be a nature to suit the condition; and there must be a condition to suit the capacity, the desires, the affections, and the tendencies of the nature.

Now, in the gospel of the grace of God, we are taught that the believer is introduced into an entirely new condition; that he is no longer viewed as in his former state of guilt and condemnation, but as in a state of perfect and everlasting justification; that the condition in which God now sees him is not only one of full pardon; but it is such that infinite holiness cannot find so much as a single stain. He has been taken out of his former condition of guilt, and placed absolutely and eternally in a new condition of unspotted righteousness. It is not, by any means, that his old condition is improved. This was utterly impossible. "That which is crooked cannot be made straight." "Can the Ethiopian change his skin, or the leopard his spots?" Nothing can be more opposed to the fundamental truth of the gospel than the theory of a gradual improvement in the sinner's condition. He is born in a certain condition, and until he is "born again" he cannot be in any other. He may try to improve. He may resolve to be better for the future – to "turn over a new leaf" – to live a different sort of life; but, all the while, he has not moved a single hair's breadth out of his real condition as a sinner. He may become "religious" as it is called, he may try to pray, he may diligently attend to ordinances, and exhibit an appearance of moral reform; but none of these things can, in the smallest degree, affect his positive condition before God.

The case is precisely similar as to the question of *nature*. How can a man alter his nature? He may make it undergo a process, he may try to subdue it, to place it under discipline; but it is nature still. "That which is born of the flesh is flesh." There must be a new nature as well as a new condition. And how is this to be had? By believing God's testimony concerning His Son. "As many as received him, to them gave he power to become the sons of God, even *to them that believe on his name*: which were born, not of blood, nor of the will of the flesh, nor of the will of man, but of God" (John 1:12, 13). Here we learn that those who believe on the name of the only-begotten Son of God, have the right or privilege of being sons of God. They are made partakers of a new nature. They have gotten eternal life. "He that believeth on the Son *hath* everlasting life" (John 3:36). "Verily, verily, I say unto you, he that *heareth* my word, and *believeth* on him that sent me, *hath* everlasting life, and shall not come into condemnation; but *is* passed from death unto life" (John 5:24). "And this *is* life eternal, that they might know thee, the only true God, and Jesus Christ, whom thou hast sent" (John 17:3). "And this is the record, that God hath given to us eternal life, and this life is in his Son." "He that hath the Son *hath* life" (1 John 5:11, 12).

Such is the plain doctrine of the Word in reference to the momentous questions of condition and nature. But on what is all this founded? How is the believer introduced into a condition of divine righteousness and made partaker of the divine nature? It all rests on the great truth that "JESUS DIED AND ROSE AGAIN." That Blessed One left the bosom of eternal love – the throne of glory – the mansions of unfading light – came down into this world of guilt and woe – took upon Him the likeness of sinful flesh; and, having perfectly exhibited and perfectly glorified God, in all the movements of His blessed life here below, He died upon the cross, under the full weight of His people's transgressions. By so doing, He divinely met all that was, or could be, against us. He magnified the law and made it honourable; and, having done so, He became a curse by hanging on the tree. Every claim was met, every enemy silenced, every obstacle removed. "Mercy and truth are met together; righteousness and peace have kissed each other." Infinite justice was satisfied, and infinite love can flow, in all its soothing and refreshing virtues, into the broken heart of the sinner; while, at the same time, the cleansing and atoning stream that flowed from the pierced side of a crucified Christ, perfectly meets all the cravings of a guilty and convicted conscience. The Lord Jesus, on the cross, stood in our place. He was our representative. He died, "the just for the unjust." "He was made sin for us" (2 Cor. 5:21; 1 Peter 3:18). He died the sinner's death, was buried, and rose again, having accomplished all. Hence, there is absolutely nothing against the believer. He is linked with Christ and stands in the same condition of righteousness. "As he is so are we in this world" (1 John 4:17).

This gives settled peace to the conscience. If I am no longer in a condition of guilt, but in a condition of justification; if God only sees me *in* Christ and as Christ, then, clearly, my portion is perfect peace. "Being justified by faith, we *have* peace with God through our Lord Jesus Christ" (Rom. 5:1). The blood of the Lamb has cancelled all the believer's guilt, blotted out his heavy debt, and given him a perfectly blank page, in the presence of that holiness which "cannot look upon sin."

But the believer has not merely found peace with God; he is made a child of God, so that he can taste the sweetness of communion with the Father and the Son, through the power of the Holy Ghost. The cross is to be viewed in two ways: first, as satisfying God's claims; secondly, as expressing God's affections. If I look at my sins in connexion with the claims of God as a Judge, I find, in the cross, a perfect settlement of those claims. God, as a Judge, has been divinely satisfied – yea, glorified, in the cross. But there is more than this. God had affections as well as claims; and, in the cross of the Lord Jesus Christ, all those affections are sweetly and touchingly told out into the sinner's ear; while, at the same time, he is made the partaker of a new nature which is capable of enjoying those affections and of having fellowship with the heart from which they flow. "For Christ also hath once suffered for sins, the just for the unjust, that he might bring us to God" (1 Peter 3:18). Thus we are not only brought into *a condition*, but unto *a Person*, even God Himself, and we are endowed with *a nature* which can delight in Him. *We also joy in God*, through our Lord Jesus Christ, by whom we have now received the atonement" (Rom. 5:11).

The purpose of Israel's deliverance

What force and beauty, therefore, can we see in those emancipating words, "Let my people go, that they may hold a feast unto me in the wilderness." "The Spirit of the Lord is upon me, because he hath anointed me to preach the gospel; he hath sent me to heal the broken-hearted, to preach deliverance to the captives, and recovering of sight to the blind, to set at liberty them that are bruised" (Luke 4:18). The glad tidings of the gospel announce full deliverance from every yoke of bondage. Peace and liberty are the boons which that gospel bestows on all who believe it, as God has declared it.

And mark, it is "that they may hold a feast to *me*." If they were to get done with Pharaoh, it was that they might begin with God. This was a great change. Instead of toiling under Pharaoh's taskmasters, they were to feast in company with Jehovah; and, although they were to pass from Egypt into the wilderness, still the divine presence was to accompany them; and if the wilderness was rough and dreary, it was the way to the land of Canaan. The divine purpose was, that they should hold a feast unto the Lord, in the wilderness; and, in order to do this, they should be "*let go*" out of Egypt.

Pharaoh's thoughts

However, Pharaoh was in no wise disposed to yield obedience to the divine mandate. "Who is the Lord," said he, "that I should obey his voice to let Israel go. I know not the Lord, neither will I let Israel go" (chap. 5:2). Pharaoh most truly expressed, in these words, his real condition. His condition was one of ignorance and consequent disobedience. Both go together. If God be not known, He cannot be obeyed; for obedience is ever founded upon knowledge. When the soul is blessed with the knowledge of God, it finds this knowledge to be life (John 17:3), and life is power; and when I get power I can act. It is obvious that one cannot act without life; and therefore it is most unintelligent to set people upon doing certain things, in order to get that by which alone they can do anything.

But Pharaoh was as ignorant of himself as he was of the Lord. He did not know that he was a poor, vile worm of the earth, and that he had been raised up for the express purpose of making known the glory of the very One whom he said he knew not (Exod. 9:16; Rom. 9:17). "And they said, The God of the Hebrews has met with us: let us go, we pray thee, three days journey into the desert, and sacrifice unto the Lord our God; lest he fall upon us with pestilence or with the sword. And the king of Egypt said unto them, Wherefore do ye, Moses and Aaron, let the people from their work? Get you unto your burdens . . . let there more work be laid upon the men, that they may labour therein; and let them not regard *vain words*" (Ver. 3-9).

What a development of the secret springs of the human heart we have here! What complete incompetency to enter into the things of God! All the divine titles and the divine revelations were, in Pharaoh's estimation, "vain words." What did he know or care about "three days journey into the wilderness," or "a feast to Jehovah?" How could he understand the need of such a journey, or the nature or object of such a feast? Impossible. He could understand burden-bearing and brick-making; these things had an air of reality about them, in his judgment; but as to anything of God, His service, or His worship, he could only regard it in the light of an idle chimera, devised by those who only wanted an excuse to make their escape from the stern realities of actual life.

Thus has it, too often, been with the wise and great of this world. They have ever been the most forward to write folly and vanity upon the divine testimonies. Hearken, for example, to the estimate which the "most noble Festus" formed of the grand question at issue between Paul and the Jews: "they had certain questions against him of their own superstition, and *of one Jesus which was dead, whom Paul affirmed to be alive*" (Acts 25:19). Alas! how little he knew what he was saying! How little he knew what was involved in the question, as to whether "Jesus" was "dead" or "alive!" He thought not of the solemn bearing of that momentous question upon himself and his friends, Agrippa and Bernice; but that did not alter the matter; he and they know somewhat more about it now, though in their passing moment of earthly glory they regarded it as a superstitious question, wholly beneath the notice of men of common sense, and only fit to occupy the disordered brain of visionary enthusiasts. Yes; the stupendous question which fixes the destiny of every child of Adam – on which is founded the present and everlasting condition of the Church and the world – which stands connected with all the divine counsels – this question was, in the judgment of Festus, a vain superstition.

Thus was it in Pharaoh's case. He knew nothing of "the Lord God of the Hebrews" – the great "I AM," and hence he regarded all that Moses and Aaron had said to him, in reference to doing sacrifice to God, as "vain words." The things of God must ever seem vain, profitless, and unmeaning, to the unsanctified mind of man. His name may be made use of as part of the flippant phraseology of a cold and formal religiousness; but He Himself is not known. His precious name, which, to a believer's heart, has wrapped up in it all that he can possibly need or desire, has no significancy, no power, no virtue for an unbeliever. All, therefore, connected with God, His words, His counsels, His thoughts, His ways, everything, in short, that treats of, or refers to, Him, is regarded as "vain words."

However, the time is rapidly approaching when it will not be thus. The judgment-seat of Christ, the terrors of the world to come, the surges of the lake of fire, will not be "vain words." Assuredly not; and it should be the great aim of all who, through grace, believe them now to be realities, to press them upon the consciences of those who, like Pharaoh, regard the making of bricks as the only thing worth thinking about – the only thing that can be called real and solid.

Alas! that even Christians should so frequently be found living in the region of sight, the region of earth, the region of nature, as to lose the deep, abiding, influential sense of the reality of divine and heavenly things. We want to live more in the region of faith, the region of heaven, the region of the "new creation." Then we should see things as God sees them, think about them as He thinks; and our whole course and character would be more elevated, more disinterested, more thoroughly separated from earth and earthly things.

Moses misunderstood by his brethren

But Moses' sorest trial did not arise from Pharaoh's judgment about his mission. The true and wholehearted servant of Christ must ever expect to be looked on, by the men of this world, as a mere visionary enthusiast. The point of view from which they contemplate him is such as to lead us to look for this judgment and none other. The more faithful he is to his heavenly Master, the more he walks in His footsteps, the more conformed he is to His image, the more likely he is to be considered, by the sons of earth, as one "beside himself." This, therefore, should neither disappoint nor discourage him. But then it is a far more painful thing when his service and testimony are misunderstood, unheeded, or rejected by those who are themselves the specific objects thereof. When such is the case, he needs to be much with God, much in the secret of His mind, much in the power of communion, to have his spirit sustained in the abiding reality of his path and service. Under such trying circumstances, if one be not fully persuaded of the divine commission, and conscious of the divine presence, he will be almost sure to break down.

Had not Moses been thus upheld, his heart must have utterly failed him when the augmented pressure of Pharaoh's power elicited from the officers of the children of Israel such desponding and depressing words as these: – "The Lord look upon you, and judge; because ye have made our savour to be abhorred in the eyes of Pharaoh, and in the eyes of his servants, to put a sword in their hand to slay us." This was gloomy enough; and Moses felt it so, for "he returned unto the Lord, and said, Lord, wherefore hast thou so evil entreated this people? Why is it that thou hast sent me? For since I came unto Pharaoh to speak in thy name, he hath done evil to this people; neither hast thou delivered thy people at all." The aspect of things had become most discouraging, at the very moment when deliverance seemed at hand; just as, in nature, the darkest hour of the night is often that which immediately precedes the dawn of the morning. Thus will it assuredly be, in Israel's history, in the latter day. The moment of most profound darkness and depressing gloom will precede the bursting of "the Sun of Righteousness" from behind the cloud, with healing in His wings, to heal eternally, "the hurt of the daughter of His people."

Encouragement for Moses

We may well question how far genuine faith, or a mortified will, dictated the "*wherefore?*" and the "*why?*" of Moses, in the above quotation. Still, the Lord does not rebuke a remonstrance drawn forth by the intense pressure of the moment. He most graciously replies, " Now shalt thou see what I will do to Pharaoh: for with a strong hand shall he let them go, and with a strong hand shall he drive them out of his land" (chap. 6:1). This reply breathes peculiar grace. Instead of reproving the petulance which could presume to call in question the unsearchable ways of the great I AM, that ever gracious One seeks to relieve the harassed spirit of His servant, by unfolding to him what He was about to do. This was worthy of the blessed God – the unupbraiding Giver of every good and every perfect gift. "He knoweth our frame; he remembereth that we are dust" (Ps. 103:14).

God reveals His name as Jehovah

Nor is it merely in His actings that He would cause the heart to find its solace, but in Himself – in His very name and character. This is full, divine, and everlasting blessedness. When the heart can find its sweet relief in God Himself – when it can retreat into the strong tower which His name affords – when it can find, in His character, a perfect answer to all its need, then truly, it is raised far above the region of the creature – it can turn away from earth's fair promises – it can place the proper value on man's lofty pretensions. The heart which is endowed with an experimental knowledge of God can not only look forth upon earth, and say "all is vanity," but it can also look straight up to Him, and say, "all my springs are in thee."

"And God spake unto Moses, and said unto him, I am the Lord: and I appeared unto Abraham, unto Isaac, and unto Jacob, by the name of God Almighty; but by my name JEHOVAH was I not known to them. And I have also established my covenant with them to give them the land of Canaan, the land of their pilgrimage, wherein they were strangers. And I have also heard the groaning of the children of Israel, whom the Egyptians keep in bondage; and I have remembered my covenant." "JEHOVAH" is the title which He takes as the Deliverer of His people, on the ground of His covenant of pure and sovereign grace He reveals Himself as the great self-existing Source of redeeming love, establishing His counsels, fulfilling His promises, delivering His elect people from every enemy and every evil. It was Israel's privilege ever to abide under the safe covert of that significant title – a title which displays God acting for His own glory, and taking up His oppressed people in order to show forth in them that glory.

"Wherefore say unto the children of Israel, I am the Lord, and I will bring you out from under the burdens of the Egyptians, and I will rid you out of their bondage, and I will redeem you with a stretched out arm, and with great judgments. And I will take you to me for a people, and I will be to you a God; and ye shall know that I am the Lord your God, which bringeth you out from under the burdens of the Egyptians. And I will bring you in unto the land concerning the which I did swear to give it unto Abraham, to Isaac, and to Jacob; and I will give it you for an heritage: I am the Lord" (ver. 6-8.). All this speaks the purest, freest, richest grace. Jehovah presents Himself to the hearts of His people as the One who was to act *in* them, *for* them, and *with* them, for the display of His own glory. Ruined and helpless as they were, He had come down to show forth His glory, to exhibit His grace, and to furnish a sample of His power, in their full deliverance. His glory and their salvation were inseparably connected. They were afterwards reminded of all this, as we read in the book of Deuteronomy. "The Lord did not set His love upon you nor choose you, because ye were more in number than any people; for ye were the fewest of all people; but because the Lord loved you, and because he would keep the oath which he had sworn unto your fathers, hath the Lord brought you out with a mighty hand, and redeemed you out of the house of bondmen, from the hand of Pharaoh king of Egypt" (Deut. 7:7, 8).

God loves us as we are

Nothing is more calculated to assure and establish the doubting, trembling heart than the knowledge that God has taken us up, *just as we are*, and in the full intelligence of what we are; and, moreover, that He can never make any fresh discovery to cause an alteration in the character and measure of His love. "Having loved his own which were in the world, he loved them unto the end" (John 13). *Whom* He loves and *as* He loves, He loves unto the end. This is an unspeakable comfort. God knew all about us – He knew the very worst of us, when He manifested His love to us in the gift of His Son. He knew what was needed, and He provided it. He knew what was due, and He paid it. He knew what was to be wrought, and He wrought it. His own requirements had to be met, and He met them. It is all His own work. Hence, we find Him saying to Israel, as in the above passage, "I will bring you out" – "I will bring you in" – "I will take you to me" – "I will give you the land" – "I am Jehovah." It was all what *He would do*, as founded upon what *He was*. Until this great truth is fully laid hold of, until it enters into the soul, in the power of the Holy Ghost, there cannot be settled peace. The heart can never be happy or the conscience at rest until one knows and believes that all divine requirements have been divinely answered.

Record of the families of Israel

The remainder of our section is taken up with a record of "the heads of their fathers' houses," and is very interesting, as showing us Jehovah coming in and numbering those that belonged to Himself, though they were still in the possession of the enemy. Israel was God's people, and He here counts up those on whom He had a sovereign claim. Amazing grace! To find an object in those who were in the midst of all the degradation of Egyptian bondage! This was worthy of God. The One who had made the worlds, who was surrounded by hosts of unfallen angels, ever ready to "do his pleasure," should come down for the purpose of taking up a number of bondslaves with whom He condescended to connect His name. He came down and stood amid the brick-kilns of Egypt, and there beheld a people groaning beneath the lash of the task-masters, and He uttered those memorable accents, "Let *my* people go;" and, having so said, He proceeded to count them up, as much as to say, "These are mine; let me see how many I have, that not one may be left behind." "He taketh up the beggar from the dunghill, to set him amongst the princes of his people, and to make him inherit the throne of glory" (1 Sam. 2).

Chapters 7-11

THE TEN PLAGUES OF EGYPT

These five chapters form one distinct section, the contents of which may be distributed into the three following divisions, namely, the ten judgments from the hand of Jehovah; the resistance of "Jannes and Jambres;" and the four objections of Pharaoh.

The judgments of the Lord on the oppressors

The whole land of Egypt was made to tremble beneath the successive strokes of the rod of God. All from the monarch on his throne to the menial at the mill, were made to feel the terrible weight of that rod. "He sent Moses his servant, and Aaron whom he had chosen. They showed his signs among them, and wonders in the land of Ham. He sent darkness and made it dark; and they rebelled not against his word. He turned their waters into blood, and slew their fish. Their land brought forth frogs in abundance, in the chambers of their kings. He spake, and there came divers sorts of flies and lice in all their coasts. He gave them hail for rain, and flaming fire in their land. He smote their vines also, and their fig-trees; and brake the trees of their coasts. He spake, and their locusts came, and the caterpillars, and that without number, and did eat up all the herbs in their land, and devoured the fruit of their ground. He smote also all the firstborn in their land, the chief of all their strength" (Ps. 105:26-36).

Here the inspired Psalmist has given a condensed view of those appalling afflictions which the hardness of Pharaoh's heart brought upon his land and upon his people. This haughty monarch had set himself to resist the sovereign will and course of the Most High God; and, as a just consequence, he was given over to judicial blindness and hardness of heart. "And the Lord hardened the heart of Pharaoh, and he hearkened not unto them, as the Lord had spoken unto Moses. And the Lord said unto Moses, Rise up early in the morning, and stand before Pharaoh: and say unto him, Thus saith the Lord God of the Hebrews, Let my people go, that they may serve me. For I will at this time send all my plagues upon thine heart, and upon thy servants, and upon thy people; that thou mayest know that there is none like me in all the earth. For now I will stretch out my hand that I may smite thee and thy people with pestilence; and thou shalt be cut off from the earth. And in very deed for this cause have I raised thee up, for to show in thee my power; and that my name may be declared throughout all the earth" (Exod. 9:12-16).

In contemplating Pharaoh and his actings, the mind is carried forward to the stirring scenes of the Book of Revelation, in which we find the last proud oppressor of the people of God bringing down upon his kingdom and upon himself the seven vials of the wrath of the Almighty. It is God's purpose that Israel shall be pre-eminent in the earth; and, therefore, every one who presumes to stand in the way of that pre-eminence must be set aside. Divine grace must find its object; and every one who would act as a barrier in the way of that grace must be taken out of the way. Whether it be Egypt, Babylon, or "the beast that was, is not, and shall be present," it matters not. Divine power will clear the channel for divine grace to flow, and eternal woe be to all who stand in the way. They shall taste, throughout the everlasting course of ages, the bitter fruit of having exalted themselves against "the Lord God of the Hebrews." He has said to His people, "no weapon that is formed against thee shall prosper," and His infallible faithfulness will assuredly make good what His infinite grace hath promised.

Thus, in Pharaoh's case, when he persisted in holding, with an iron grasp, the Israel of God, the vials of divine wrath were poured forth upon him; and the land of Egypt was covered, throughout its entire length and breadth, with darkness, disease, and desolation. So will it be, by and by, when the last great oppressor shall emerge from the bottomless pit, armed with Satanic power, to crush beneath his "foot of pride" the favoured objects of Jehovah's choice. His throne shall be overturned, his kingdom devastated by the seven last plagues, and, finally, he himself plunged, not in the Red Sea, but "in the lake that burneth with fire and brimstone" (comp. Rev. 17:8; 20:10).

Not one jot or one tittle of what God has promised to Abraham, Isaac, and Jacob, shall fail. He will accomplish all. Notwithstanding all that has been said and done to the contrary, God remembers His promises, and He will fulfil them. They are all "yea and amen in Christ Jesus." Dynasties have risen and acted on the stage of this world; thrones have been erected on the apparent ruins of Jerusalem's ancient glory; empires have flourished for a time, and then fallen to decay; ambitious potentates have contended for the possession of "the land of promise" – all these things have taken place; but Jehovah has said concerning Palestine," the land shall not be sold for ever: for the land is mine" (Lev. 25:23). No one, therefore, shall ever finally possess that land but Jehovah Himself, and He will inherit it through the seed of Abraham. One plain passage of scripture is quite sufficient to establish the mind in reference to this or any other subject. The land of Canaan is for the seed of Abraham, and the seed of Abraham for the land of Canaan; nor can any power of earth or hell ever reverse this divine order. The eternal God has pledged His word, and the blood of the everlasting covenant has flowed to ratify that word. Who, then, shall make it void? "Heaven and earth shall pass away, but that word shall never pass away." Truly, "there is none like unto the God of Jeshurun, who rideth upon the heaven in thy help, and in his excellency on the sky. The eternal God is thy refuge, and underneath are the everlasting arms, and he shall thrust out the enemy from before thee; and shall say, Destroy them. Israel then shall dwell in safety alone: the fountain of Jacob shall be upon a land of corn and wine; also his heavens shall drop down dew. Happy art thou, O Israel: who is like unto thee, O people saved by the Lord, the shield of thy help, and who is the sword of thy excellency! and thine enemies shall be found liars unto thee; and thou shalt tread upon their high places" (Deut. 33:26-29).

The opposition of the magicians

We shall now consider, in the second place, the opposition of "Jannes and Jambres," the magicians of Egypt. We should not have known the names of these ancient opposers of the truth of God, had they not been recorded by the Holy Ghost, in connexion with "the perilous times" of which the Apostle Paul warns his son Timothy. It is important that the Christian reader should clearly understand the real nature of the opposition given to Moses by those magicians, and in order that he may have the subject fully before him, I shall quote the entire passage from St. Paul's Epistle to Timothy. It is one of deep and awful solemnity.

"This know, also, that in the last days perilous times shall come. For men shall be lovers of their own selves, covetous, boasters, proud, blasphemers, disobedient to parents, unthankful, unholy, without natural affection, truce-breakers, false accusers, incontinent, fierce, despisers of those that are good, traitors, heady, high minded, lovers of pleasures rather than lovers of God; having a form of godliness, but denying the power thereof: from such turn away. For of this sort are they which creep into houses, and lead captive silly women laden with sins, led away with divers lusts, ever learning, and never able to come to the knowledge of the truth. Now as Jannes and Jambres withstood Moses, so do these also resist the truth: men of corrupt minds, reprobate concerning the faith. But they shall proceed no further: for their folly shall be manifest unto all, as theirs also was" (2 Tim. 3:1-9).

Now, it is peculiarly solemn to mark the nature of this resistance to the truth. The mode in which "Jannes and

Jambres withstood Moses" was simply by imitating, so far as they were able, whatever he did. We do not find that they attributed his actings to a false or evil energy, but rather that they sought to neutralise their power upon the conscience, by doing the same things. What Moses did they could do, so that, after all there was no great difference. One was as good as the other. A miracle is a miracle. If Moses wrought miracles to get the people out of Egypt, they could work miracles to keep them in; so where was the difference?

From all this we learn the solemn truth that the most Satanic resistance to God's testimony, in the world, is offered by those who, though they imitate the effects of the truth, have but "the form of godliness," and "deny the power thereof." Persons of this class can do the same things, adopt the same habits and forms, use the same phraseology, profess the same opinions as others. If the true Christian, constrained by the love of Christ, feeds the hungry, clothes the naked, visits the sick, circulates the scriptures, distributes tracts, supports the gospel, engages in prayer, sings praise, preaches the gospel, the formalist can do every one of these things; and this, be it observed, is the special character of the resistance offered to the truth "in the last days" – this is the spirit of "Jannes and Jambres." How needful to understand this! How important to remember that, "*as* Jannes and Jambres withstood Moses, *so* do" those self-loving, world-seeking, pleasure-hunting professors, "resist the truth!" They would not be without "a form of godliness;" but, while adopting "the form," because it is customary, they hate "the power," because it involves self-denial. "The power" of godliness involves the recognition of God's claims, the implanting of His kingdom in the heart, and the consequent exhibition thereof in the whole life and character; but the formalist knows nothing of this. "The power" of godliness could never comport with any one of those hideous features set forth in the foregoing quotation; but "the form," while it covers them over, leaves them wholly unsubdued; and this the formalist likes. He does not want his lusts subdued, his pleasures interfered with, his passions curbed, his affections governed, his heart purified. He wants just as much religion as will enable him "to make the best of both worlds." He knows nothing of giving up the world that is, because of having found "the world to come."

In marking the forms of Satan's opposition to the truth of God, we find that his method has ever been, first, to oppose it by open violence; and then, if that did not succeed, to corrupt it by producing a counterfeit. Hence, he first sought to slay Moses, (chap. 2:15), and having failed to accomplish his purpose, he sought to imitate his works.

Thus, too, has it been in reference to the truth committed to the Church of God. Satan's early efforts showed themselves in connexion with the wrath of the chief priests and elders, the judgment-seat, the prison, and the sword. But, in the passage just quoted from 2 Timothy, we find no reference to any such agency. Open violence has made way for the far more wily and dangerous instrumentality of a powerless form, an empty profession, a human counterfeit. The enemy, instead of appearing with the sword of persecution in his hand, walks about with the cloak of profession on his shoulders. He professes and imitates that which he once opposed and persecuted; and, by so doing, gains most appalling advantages, for the time being. The fearful forms of moral evil which, from age to age, have stained the page of human history, instead of being found only where we might naturally look for them, amid the dens and caves of human darkness, are to be found carefully arranged beneath the drapery of a cold, powerless, uninfluential profession; and this is one of Satan's grand masterpieces.

That man, as a fallen, corrupt creature, should love himself, be covetous, boastful, proud, and the like, is natural; but that he should be all these, beneath the fair covering of "a form of godliness," marks the special energy of Satan in his resistance to the truth in "the last days." That man should stand forth in the bold exhibition of those hideous vices, lusts, and passions, which are the necessary results of departure from the source of infinite holiness and purity, is only what might be expected, for man will be what he is to the end of the chapter. But on the other hand, when we find the holy name of the Lord Jesus Christ connected with man's wickedness and deadly evil – when we find holy principles connected with unholy practices – when we find all the characteristics of Gentile corruption, referred to in the first chapter of Romans, associated with "a form of godliness," then, truly, we may say, these are the terrible features of "the last days" – this is the resistance of "Jannes and Jambres."

However, there were only three things in which the magicians of Egypt were able to imitate the servants of the true and living God, namely, in turning their rods into serpents (chap. 7:12), turning the water into blood (chap. 7:22), and bringing up the frogs (chap. 8: 7); but, in the fourth, which involved the exhibition of life, in connexion with the display of nature's humiliation, they were totally confounded, and obliged to own, " this is the finger of God" (chap. 8:16-19). Thus it is also with the latter-day resisters of the truth. All that they do is by the direct energy of Satan, and lies within the range of his power. Moreover, its specific object is to "resist the truth."

The three things which "Jannes and Jambres" were able to accomplish were characterised by Satanic energy, death, and uncleanness; that is to say, the serpents, the blood, and the frogs. Thus it was they "withstood Moses;" and "so do these also resist the truth," and hinder its moral weight and action upon the conscience. There is nothing which so tends to deaden the power of truth as the fact that persons who are not under its influence at all, do the self-same things as those who are. This is Satan's agency just now. He seeks to have all regarded as Christians. He would fain make us believe ourselves surrounded by "a Christian world;" but it is counterfeit Christianity, which, so far from being a testimony to the truth, is designed by the enemy of the truth, to withstand its purifying and elevating influence.

In short, the servant of Christ and the witness for the truth is surrounded, on all sides, by the spirit of "Jannes and Jambres;" and it is well for him to remember this – to know thoroughly the evil with which he has to grapple – to bear in mind that it is Satan's imitation of God's reality, produced, not by the wand of an openly-wicked magician, but by the actings of false professors, who have "a form of godliness, but deny the power thereof," who do things apparently right and good, but who have neither the life of Christ in their souls, the love of God in their hearts, nor the power of the word in their consciences.

"But," adds the inspired apostle, "they shall proceed no further, for their folly shall be manifested unto all, as theirs also was." Truly the "folly" of "Jannes and Jambres" was manifest unto all, when they not only failed to imitate the further actings of Moses and Aaron, but actually became involved in the judgments of God. This is a solemn point. The folly of all who are merely possessed of the form will, in like manner, be made manifest. They will not only be quite unable to imitate the full and proper effects of divine life and power, but they will themselves become the subjects of those judgments which will result from the rejection of that truth which they have resisted.

Will any one say that all this has no voice for a day of powerless profession? Assuredly, it has. It should speak to each conscience in living power; it should tell on each heart, in accents of impressive solemnity. It should lead each one to enquire seriously whether he is testifying for the truth, by walking in the power of godliness, or hindering it, and neutralising its action, by having only the form. The effect of the power of godliness will be seen by our "continuing in the things which we have learned." None will continue, save those who are taught of God; those, by the power of the Spirit of God, have drunk in divine principle, at the pure fountain of inspiration.

Blessed be God, there are many such throughout the various sections of the professing Church. There are many, here and there, whose consciences have been bathed in the atoning blood of "the Lamb of God," whose hearts beat high with genuine attachment to His Person, and whose spirits are cheered by "that blessed hope" of seeing Him as He is, and of being eternally conformed to His image. It is encouraging to think of such. It is an unspeakable mercy to have fellowship with those who can give a reason of the hope that is in them, and for the position which they occupy. May the Lord add to their number daily. May the power of godliness spread far and wide in these last days, so that a bright and well-sustained testimony may be raised to the name of Him who is worthy.

PHARAOH'S OBJECTIONS TO ISRAEL'S LEAVING

The third point in our section yet remains to be considered, namely, Pharaoh's four subtle objections to the full deliverance and complete separation of God's people from the land of Egypt.

The first objection

The first of these we have in chapter 8:25. "And Pharaoh called for Moses and Aaron, and said, Go ye, *sacrifice to your God in the land.*" It is needless to remark here, that whether the magicians withstood, or Pharaoh objected, it was in reality, Satan that stood behind the scenes; and his manifest object, in this proposal of Pharaoh, was to hinder the testimony to the Lord's name – a testimony connected with the thorough separation of His people from Egypt. There could, evidently, be no such testimony had they remained in Egypt, even though they were to sacrifice to Him. They would have taken common ground with the uncircumcised Egyptians, and put Jehovah on a level with the gods of Egypt.

In this case an Egyptian could have said to an Israelite, "I see no difference between us; you have your worship and we have ours; it is all alike."

As a matter of course, men think it quite right for every one to have a religion, let it be what it may. Provided we are sincere, and do not interfere with our neighbour's creed, it does not matter what shape our religion may happen to wear. Such are the thoughts of men in reference to what they call religion; but it is very obvious that the glory of the name of Jesus finds no place in all this. The demand for separation is that which the enemy will ever oppose, and which the heart of man cannot understand. The heart may crave religiousness because conscience testifies that all is not right; but it craves the world as well. It would like to "sacrifice to God in the land;" and Satan's object is gained when people accept of a worldly religion, and refuse to "come out and be separate" (2 Cor. 6). His unvarying purpose, from the beginning, has been to hinder the testimony to God's name on the earth. Such was the dark tendency of the proposal, "Go ye, sacrifice to your God in the land." What a complete damper to the testimony, had this proposal been acceded to! God's people in Egypt and God Himself linked with the idols of Egypt! Terrible blasphemy!

Reader, we should deeply ponder this. The effort to induce Israel to worship God in Egypt reveals a far deeper principle than we might, at first sight, imagine. The enemy would rejoice, at any time, by any means, or under any circumstances, to get even the semblance of divine sanction for the world's religion. He has no objection to such religion. He gains his end as effectually by what is termed "the religious world" as by any other agency; and, hence, when he can succeed in getting a true Christian to accredit the religion of the day, he gains a grand point. As a matter of actual fact, one knows that nothing elicits such intense indignation as the divine principle of separation from this present evil world. You may hold the same opinions, preach the same doctrines, do the same work; but if you only attempt, in ever so feeble a manner, to act upon the divine commands, "from such turn away" (2 Tim. 3:5), and "come out from among them" (2 Cor. 6:17), you may reckon assuredly upon the most vigorous opposition. Now how is this to be accounted for? Mainly by the fact that Christians, in separation from this world's hollow religiousness, bear a testimony for Christ which they never can bear while connected with it.

There is a very wide difference between human religion and Christ. A poor, benighted Hindu might talk to you of his religion, but he knows nothing of Christ. The apostle does not say, "if there be any consolation in religion;" though, doubtless, the votaries of each kind of religion find what they deem consolation therein. Paul, on the other hand, found his consolation in Christ, having fully proved the worthlessness of religion, and that too, in its fairest and most imposing form (comp. Gal. 1:13, 14; Phil. 3:4-11).

True, the Spirit of God speaks to us of "pure religion and undefiled;" but the unregenerate man cannot, by any means, participate therein; for how could he possibly take part in anything that is "pure and undefiled?" This religion is from heaven, the source of all that is pure and lovely; it is exclusively before the eye of "God and the Father;" it is for the exercise of the functions of that new nature, with which all are endowed who believe on the name of the Son of God (John 1:12, 13; James 1:18; 1 Peter 1:23; 1 John 5:1) Finally, it ranges itself under the two comprehensive heads of active benevolence and personal holiness; "To visit the fatherless and widows in their affliction, and to keep himself unspotted from the world" (James 1:27).

Now if you go through the entire catalogue of the genuine fruits of Christianity, you will find them all classed under these two heads; and it is deeply interesting to observe that, whether we turn to the eighth of Exodus or to the first of James, we find separation from the world put forward as an indispensable quality in the true service of God. Nothing could be acceptable before God – nothing could receive from His hand the stamp of "pure and undefiled," which was polluted by contact with an "evil world." "Come out from among them, and be ye separate, saith the Lord, and touch not the unclean thing; and I will receive you, and will be a father unto you, and ye shall be my sons and daughters, saith the Lord Almighty" (2 Cor. 6:17, 18).

There was no meeting-place for Jehovah and His redeemed in Egypt; yea, with them, redemption and separation from Egypt were one and the same thing. God had said, "I am come down to deliver them," and nothing short of this could either satisfy or glorify Him. A salvation which would have left them still in Egypt, could not possibly be God's salvation. Moreover, we must bear in mind that Jehovah's purpose, in the salvation of Israel, as well as in the destruction of Pharaoh, was, that "His name might be declared throughout all the earth;" and what declaration could there be of that name or character, were His people to attempt to worship Him in Egypt? Either none whatever or an utterly false one. Wherefore, it was essentially necessary, in order to the full and faithful declaration of God's character, that His people should be wholly delivered and completely separated from Egypt, and it is as essentially necessary now, in order to a clear and unequivocal testimony for the Son of God, that all who are really His should be separated from this present world. Such is the will of God; and for this end Christ gave Himself. "Grace unto you, and peace from God the Father, and our Lord Jesus Christ, who gave himself for our sins, that he might deliver us from this present evil world, according to the will of God and our Father: to whom be glory for ever and ever. Amen" (Gal. 1:3-5).

The Galatians were beginning to accredit a carnal and worldly religion – a religion of ordinances – a religion of "days, and months, and times, and years;" and the apostle commences his epistle by telling them that the Lord Jesus Christ gave Himself for the purpose of delivering His people from that very thing. God's people must be separate, not, by any means, on the ground of their superior personal sanctity, but because they are His people, and in order that they may rightly and intelligently answer His gracious end in taking them into connexion with Himself, and attaching His name to them. A people, still amid the defilements and abominations of Egypt, could not have been a witness for the Holy One; nor can any one, now, while mixed up with the defilements of a corrupt worldly religion, possibly be a bright and steady witness for a crucified and risen Christ.

The three days' journey and the true position of the believer outside the world

The answer given by Moses to Pharaoh's first objection was a truly memorable one. "And Moses said, It is not meet so to do; for we shall sacrifice the abomination of the Egyptians to the Lord our God; lo, shall we sacrifice the abomination of the Egyptians before their eyes, and will they not stone us? We will go three days' journey into the wilderness, and sacrifice to the Lord our God, as he shall command us" (chap. 8:26, 27). Here is true separation from Egypt – "three days journey." Nothing less than this could satisfy faith. The Israel of God must be separated from the land of death and darkness, in the power of resurrection. The waters of the Red Sea must roll between God's redeemed and Egypt, ere they can properly sacrifice to Jehovah. Had they remained in Egypt, they would have to sacrifice to the Lord the very objects of Egypt's abominable worship.[4] This would never do. There could be no tabernacle, no temple, no altar, in Egypt. It had no site, throughout its entire limits, for anything of that kind. In point of fact, as we shall see further on, Israel never presented so much as a single note of praise, until the whole congregation stood, in the full power of an accomplished redemption, on Canaan's side of the Red Sea. Exactly so is it now. The believer must know where the death and resurrection of the Lord Jesus Christ have, for ever, set him, ere he can be an intelligent worshipper, an acceptable servant, or an effectual witness.

It is not a question of being a child of God, and, as such, a saved person. Many of the children of God are very far from knowing the full results, as regards themselves, of the death and resurrection of Christ. They do not apprehend the precious truth, that the death of Christ has made an end of their sins for ever, and that they are the happy partakers of His resurrection life, with which sin can have nothing whatever to do. Christ became a curse for us, not, as some would teach us, by being born under the curse of a broken law, but by hanging on a tree (compare attentively Deut. 21:23; Gal. 3:13). We were under the curse, because we had not kept the law; but Christ, the perfect Man, having magnified the law and made it honourable, by the very fact of His obeying it perfectly, became a curse for us, by hanging on the tree. Thus, in His life He magnified God's law; and in His death He bore our curse. There is, therefore, now, no guilt, no curse, no wrath, no condemnation for the believer; and, albeit, he must be manifested before the judgment-seat of Christ, he will find that judgment-seat every whit as friendly by and by, as the mercy-seat is now. It will make manifest the truth of his condition, namely, that there is nothing against him; what he is, it is God "that hath wrought him." He is God's workmanship. He was taken up in a state of death and condemnation, and made just what God would have him to be. The Judge Himself has put away all his sins, and is his righteousness, so that the judgment-seat cannot but be friendly to him; yea, it will be the full, public, authoritative declaration to heaven, earth, and hell, that the one who is washed from his sins in the blood of the Lamb, is as clean as God can make him (see John 5:24; Rom. 8:1; 2 Cor. 5:5, 10, 11; Eph. 2:10.). All that had to be done, God Himself has done it. He surely will not condemn His own work. The righteousness that was required, God Himself has provided it. He, surely, will not find any flaw therein. The light of the judgment seat will be bright enough to disperse every mist and cloud which might tend to obscure the matchless glories and eternal virtues which belong to the cross, and to show that the believer is "clean every whit" (John 13:10; John 15:3; Eph. 5:27).

It is because these foundation-truths are not laid hold of in the simplicity of faith that many of the children of God complain of their lack of settled peace – the constant variation in their spiritual condition – the continual ups and downs in their experience. Every doubt in the heart of a Christian is a dishonour done to the word of God and the sacrifice of Christ. It is because he does not, even now, bask in the light which shall shine from the judgment-seat, that he is ever afflicted with a doubt or a fear. And yet those things which so many have to deplore – those fluctuations and waverings are but trifling consequences, comparatively, inasmuch as they merely affect their experience. The effect produced upon their worship, their service, and their testimony, is far more serious, inasmuch as the Lord's honour is concerned. But, alas! this latter is but little thought of, generally speaking, simply because personal salvation is the grand object – the aim and end, with the majority of professing Christians. We are prone to look upon everything that affects ourselves as *essential*; whereas, all that merely affects the glory of Christ in and by us is counted *non-essential*.

However, it is well to see with distinctness, that the same truth which gives the soul settled peace, puts it also into the position of intelligent worship, acceptable service, and effectual testimony. In the fifteenth chapter of 1 Corinthians, the apostle sets forth the death and resurrection of Christ as the grand foundation of everything. "Moreover, brethren, I declare unto you the gospel which I preached unto you, which also ye have received, and wherein ye stand; by which also ye are saved, if ye keep in memory what I preached unto you, unless ye have believed in vain. For I delivered unto you first of all that which I also received, how that Christ died for our sins according to the scriptures, and that he was buried, and that he rose again the third day according to the scriptures" (ver. 1-4). Here is the gospel, in one brief and comprehensive statement. A dead and risen Christ is the ground-work of salvation. "He was delivered for our offences, and raised again for our justification" (Rom. 4:25). To see Jesus, by the eye of faith, nailed to the cross, and seated on the throne, must give solid peace to the conscience and perfect liberty to the heart. We can look into the tomb and see it empty; we can look up to the throne, and see it occupied, and go on our way rejoicing. The Lord Jesus settled everything on the cross on behalf of His people; and the proof of this settlement is that He is now at the right hand of God. A risen Christ is the eternal proof of an accomplished redemption; and if redemption is an accomplished fact, the believer's peace is a settled reality. We did not make peace and never could make it; indeed, any effort on our part to make peace could only tend more fully to manifest us as *peace-breakers*. But Christ, having made peace by the blood of His cross, has taken His seat on high, triumphant over every enemy. By Him God preaches peace. The word of the gospel conveys this peace; and the soul that believes the gospel has peace – settled peace before God, for Christ is his peace (see Acts 10:36; Rom. 5:1; Eph. 2:14; Col. 1:20). In this way, God has not only satisfied His own claims, but, in so doing, He has found out a divinely-righteous vent through which His boundless affections may flow down to the guiltiest of Adam's guilty progeny.

Then, as to the practical result of all this. The cross of Christ has not only put away the believer's sins, but also dissolved for ever his connexion with the world; and, on the ground of this, he is privileged to regard the world as a crucified *thing*, and to be regarded by it as a crucified one. Thus it stands with the believer and the world. It is crucified to him and he to it. This is the real, dignified position of every true Christian. The world's judgment about Christ was expressed in the position in which it deliberately placed Him. It got its choice as to whether it would have a murderer or Christ. It allowed the murderer to go free, but nailed Christ to the cross, between two thieves. Now, if the believer walks in the footprints of Christ – if he drinks into, and manifests, His spirit, he will occupy the very same place in the world's estimation; and, in this way, he will not merely know that, as to standing before God, he is crucified with Christ, but be led to realise it in his walk and experience every day.

But while the cross has thus effectually cut the connexion between the believer and the world, the resurrection has brought him into the power of new ties and associations. If, in the cross, we see the world's judgment about Christ, in resurrection we see God's judgment. The world crucified Him; but "God hath highly exalted him." Man gave Him the very lowest, God the very highest, place; and, inasmuch as the believer is called into full fellowship with God, in his thoughts about Christ, he is enabled to turn the tables upon the world, and look upon it as a crucified thing. If, therefore, the believer is on one cross and the world on another, the moral distance between the two is vast indeed. And if it is vast in principle, so should it be in practice. The world and the Christian should have absolutely nothing in common; nor will they, except so far as he denies his Lord and Master. The believer proves himself false to Christ, to the very same degree that he has fellowship with the world.

All this is plain enough; but, my beloved Christian reader, where does it put us as regards this world? Truly, it puts us outside and that completely. We are dead to the world and alive with Christ. We are at once partakers of His rejection by earth and His acceptance in heaven; and the joy of the latter makes us count as nothing the trial connected with the former. To be cast out of earth, without knowing that I have a place and a portion on high, would be intolerable; but when the glories of heaven fill the soul's vision, a little of earth goes a great way.

But some may feel led to ask, "What is the world?" It would be difficult to find a term more inaccurately defined than "world," or "worldliness;" for we are generally disposed to make worldliness begin a point or two above where we are ourselves. The Word of God, however, has, with perfect precision, defined what "the world" is, when it marks it as that which is "not of the Father." Hence, the deeper my fellowship with the Father, the keener will be my sense of what is worldly. This is the divine way of teaching. The more you delight in the Father's love, the more you reject the world. But who reveals the Father? The Son. How? By the power of the Holy Ghost. Wherefore, the more I am enabled, in the power of an ungrieved Spirit, to drink in the Son's revelation of the Father, the more accurate does my judgment become as to what is of the world. It is as the limits of God's kingdom expand in the heart, that the judgment as to worldliness becomes refined. You can hardly attempt to define worldliness. It is, as some one has said, "shaded off gradually from white to jet black." This is most true. You cannot place a bound and say, "here is where worldliness begins;" but the keen and exquisite sensibilities of the divine nature recoil from it; and all we need is, to walk in the power of that nature, in order to keep aloof from every form of worldliness. "Walk in the Spirit, and ye shall not fulfil the lusts of the flesh." Walk with God, and ye shall not walk with the world. Cold distinctions and rigid rules will avail nothing. The power of the divine life is what we want. We want to understand the meaning and spiritual application of the "three days' journey into the wilderness" whereby we are separated for ever, not only from Egypt's brick-kilns and taskmasters, but also from its temples and altars.

The second objection

Pharaoh's second objection partook very much of the character and tendency of the first. "And Pharaoh said, I will let you go, that ye may sacrifice to the Lord your God in the wilderness; *only ye shall not go very far away*" (chap. 8:28). If he could not keep them *in* Egypt, he would at least seek to keep them *near* it, so that he might act upon them by its varied influences. In this way, they might be brought back again, and the testimony more effectually quashed than if they had never left Egypt at all. There is always much more serious damage done to the cause of Christ by persons seeming to give up the world and returning to it again, than if they had remained entirely of it; for they virtually confess that, having tried heavenly things, they have discovered that earthly things are better and more satisfying.

Nor is this all. The moral effect of truth upon the conscience of unconverted people is sadly interfered with, by the example of professors going back again into those things which they seemed to have left. Not that such cases afford the slightest warrant to any one for the rejection of God's truth, inasmuch as each one is personally responsible and will have to give account of himself to God. Still, however, the effect in this, as well as in everything else, is bad. "For if after they have escaped the pollutions of the world, through the knowledge of the Lord and Saviour Jesus Christ, they are again entangled therein and overcome, the latter end is worse with them than the beginning. For it would have been better for them not to have known the way of righteousness than, after they have known it, to turn from the holy commandment delivered unto them (2 Peter 2:20, 21).

Wherefore, if people do not "go very far away," they had better not go at all. The enemy knew this well; and hence his second objection. The maintenance of a border position suits his purpose amazingly. Those who occupy this ground are neither one thing nor the other; and, in point of fact, whatever influence they possess, tells entirely in the wrong direction.

It is deeply important to see that Satan's design, in all these objections, was to hinder that testimony to the name of the God of Israel, which could only be rendered by a "three days' journey into the wilderness." This was, in good truth, going "very far away." It was much farther than Pharaoh could form any idea of, or than he could follow them. And oh! how happy it would be if all who profess to set out from Egypt would really, in the spirit of their minds and in the tone of their character, go thus far away from it! if they would intelligently recognise the cross and grave of Christ as forming the boundary between them and the world! No man, in the mere energy of nature, can take this ground. The Psalmist could say," Enter not into judgment with thy servant, for in thy sight shall no man living be justified" (Ps. 143:2). So also is it with regard to true and effectual separation from the world. "*No man living*" can enter into it. It is only as "*dead* with Christ," and "risen again with him, through faith of the operation of God," that any one can either be "justified" before God, or separated from the world. This is what we may call going "very far away." May all who profess and call themselves Christians go thus far! Then will their lamp yield a steady light. Then would their trumpet give a certain sound. Their path would be elevated; their experience deep and rich. Their peace would flow as a river; their affections would be heavenly and their garments unspotted. And, far above all, the name of the Lord Jesus Christ would be magnified in them, by the power of the Holy Ghost, according to the will of God their Father.

The third objection

The third objection demands our most special attention. "And Moses and Aaron were brought again unto Pharaoh: and he said unto them, Go, serve the Lord your God; but who are they that shall go? And Moses said, We will go with our young and with our old, with our sons and with our daughters, with our flocks and with our herds, will we go: for we must hold a feast unto the Lord. And he said unto them, Let the Lord be so with you, as I will let you go and your little ones: look to it; for evil is before you. Not so; go now ye that are men, and serve the Lord; for that ye did desire. And they were driven out from Pharaoh's presence" (chap. 10:8-11). Here again we have the enemy aiming a deadly blow at the testimony to the name of the God of Israel. Parents in the wilderness and their children in Egypt! Terrible anomaly! This would only have been a half deliverance, at once useless to Israel and dishonouring to Israel's God. This could not be. If the children remained in Egypt, the parents could not possibly be said to have left it, inasmuch as their children were part of themselves. The most that could be said in such a case was, that in part they were serving Jehovah, and in part Pharaoh. But Jehovah could have no part with Pharaoh. He should either have all or nothing. This is a weighty principle for Christian parents. May we lay it deeply to heart! It is our happy privilege to count on God for our children, and to "bring them up in the nurture and admonition of the Lord" (Eph. 6). We should not be satisfied with any other portion for "our little ones" than that which we ourselves enjoy.

The fourth objection

Pharaoh's fourth and last objection had reference to the flocks and herds. "And Pharaoh called unto Moses, and said, Go ye, serve the Lord; only let your flocks and herds be stayed: let your little ones also go with you" (chap. 10:24). With what perseverance did Satan dispute every inch of Israel's way out of the land of Egypt! He first sought to keep them *in* the land, then to keep them *near* the land, next to keep part of themselves in the land, and, finally, when he could not succeed in any of these three, he sought to send them forth without any ability to serve the Lord. If he could not keep the servants, he would seek to keep their ability to serve, which would answer much the same end. If he could not induce them to sacrifice in the land, he would send them out of the land without sacrifices.

In Moses' reply to this last objection, we are furnished with a fine statement of the Lord's paramount claim upon His people and all pertaining to them. "And Moses said, Thou must give us also sacrifices and burnt offerings, that we may sacrifice unto the Lord our God. Our cattle also shall go with us; *there shall not an hoof be left behind:* for thereof must we take to serve the Lord our God; and we know not with what we must serve the Lord until we come thither" (ver. 25, 26). It is only when the people of God take their stand, in simple childlike faith, upon that elevated ground, on which death and resurrection set them, that they can have anything like an adequate sense of His claims upon them. "We know not with what we must serve the Lord until we come thither."

That is, they had no knowledge of the divine claim or their responsibility, until they had gone "three days' journey." These things could not be known amid the dense and polluted atmosphere of Egypt. Redemption must be known as an accomplished fact, ere there can be any just or full perception of responsibility. All this is perfect and beautiful. "If any man will do his will, he shall know of the doctrine." I must be up out of Egypt, in the power of death and resurrection, and then, but not until then, shall I know what the Lord's service really is. It is when we take our stand, by faith, in that "large room," that wealthy place into which the precious blood of Christ introduces us; when we look around us and survey the rich, rare, and manifold results of redeeming love; when we gaze upon the Person of Him who has brought us into this place, and endowed us with these riches, then we are constrained to say, in the language of one of our own poets,

> "Were the whole realm of nature mine,
> That were an offering far too small;
> Love so amazing, so divine,
> Demands my heart, my life, my all."

"There shall not an hoof be left behind." Noble words! Egypt is not the place for anything that pertains to God's redeemed. He is worthy of all, "body, soul, and spirit;" all we are and all we have belongs to Him. "We are not our own, we are bought with a price;" and it is our happy privilege to consecrate ourselves and all that we possess to Him whose we are, and whom we are called to serve. There is nought of a legal spirit in this. The words, "until we come thither," furnish a divine guard against this horrible evil. We have travelled the "three days' journey," ere a word concerning sacrifice can be heard or understood. We are put in full and undisputed possession of resurrection life and eternal righteousness. We have left that land of death and darkness; we have been brought to God Himself, so that we may enjoy Him, in the energy of that life with which we are endowed, and in the sphere of righteousness in which we are placed: thus it is our joy to serve. There is not an affection in the heart of which He is not worthy; there is not a sacrifice in all the flock too costly for His altar. The more closely we walk with Him, the more we shall esteem it to be our meat and drink to do His blessed will. The believer counts it his highest privilege to serve the Lord. He delights in every exercise and every manifestation of the divine nature. He does not move up and down with a grievous yoke upon his neck, or an intolerable weight upon his shoulder. The yoke is broken "because of the anointing," the burden has been for ever removed, by the blood of the cross, while he himself walks abroad, "redeemed, regenerated, and disenthralled," in pursuance of those soul-stirring words, "LET MY PEOPLE GO."

NOTE. We shall consider the contents of chapter 11 in connexion with the security of Israel, under the shelter of the blood of the paschal lamb.

---

[4] The word "abomination" has reference to that which the Egyptians worshipped.

Chapter 12

THE PASSOVER AND THE LAST PLAGUE

The hardening of Pharaoh

"And the Lord said unto Moses, Yet will I bring one plague more upon Pharaoh, and upon Egypt; afterwards he will let you go hence: when he shall let you go, he shall surely thrust you out hence altogether" (chap. 11:1). One more heavy blow must fall upon this hard-hearted monarch and his land, ere he will be compelled to let go the favoured objects of Jehovah's sovereign grace.

How utterly vain it is for man to harden and exalt himself against God; for, truly, He can grind to powder the hardest heart, and bring down to the dust the haughtiest spirit. "Those that walk in pride he is able to abase" (Dan. 4:37). Man may fancy himself to be something; he may lift up his head, in pomp and vain glory, as though he were his own master. Vain man – how little he knows of his real condition and character. He is but the tool of Satan, taken up and used by him, in his malignant efforts to counteract the purposes of God. The most splendid intellect, the most commanding genius, the most indomitable energy, if not under the direct control of the Spirit of God, are but so many instruments in Satan's hand to carry forward his dark designs. No man is his own master; he is either governed by Christ or governed by Satan. The king of Egypt might fancy himself to be a free agent, yet was he but a tool in the hands of another. Satan was behind the throne; and, as the result of Pharaoh's having set himself to resist the purposes of God, he was judicially handed over to the blinding and hardening influence of his self-chosen master.

This will explain to us an expression occurring very frequently throughout the earlier chapters of this book. "The Lord hardened Pharaoh's heart." There is no need, whatever, for any one to seek to avoid the full, plain sense of this most solemn statement. If man resists the light of divine testimony, he is shut up to judicial blindness and hardness of heart. God leaves him to himself, and then Satan comes in and carries him headlong to perdition. There was abundant light for Pharaoh, to show him the extravagant folly of his course in seeking to detain those whom God had commanded him to let go. But the real disposition of his heart was to act against God, and therefore God left him to himself, and made him a monument for the display of His glory "through all the earth." There is no difficulty in this to any, save those whose desire is to argue against God – "to rush upon the thick bosses of the shield of the Almighty" – to ruin their own immortal souls.

God gives people, at times, according to the real bent of their hearts' desire. "... because of this, God shall send them strong delusion, that they should believe a lie; that they all might be damned who believed not the truth, but *had pleasure in unrighteousness*" (2 Thess. 2:11, 12). If men will not have the truth when it is put before them, they shall, assuredly, have a lie. If they will not have Christ, they shall have Satan; if they will not have heaven, they shall have hell.[5] Will the infidel mind find fault with this? Ere it does so, let it prove that all who are thus judicially dealt with have fully answered their responsibilities. Let it, for instance, prove, in Pharaoh's case, that he acted, in any measure, up to the light he possessed. The same is to be proved in every case. Unquestionably, the task of proving rests on those who are disposed to quarrel with God's mode of dealing with the rejecters of His truth. The simple-hearted child of God will justify Him, in view of the most inscrutable dispensations; and even if he cannot meet and satisfactorily solve the difficult questions of a sceptical mind, he can rest perfectly satisfied with this word, "Shall not the Judge of all the earth do right?" There is far more wisdom in this method of settling an apparent difficulty, than in the most elaborate argument; for it is perfectly certain that the heart which is in a condition to "reply against God," will not be convinced by the arguments of man.

The destruction of the firstborn

However, it is God's prerogative to answer all the proud reasonings, and bring down the lofty imaginations of the human mind. He can write the sentence of death upon nature, in its fairest forms. "It is appointed unto men once to die." This cannot be avoided. Man may seek to hide his humiliation in various ways; to cover his retreat through the valley of death, in the most heroic manner possible; to call the last humiliating stage of his career by the most honourable titles he can devise; to gild the bed of death with a false light; to adorn the funeral procession and the grave with the appearance of pomp, pageantry, and glory; to raise above the mouldering ashes a splendid monument, on which are engraven the records of human shame. All these things he may do; but death is death after all, and he cannot keep it off for a moment, or make it anything else than what it is, namely, "the wages of sin."

The foregoing thoughts are suggested by the opening verse of chap. 11. "One plague more!" Solemn word! It signed the death-warrant of Egypt's firstborn – "the chief of all their strength." "And Moses said, Thus saith the Lord, About midnight will I go out into the midst of Egypt; and all the firstborn in the land of Egypt shall die, from the firstborn of Pharaoh that sitteth upon his throne, even unto the firstborn of the maidservant that is behind the mill; and all the firstborn of beasts. And there shall be a great cry throughout all the land of Egypt, such as there was none like it, nor shall be like it any more" (chap. 11:4-6). This was to be the final plague –

death in every house. "But against any of the children of Israel shall not a dog move his tongue, against man or beast; that ye may know how that the Lord doth put a difference between the Egyptians and Israel." It is the Lord alone who can "put a difference" between those who are His and those who are not. It is not our province to say to any one, "stand by thyself, I am holier than thou:" this is the language of a Pharisee. "But when God puts a difference" we are bound to enquire what that difference is; and, in the case before us, we see it to be a simple question of *life or death*. This is God's grand "difference." He draws a line of demarcation, and on one side of this line is "life," on the other "death." Many of Egypt's firstborn might have been as fair and attractive as those of Israel, and much more so; but Israel had life and light, founded upon God's counsels of redeeming love, established, as we shall see presently, by the blood of the lamb. This was Israel's happy position; while, on the other hand, throughout the length and breadth of the land of Egypt, from the monarch on the throne to the menial behind the mill, nothing was to be seen but death; nothing to be heard but the cry of bitter anguish, elicited by the heavy stroke of Jehovah's rod. God can bring down the haughty spirit of man. He can make the wrath of man to praise Him, and restrain the remainder. "And all these thy servants shall come down unto me, and bow down themselves unto me, saying, Get thee out and all the people that follow thee: and after that I will go out." God will accomplish His own ends. His schemes of mercy must be carried out at all cost, and confusion of face must be the portion of all who stand in the way. "O! give thanks unto the Lord; for he is good: for His mercy endureth for ever . . . To him that smote Egypt in their first-born: for his mercy endureth for ever: and brought out Israel from among them; for his mercy endureth for ever: with a strong hand, and with a stretched-out arm; for his mercy endureth for ever" (Psalm 136).

The beginning of months

"And the Lord spake unto Moses and Aaron in the land of Egypt, saying, This month shall be unto you the beginning of months: it shall be the first month of the year to you" (chap. 12:1, 2). There is, here, a very interesting change in the order of time. The common or civil year was rolling on in its ordinary course, when Jehovah interrupted it in reference to His people, and thus, in principle, taught them that they were to begin a new era in company with Him. Their previous history was, henceforth, to be regarded as a blank. Redemption was to constitute the first step in *real life*.

This teaches a plain truth. A man's life is really of no account until he begins to walk with God, in the knowledge of full salvation and settled peace, through the precious blood of the Lamb. Previous to this he is, in the judgment of God, and in the language of scripture, "dead in trespasses and sins;" "alienated from the life of God." His whole history is a complete blank, even though, in man's account, it may have been one uninterrupted scene of bustling activity. All that which engages the attention of the man of this world, the honours, the riches, the pleasures, the attractions, of life, so called – all, when examined in the light of the judgment of God, when weighed in the balances of the sanctuary, must be accounted as a dismal blank, a worthless void, utterly unworthy of a place in the records of the Holy Ghost. "He that believeth not the Son shall not see life" (John 3:36). Men speak of "seeing life," when they launch forth into society, travel hither and thither, and see all that is to be seen; but they forget that the only true, the only real, the only divine way to " see life," is to "believe on the Son of God."

How little do men think of this! They imagine that "real life" is at an end when a man becomes a Christian, in truth and reality, not merely in name and outward profession; whereas God's word teaches us that it is only then we can see life and taste true happiness. "He that hath the Son hath life" (1 John 5:12). And, again, " Happy is he whose transgression is forgiven, whose sin is covered" (Ps. 32:1). We can get life and happiness *only* in Christ. Apart from Him, all is death and misery, in Heaven's judgment, whatever the outward appearance may be. It is when the thick vail of unbelief is removed from the heart, and we are enabled to behold, with the eye of faith, the bleeding Lamb, bearing our heavy burden of guilt upon the cursed tree, that we enter upon the path of life, and partake of the cup of divine happiness – a life which begins at the cross, and flows onward into an eternity of glory – a happiness which, each day, becomes deeper and purer, more connected with God and founded on Christ, until we reach its proper sphere, in the presence of God and the Lamb. To seek life and happiness in any other way, is vainer work by far than seeking to make bricks without straw.

True, the enemy of souls spreads a gilding over this passing scene, in order that men may imagine it to be all gold. He sets up many a puppet-show to elicit the hollow laugh from a thoughtless multitude, who will not remember that it is Satan who is in the box, and that his object is to keep them from Christ, and drag them down into eternal perdition. There is nothing real, nothing solid, nothing satisfying, but in Christ. Outside of Him, "all is vanity and vexation of spirit." In Him alone true and eternal joys are to be found; and we only begin to live when we begin to live *in*, live *on*, live *with*, and live *for* Him. "This month shall be unto you the beginning of months: it shall be the first month of the year to you." The time spent in the brick-kilns and by the flesh-pots must be ignored. It is, henceforth, to be of no account save that the remembrance thereof should, ever and anon, serve to quicken and deepen their sense of what divine grace had accomplished on their behalf.

The Passover Lamb

"Speak ye unto all the congregation of Israel, saying, In the tenth day of this month they shall take to them every man a lamb according to the house of their fathers, a lamb for an house . . . Your lamb shall be without blemish, a male of the first year; ye shall take it out from the sheep or from the goats: and ye shall keep it up until the fourteenth day of the same month; and the whole assembly of the congregation of Israel shall kill it in the evening." Here we have the redemption of the people founded upon the blood of the lamb, in pursuance of God's eternal purpose. This imparts to it all its divine stability. Redemption was no after-thought with God. Before the world was, or Satan, or sin – before ever the voice of God was heard breaking the silence of eternity, and calling worlds into existence, He had His deep counsels of love; and these counsels could never find a sufficiently solid basis in creation. All the blessings, the privileges, and the dignities of creation were founded upon a creature's obedience, and the moment that failed, all was gone. But, then, Satan's attempt to mar creation only opened the way for the manifestation of God's deeper purposes of redemption.

This beautiful truth is typically presented to us in the circumstance of the lamb's being "kept up" from the "tenth" to "the fourteenth day." That this lamb pointed to Christ is unquestionable. First Corinthians 5:7, settles the application of this interesting type beyond all question; "For even Christ our passover is sacrificed for us." We have, in the first epistle of Peter, an allusion to the keeping up of the lamb: "Forasmuch as ye know that ye were not redeemed with corruptible things, as silver and gold, from your vain conversation, received by tradition from your fathers; but with the precious blood of Christ, as of a lamb without blemish and without spot: who verily was *foreordained before the foundation of the world*, but was *manifest in these last times for you* (chap. 1:18-20).

All God's purposes, from everlasting, had reference to Christ; and no effort of the enemy could possibly interfere with those counsels: yea, his efforts only tended to the display of the unfathomable wisdom and immovable stability thereof. If the "Lamb without blemish and without spot" was "foreordained before the foundation of the world," then, assuredly, redemption must have been in the mind of God before the foundation of the world. The Blessed One had not to pause in order to devise some plan to remedy the terrible evil which the enemy had introduced into His fair creation. No, He had only to bring forth, from the unexplored treasury of His precious counsels, the truth concerning the spotless Lamb, who was foreordained from everlasting, and to be "manifest in these last times for us."

There was no need for the blood of the Lamb in creation, as it came fresh from the hand of the Creator, exhibiting in every stage, and every department of it, the beauteous impress of His hand – "the infallible proofs" of "His eternal power and Godhead" (Rom. 1). But when, "by one man," sin was introduced into the world, then came out the higher, richer, fuller, deeper thought of redemption by the blood of the Lamb. This glorious truth first broke through the thick clouds which surrounded our first parents, as they retreated from the garden of Eden; its glimmerings appear in the types and shadows of the Mosaic economy; it burst upon the world in full brightness, when "the dayspring from on high" appeared in the Person of " God manifest in the flesh;" and its rich and rare results will be realised when the white-robed, palm-bearing multitude shall cluster round the throne of God and the Lamb, and the whole creation shall rest beneath the peaceful sceptre of the Son of David.

Now, the lamb taken on the tenth day, and kept up until the fourteenth day, shows us Christ foreordained of God, from eternity, but manifest for us, in time. God's eternal purpose in Christ becomes the foundation of the believer's peace. Nothing short of this would do. We are carried back far beyond creation, beyond the bounds of time, beyond the entrance in of sin, and everything that could possibly affect the ground-work of our peace. The expression, "foreordained before the foundation of the world," conducts us back into the unfathomed depths of eternity, and shows us God forming His own counsels of redeeming love, and basing them all upon the atoning blood of His own precious, spotless Lamb.

Christ was ever the primary thought in the divine mind; and, hence, the moment He began to speak or act, He took occasion to shadow forth that One who occupied the highest place in His counsels and affections; and, as we pass along the current of inspiration, we find that every ceremony, every rite, every ordinance, and every sacrifice pointed forward to "the Lamb of God that taketh away the sin of the world," and not one more strikingly than the Passover. The paschal lamb, with all the attendant circumstances, forms one of the most profoundly interesting and deeply instructive types of Scripture.

In the interpretation of Exodus 12 we have to do with *one* assembly and *one* sacrifice. "The whole assembly of the congregation of Israel shall kill *it* in the evening" (ver. 6). It is not so much a number of families with several lambs – a thing quite true in itself – as one assembly and one lamb. Each house was but the local expression of the whole assembly gathered round the lamb. The antitype of this we have in the whole Church of God, gathered by the Holy Ghost, in the name of Jesus, of which each separate assembly, wherever convened, should be the local expression.

The blood of the Lamb

"And they shall take of the blood, and strike it on the two side posts, and on the upper door posts of the houses, wherein they shall eat it. And they shall eat the flesh in that night, roast with fire, and unleavened bread; and with bitter herbs they shall eat it. Eat not of it raw, nor sodden at all with water, but roast with fire; his head with his legs, and with the purtenance thereof" (ver. 7-9). We have to contemplate the paschal lamb in two aspects, namely, as the ground of peace and the centre of unity. The blood on the lintel secured Israel's peace. "When I see the blood, I will pass over you" (ver. 13). There was nothing more required, in order to enjoy settled peace, in reference to the destroying angel, than the application of the blood of sprinkling. Death had to do its work in every house throughout the land of Egypt. "It is appointed unto men once to die." But God, in His great mercy, found an unblemished substitute for Israel on which the sentence of death was executed. Thus God's claims and Israel's need were met by one and the same thing, namely, the blood of the lamb. That blood outside proved that *all* was perfectly, because divinely, settled; and therefore perfect peace reigned within. A shade of doubt in the bosom of an Israelite, would have been a dishonour offered to the divinely-appointed ground of peace – the blood of atonement.

True it is that each one within the blood-sprinkled door would, necessarily, feel that were he to receive his due reward, the sword of the destroyer should, most assuredly, find its object in him; but then the lamb was treated in his stead. This was the solid foundation of his peace. The judgment that was due to him fell upon a divinely-appointed victim; and believing this, he could feed in peace within. A single doubt would have made Jehovah a liar; for He had said, "when *I* see the *blood*, I will pass over you." This was enough. It was no question of personal worthiness. Self had nothing whatever to do in the matter. All under the cover of the blood were safe. They were not merely in a salvable state, they were *saved*. They were not hoping or praying to be saved, they knew it as an assured fact, on the authority of that word which shall endure throughout all generations. Moreover, they were not partly saved and partly exposed to judgment; they were wholly saved. The blood of the lamb and the word of the Lord formed the foundation of Israel's peace on that terrible night in which Egypt's firstborn were laid low. If an hair of an Israelite's head could be touched, it would have proved Jehovah's word void, and the blood of the lamb valueless.

It is most needful to be simple and clear as to what constitutes the ground of a sinner's peace, in the presence of God. So many things are mixed up with the finished work of Christ, that souls are plunged into darkness and uncertainty, as to their acceptance. They do not see the absolutely-settled character of redemption through the blood of Christ, in its application to themselves. They seem not to be aware that full forgiveness of sins rests upon the simple fact that a full atonement has been offered – a fact attested in the view of all created intelligence, by the resurrection of the sinner's Surety from the dead. They know that there is no other way of being saved but by the blood of the cross – but the devils know this, yet it avails them nought. What is so much needed is to know that *we are saved*. The Israelite not merely knew that there was safety in the blood; he knew that *he* was *safe*. And why safe? Was it because of anything that he had done, or felt, or thought? By no means, but because God had said, "when I see the blood I will pass over you." He rested upon God's testimony. He believed what God said, because God said it. "He set to his seal that God was true."

And, observe, my reader, it was not upon his own thoughts, feelings, or experiences, respecting the blood, that the Israelite rested. This would have been a poor sandy foundation to rest upon. His thoughts and feelings might be deep or they might be shallow; but deep or shallow, they had nothing to do with the ground of his peace. It was not said, "when *you* see the blood, and value it as you ought, I will pass over you." This would have been sufficient to plunge him in dark despair about himself, inasmuch as it was quite impossible that the human mind could ever sufficiently appreciate the precious blood of the Lamb. What gave peace was the fact that Jehovah's eye rested upon the blood, and that He knew its worth. This tranquillized the heart. The blood was outside, and the Israelite inside, so that he could not possibly see it; but God saw it, and that was quite enough.

The work of Christ for us

The application of this to the question of a sinner's peace is very plain. The Lord Jesus Christ, having shed His precious blood, as a perfect atonement for sin, has taken it into the presence of God, and sprinkled it there; and God's testimony assures the believing sinner, that everything is settled on his behalf – settled not by his estimate of the blood, but by the blood itself which God estimates so highly, that because of it, without a single jot or tittle added thereto, He can righteously forgive all sin, and accept the sinner as perfectly righteous in Christ. How can any one ever enjoy settled peace, if his peace depends upon his estimate of the blood? Impossible. The loftiest estimate which the human mind can form of the blood must fall infinitely short of its divine preciousness; and, therefore, if our peace were to depend upon our valuing it as we ought, we could no more enjoy settled peace than if we were seeking it by "works of law." There must either be a sufficient ground of peace in the blood *alone*, or we can never have peace. To mix up our estimate with it, is to upset the entire fabric of Christianity, just as effectually as if we were to conduct the sinner to the foot of mount Sinai, and put him under a covenant of works. Either Christ's atoning sacrifice is sufficient or it is not. If it is sufficient, why those doubts and fears? The words of our *lips* profess that the work is finished; but the doubts and fears of the *heart* declare that it is not. Every one who doubts his full and everlasting forgiveness, denies, so far as he is concerned, the completeness of the sacrifice of Christ.

But there are very many who would shrink from the idea of deliberately and avowedly calling in question the efficacy of the blood of Christ, who, nevertheless, have not settled peace. Such persons profess to be quite assured of the sufficiency of the blood, *if* only *they* were sure of an interest therein – *if only* they had the right kind of faith. There are many precious souls in this unhappy condition. They are occupied with their interest and their faith, instead of with Christ's blood, and God's word. In other words, they are looking in at self, instead of out at Christ. This is not faith; and, as a consequence, they have not peace. An Israelite within the blood-stained lintel could teach such souls a most seasonable lesson. He was not saved by his interest in, or his thoughts about, the blood, but simply by the blood. No doubt, he had a blessed interest in it; and he would have his thoughts, likewise; but, then, God did not say, "When I see your interest in the blood, I will pass over you." Oh! no; THE BLOOD, in all its solitary dignity and divine efficacy, was set before Israel; and had they attempted to place even a morsel of unleavened bread beside the blood, as a ground of security, they would have made Jehovah a liar, and denied the sufficiency of His remedy.

The work of the Holy Spirit in us

We are ever prone to look at something in or connected with ourselves as necessary, in order to make up, with the blood of Christ, the groundwork of our peace. There is a sad lack of clearness and soundness on this vital point, as is evident from the doubts and fears with which so many of the people of God are afflicted. We are apt to regard the fruits of the Spirit *in* us, rather than the work of Christ *for* us, as the foundation of peace. We shall see, presently, the place which the work of the Holy Spirit occupies in Christianity; but it is never set forth in Scripture as being that on which our peace reposes. The Holy Ghost did not make peace, but Christ did. The Holy Ghost is not said to be our peace, but Christ is. God did not send preaching peace by the Holy Ghost, but by Jesus Christ (compare Acts 10:36; Eph. 2:14, 17; Col. 1:20). My reader cannot be too simple in his apprehension of this important distinction. It is the blood of Christ which gives peace, imparts perfect justification, divine righteousness, purges the conscience, brings us into the holiest of all, justifies God in receiving the believing sinner, and constitutes our title to all the joys, the dignities, and the glories of heaven (see Rom. 3:24-26; 5:9; Eph. 2:13-18; Col. 1:20-22; Heb. 9:14; 10:19; 1 Peter 1:19; 2:24; 1 John 1:7; Rev. 7:14-17).

It will not, I fondly hope, be supposed that, in seeking to put "the precious blood of Christ" in its divinely-appointed place, I would write a single line which might seem to detract from the value of the Spirit's operations. God forbid. The Holy

Ghost reveals Christ; makes us to know, enjoy, and feed upon Christ; He bears witness to Christ; He takes of the things of Christ and shows them unto us. He is the power of communion, the seal, the witness, the earnest, the unction. In short, His blessed operations are absolutely essential. Without Him, we can neither see, hear, know, feel, experience, enjoy, nor exhibit anything of Christ. This is plain. The doctrine of the Spirit's operations is clearly laid down in the word, and is understood and admitted by every true and rightly instructed Christian.

Yet, notwithstanding all this, the work of the Spirit is not the ground of peace; for, if it were, we could not have settled peace until Christ's coming, inasmuch as the work of the Spirit, in the Church, will not, properly speaking, be complete till then. He still carries on His work in the believer. "He maketh intercession with groanings which cannot be uttered" (Rom. 8). He labours to bring us up to the predestinated standard, namely, perfect conformity, in all things, to the image of "the Son." He is the sole Author of every right desire, every holy aspiration, every pure affection, every divine experience, every sound conviction; but, clearly, His work *in* us will not be complete until we have left this present scene and taken our place with Christ in the glory. Just as, in the case of Abraham's servant, his work was not complete, in the matter of Rebecca, until he had presented her to Isaac.

Not so the work of Christ *for* us. That is absolutely and eternally complete. He could say, "I have finished the work which thou gavest me to do" (John 17:4). And, again, "It is finished" (John 19:30). The Holy Ghost cannot yet say He has finished His work. As the true Vicar of Christ upon earth, He still labours amid the varied hostile influences which surround the sphere of His operations. He works in the hearts of the people of God to bring them up, practically and experimentally, to the divinely appointed standard. But He never teaches a soul to lean on His work for peace in the presence of God. His office is to speak of Jesus. "He," says Christ, "shall receive of mine and shall shew it unto you" (John 16:13, 14). If, then, it is only by the Spirit's teaching that any one can understand the true ground of peace, it is obvious that He can only present Christ's work as the foundation on which the soul must rest for ever; yea, it is in virtue of that work that He takes up His abode and carries on His marvellous operations in the believer. He is not our title, though He reveals that title and enables us to understand and enjoy it.

The death of Christ, the sole ground of our salvation

Hence, therefore, the paschal lamb, as the ground of Israel's peace, is a marked and beautiful type of Christ as the ground of the believer's peace. There was nothing to be added to the blood on the lintel; neither is there anything to be added to the blood on the mercy-seat. The "unleavened bread" and "bitter herbs" were necessary, but not as forming, either in whole or in part, the ground of peace. They were for the inside of the house and formed the characteristics of the communion there; but THE BLOOD OF THE LAMB WAS THE FOUNDATION OF EVERYTHING. It saved them from death and introduced them into a scene of life, light, and peace. It formed the link between God and His redeemed people. As a people linked with God, on the ground of accomplished redemption, it was their high privilege to meet certain responsibilities; but these responsibilities did not form the link, but merely flowed out of it.

And I would further remind my reader that the obedient *life* of Christ is not set forth in Scripture as the procuring cause of our forgiveness. It was His death upon the cross that opened those everlasting floodgates of love which else should have remained pent up for ever. If he had remained to this very hour, going through the cities of Israel, "doing good," the veil of the temple would continue unrent, to bar the worshipper's approach to God. It was His death that rent that mysterious curtain "from top to bottom." It is "by *His stripes*," not by His obedient life, that "we are healed;" and those "stripes" He endured *on the cross*, and nowhere else. His own words, during the progress of His blessed life, are quite sufficient to settle this point. "I have a baptism to be baptised with; and how am I straitened till it be accomplished" (Luke 12:50). To what does this refer but to His death upon the cross, which was the accomplishment of His baptism and the opening up of a righteous vent through which His love might freely flow out to the guilty sons of Adam? Again, He says, "except a corn of wheat fall into the ground and die it abideth alone" (John 12:24). He was that precious "corn of wheat:" and He should have remained for ever "alone," even though incarnate, had He not, by His death upon the accursed tree, removed out of the way everything that could have hindered the union of his people with Him in resurrection. "If it die, it bringeth forth much fruit."

My reader cannot too carefully ponder this subject. It is one of immense weight and importance. He has to remember two points in reference to this entire question, namely, that there could be no union with Christ, save in resurrection; and that Christ *only* suffered for sins on the cross. We are not to suppose that incarnation was, by any means, Christ taking us into union with Himself. This could not be. How could sinful flesh be thus united? The body of sin had to be destroyed by death. Sin had to be put away, according to the divine requirement; all the power of the enemy had to be abolished. How was all this to be done? Only by the precious, spotless Lamb of God submitting to the death of the cross. "It became him, for whom are all things, and by whom are all things, in bringing many sons unto glory, to make the captain of their salvation perfect *through sufferings*" (Heb. 2:10). "Behold, I cast out devils, and I do cures today and tomorrow, and *the third day I shall be perfected*" (Luke 13:32). The expressions "perfect" and "perfected" in the above passages do not refer to Christ in His own Person abstractedly, for He was perfect from all eternity, as Son of God; and as to His humanity, He was absolutely perfect likewise. But then, as "the captain of salvation" – as "bringing many sons unto glory" – as "bringing forth much fruit" – as associating a redeemed people *with* Himself, He had to reach "the third day" in order to be "perfected." He went down *alone* into the "horrible pit, and miry clay;" but, directly He plants His "foot on the rock" of resurrection, He associates with Himself the "many sons." (Ps. 40:1-3). He fought the fight alone; but, as the mighty Conqueror, He scatters around Him, in rich profusion, the spoils of victory, that we might gather them up and enjoy them for ever.

Moreover, we are not to regard the cross of Christ as a mere circumstance in a life of sin-bearing. It was *the* grand and only scene of sin-bearing. "His own self bare our sins in his own body on the tree." (1 Peter 2:14). He did not bear them anywhere else. He did not bear them in the manger, nor in the wilderness, nor in the garden; but ONLY "ON THE TREE." He never had anything to say to sin, save on the cross; and there He bowed His blessed head, and yielded up His precious life, under the accumulated weight of His people's sins. Neither did He ever suffer at the hand of God save on the cross; and there Jehovah hid His face from Him because He was "made sin" (2 Cor. 5).

The above train of thought, and the various passages of scripture referred to, may, perhaps, enable my reader to enter more fully into the divine power of the words, *"when I see the blood* I will pass over you." The lamb needed to be without blemish, no doubt, for what else could meet the holy eye of Jehovah? But, had the blood not been shed, there could have been no passing over, for "without shedding of blood is no remission" (Heb. 9:22). This subject will, the Lord permitting, come more fully and appropriately before us in the types of Leviticus. It demands the prayerful attention of every one who loves our Lord Jesus Christ in sincerity.

A centre of gathering for Israel

We shall now consider the second aspect of the Passover, as the centre round which the assembly was gathered, in peaceful, holy, happy fellowship. Israel, saved by the blood, was one thing; and Israel, feeding on the lamb, was quite another. They were saved *only* by the blood; but the object round which they were gathered was, manifestly, the roasted lamb. This is not, by any means, a distinction without a difference. The blood of the Lamb forms the foundation both of our connexion with God, and our connexion with one another. It is as those who are washed in that blood, that we are introduced to God and to one another. Apart from the perfect atonement of Christ, there could obviously be no fellowship either with God or His assembly. Still we must remember that it is to a living Christ in heaven that believers are gathered by the Holy Ghost. It is with a living Head we are connected – to "a living stone" we have come. He is our centre. Having found peace, through His blood, we own Him as our grand gathering point and connecting link. "Where two or three are gathered together in my name there am I in the midst of them" (Matt. 18:20). The Holy Ghost is the only Gatherer; Christ Himself is the only object to which we are gathered; and our assembly, when thus convened, is to be characterised by holiness, so that the Lord our God may dwell among us. The Holy Ghost can only gather to Christ. He cannot gather to a system, a name, a doctrine, or an ordinance. He gathers to a Person, and that Person is a glorified Christ in heaven. This must stamp a peculiar character on God's assembly. Men may associate, on any ground, round any centre, or for any object they please; but, when the Holy Ghost associates, it is on the ground of accomplished redemption, around the Person of Christ, in order to form a holy dwelling place for God (1 Cor. 3:16, 17; 6:19; Eph. 2:21, 22; 1 Peter 2:4, 5).

The ordinance of the Passover

We shall now look in detail at the principles brought before us in the paschal feast. The assembly of Israel, as under the cover of the blood, was to be ordered by Jehovah in a manner worthy of Himself. In the matter of safety from judgment, as we have already seen, nothing was needed but the blood; but in the fellowship which flowed out of this safety, other things were needed which could not be neglected with impunity.

And first, then, we read, "They shall eat the flesh in that night, roast with fire, and unleavened bread; and with bitter herbs they shall eat it. Eat not of it raw, nor sodden at all with water, but roast with fire; his head with his legs, and with the purtenance thereof" (ver. 8, 9). The lamb, round which the congregation was assembled, and on which it feasted, was a roasted lamb – a lamb which had undergone the action of fire. In this we see "Christ our Passover" presenting Himself to the action of the fire of divine holiness and judgment which found in Him a perfect material. He could say, "Thou hast proved mine heart; thou hast visited me in the night; thou hast tried me and shalt find nothing; I am purposed that my mouth shall not transgress" (Ps. 17:3). All in Him was perfect. The fire tried Him and there was no dross. "His head with his legs, and with the purtenance thereof." That is to say, the seat of His understanding; His outward walk with all that pertained thereto – all was submitted to the action of the fire, and all was entirely perfect. The process of roasting was therefore deeply significant, as is every circumstance in the ordinances of God. Nothing should be passed over, because all is pregnant with meaning.

"Eat not of it raw, nor sodden at all with water." Had it been eaten thus, there would have been no expression of the great truth which it was the divine purpose to shadow forth; namely, that our paschal Lamb was to endure, on the cross, the fire of Jehovah's righteous wrath – a truth of infinite preciousness to the soul. We are not merely under the eternal shelter of the blood of the Lamb, but we feed, by faith, upon the Person of the Lamb. Many of us come short here. We are apt to rest satisfied with being saved by what Christ has done for us, without cultivating holy communion with Himself. His loving heart could never be satisfied with this. He has brought us nigh to Himself, that we might enjoy Him, that we might feed on Him, and delight in Him. He presents Himself to us as the One who has endured, to the uttermost, the intense fire of the wrath of God, that He may, in this wondrous character, be the food of our ransomed souls.

The unleavened bread

But how was this lamb to be eaten? "With unleavened bread and bitter herbs." Leaven is, invariably, used, throughout scripture, as emblematical of evil. Neither in the Old nor in the New Testament is it ever used to set forth anything pure, holy, or good. Thus, in this chapter, "the feast of unleavened bread" is the type of that practical separation from evil which is the proper result of being washed from our sins in the blood of the Lamb, and the proper accompaniment of communion with His sufferings. Nought but perfectly unleavened bread could at all comport with a roasted lamb. A single particle of that which was the marked type of evil, would have destroyed the moral character of the entire ordinance. How could we connect any species of evil with our fellowship with a suffering Christ? Impossible. All who enter by the power of the Holy Ghost, into the meaning of the cross will, assuredly, by the same power, put away leaven from all their borders. "For even Christ our Passover is sacrificed for us: *therefore* let us keep the feast, not with old leaven, neither with the leaven of malice and wickedness; but with the unleavened bread of sincerity and truth" (1 Cor. 5:7, 8). The feast spoken of in this passage is that which, in the life and conduct of the Church, corresponds with the feast of unleavened bread. This latter lasted "seven days;" and the Church collectively, and the believer individually, are called to walk in practical holiness, during the seven days, or entire period, of their course here below; and this, moreover, as the direct result of being washed in the blood, and having communion with the sufferings of Christ.

The Israelite did not put away leaven in order to be saved, but because he was saved; and if he failed to put away leaven, it did not raise the question of security through the blood, but simply of fellowship with the assembly. "Seven days shall there be no leaven found in your houses: for whosoever eateth that which is leavened, even that soul shall be cut off from the congregation of Israel, whether he be a stranger, or born in the land" (ver. 19). The cutting off of an Israelite from the congregation answers precisely to the suspension of a Christian's fellowship, if he be indulging in that which is contrary to the holiness of the divine presence. God cannot tolerate evil. A single unholy thought will interrupt the soul's communion; and until the soil contracted by any such thought is got rid of by confession, founded on the advocacy of Christ, the communion cannot possibly be restored (See 1 John 1:5-10). The true-hearted Christian rejoices in this. He can ever "give thanks at the remembrance of God's holiness." He would not, if he could, lower the standard a single hair's breadth. It is his exceeding joy to walk in company with one who will not go on, for a moment, with a single jot or tittle of "leaven."

Blessed be God, we know that nothing can ever snap asunder the link which binds the true believer to Him. We are "saved in the Lord," not with a temporary or conditional, but "with an everlasting salvation." But then salvation and communion are not the same thing. Many are saved, who do not know it; and many, also, who do not enjoy it. It is quite impossible that I can enjoy a blood-stained lintel if I have leavened borders. This is an axiom in the divine life. May it be written on our hearts! Practical holiness, though not the basis of our *salvation*, is intimately connected with our *enjoyment* thereof. An Israelite was not saved by unleavened bread, but by the blood; and yet leaven would have cut him off from communion. And as to the Christian, he is not saved by his practical holiness, but by the blood; but if he indulges in evil, in thought, word, or deed, he will have no true enjoyment of salvation, and no true communion with the Person of the Lamb.

This, I cannot doubt, is the secret of much of the spiritual barrenness and lack of settled peace which one finds amongst the children of God. They are not cultivating holiness; they are not keeping "the feast of unleavened bread." The blood is on the lintel, but the leaven within their borders keeps them from enjoying the security which the blood provides. The allowance of evil destroys our fellowship, though it does not break the link which binds our souls eternally to God. Those who belong to God's assembly must be holy. They have not only been delivered from the guilt and consequences of sin, but also from the practice of it, the power of it, and the love of it. The very fact of being delivered by the blood of the paschal lamb, rendered Israel responsible to put away leaven from all their quarters. They could not say, in the frightful language of the antinomian, "now that we are delivered, we may conduct ourselves as we please." By no means. If they were saved *by grace*, they were saved *to holiness*. The soul that can take occasion, from the freedom of divine grace, and the completeness of the redemption which is in Christ Jesus, to "continue in sin," proves very distinctly that he understands neither the one nor the other.

Grace not only saves the soul with an everlasting salvation, but also imparts a nature which delights in everything that belongs to God, because it is divine. We are made partakers of the divine nature, which cannot sin, because it is born of God. To walk in the energy of this nature is, in reality, to "keep" the feast of unleavened bread. There is no "old leaven" nor "leaven of malice and wickedness" in the new nature, because it is of God, and God is holy, and "God is love." Hence it is evident that we do not put away evil from us in order to better our old nature, which is irremediable; nor yet to obtain the new nature, but because we have it. We have life, and, in the power of that life, we put away evil. It is only when we are delivered from the guilt of sin that we can understand or exhibit the true power of holiness. To attempt it in any other way is hopeless labour. The feast of unleavened bread can only be kept beneath the perfect shelter of the blood.

The bitter herbs

We may perceive equal significancy and moral propriety in that which was to accompany the unleavened bread, namely, the "bitter herbs." We cannot enjoy communion with the sufferings of Christ, without remembering what it was which rendered those sufferings needful, and this remembrance must necessarily produce a chastened and subdued tone of spirit, which is aptly expressed by the bitter herbs in the paschal feast. If the roasted lamb expressed Christ's endurance of the wrath of God in His own Person, on the cross, the bitter herbs express the believer's recognition of the truth that He "suffered *for us*." "The chastisement of our peace was upon him, and with his stripes we are healed" (Is 53:5). It is well, owing to the excessive levity of our hearts, to understand the deep meaning of the bitter herbs. Who can read such Psalms as the 6, 22, 38, 49, 88, and 109, and not enter, in some measure, into the meaning of the unleavened bread with bitter herbs? Practical holiness of life with deep subduedness of soul must flow from real communion with Christ's suffering, for it is quite impossible that moral evil and levity of spirit can exist in view of those sufferings.

But, it may be asked, is there not a deep joy for the soul in the consciousness that Christ has borne our sins; that He has fully drained, on our behalf, the cup of God's righteous wrath? Unquestionably. This is the solid foundation of all our joy. But can we ever forget that it was for "*our sins*" He suffered? Can we ever lose sight of the soul-subduing truth that the blessed Lamb of God bowed His head beneath the weight of our transgressions? Surely not. We must eat our lamb with bitter herbs, which, be it remembered, do not set forth the tears of a worthless and shallow sentimentality, but the deep and real experiences of a soul that enters, with spiritual intelligence and power, into the meaning and into the practical effect of the cross.

In contemplating the cross, we find in it that which cancels all our guilt. This imparts sweet peace and joy. But we find in it also the complete setting aside of nature, the crucifixion of "the flesh," the death of "the old man" (see Rom. 6:6; Gal. 2:20; 6:14; Col 2:11). This, in its practical results, will involve much that is "bitter" to nature. It will call for self-denial, the mortification of our members which are on the earth (Col. 3:5), the reckoning of self to be dead indeed unto sin (Rom. 6). All these things may seem terrible to look at; but when one gets inside the bloodstained door-post he thinks quite differently. The very herbs which, to an Egyptian's taste, would, no doubt, have seemed so bitter, formed an integral part of Israel's redemption *feast*. Those who are redeemed by the blood of the Lamb, who know the joy of fellowship with Him, esteem it a "feast" to put away evil and to keep nature in the place of death.

Nothing remaining

"And ye shall let nothing of it remain until the morning; and that which remaineth of it until the morning ye shall burn with fire" (ver. 10). In this command, we are taught that the communion of the congregation was, in no wise, to be separated from the sacrifice on which that communion was founded. The heart must ever cherish the vivid remembrance that all true fellowship is inseparably connected with accomplished redemption. To think of having communion *with God*, on any other ground is to imagine that He could have fellowship with our evil; and to think of fellowship *with man*, on any other ground, is but to form an unholy club, from which nothing could issue but confusion and iniquity. In a word, all must be founded upon, and inseparably linked with, the blood. This is the simple meaning of eating the paschal lamb the same night on which the blood was shed. The fellowship must not be separated from its foundation.

What a beauteous picture, then, we have in the blood-sheltered assembly of Israel, feeding peacefully on the roasted lamb, with unleavened bread and bitter herbs! No fear of judgment, no fear of the wrath of Jehovah, no fear of the terrible hurricane of righteous vengeance which was sweeping vehemently over the land of Egypt, at the midnight hour. All was profound peace within the blood-stained lintel. They had no need to fear anything from without; and nothing within could trouble them, save leaven, which would have proved a death-blow to all their peace and blessedness. What a picture for the Church! What a picture for the Christian! May we gaze upon it with an enlightened eye and a teachable spirit!

The loins girded and shoes on the feet

However, we are not yet done with this most instructive ordinance. We have been looking at Israel's *position*, and Israel's *food*, let us now look at Israel's *habit*.

"And thus shall ye eat it; with your loins girded, your shoes on your feet, and your staff in your hand; and ye shall eat it in haste; it is the Lord's Passover" (ver. 11). They were to eat it as a people prepared to leave behind them the land of death and darkness, wrath and judgment, to move onward toward the land of promise – their destined inheritance. The blood which had preserved them from the fate of Egypt's firstborn was also the foundation of their deliverance from Egypt's bondage; and they were now to set out and walk with God toward the land that flowed with milk and honey. True, they had not yet crossed the Red Sea; they had not yet gone the "three days' journey." Still they were, in principle, a redeemed people, a separated people, a pilgrim people, an expectant people, a dependent people; and their entire habit was to be in keeping with their present position and future destiny. The girded loins bespoke intense separation from all around them, together with a readiness to serve. The shod feet declared their preparedness to leave that scene; while the staff was the expressive emblem of a pilgrim people, in the attitude of leaning on something outside themselves. Precious characteristics! Would that they were more exhibited by every member of God's redeemed family.

Beloved Christian reader, let us "meditate on these things."

We have tasted, through grace, the cleansing efficacy of the blood of Jesus; as such it is our privilege to feed upon His adorable Person and delight ourselves in His "unsearchable riches;" to have fellowship in His sufferings and be made conformable to His death. Oh! let us, therefore, be seen with the unleavened bread and bitter herbs, the girded loins, the shoes and staff. In a word, let us be marked as a holy people, a crucified people, a watchful and diligent people – a people manifestly "on our way to God" – on our way to glory – "bound for the kingdom." May God grant us to enter into the depth and power of all these things; so that they may not be mere theories in our intellects – mere principles of scriptural knowledge and interpretation; but living, divine realities, known by experience, and exhibited in the life, to the glory of God.

And if a stranger will keep the Passover

We shall close this section by glancing, for a moment, at verses 43-49. Here we are taught that while it was the place and privilege of every true Israelite to eat the Passover, yet no uncircumcised stranger should participate therein. "There shall no stranger eat thereof . . . all the congregation of Israel shall keep it." Circumcision was necessary ere the Passover could be eaten. In other words, the sentence of death must be written upon nature ere we can intelligently feed upon Christ, either as the ground of peace or the centre of unity. Circumcision has its antitype in the cross. The male alone was circumcised. The female was represented in the male. So, in the cross, Christ represented His Church, and, hence, the Church is crucified with Christ; nevertheless, she lives by the life of Christ, known and exhibited on earth, through the power of the Holy Ghost. "And when a stranger shall sojourn with thee, and will keep the Passover unto the Lord, let all his males be circumcised, and then let him come near and keep it; and he shall be as one that is born in the land: for no uncircumcised person shall eat thereof." "They that are in the flesh cannot please God" (Rom. 8:8).

The ordinance of circumcision formed the grand boundary line between the Israel of God and all the nations that were upon the face of the earth; and the cross of the Lord Jesus Christ forms the boundary between the church and the world. It matters not, in the smallest degree, what advantages of person or position a man possessed, he could have no part with Israel until he submitted to that flesh-cutting operation. A circumcised beggar was nearer to God than an uncircumcised king. So, also, now, there can be no participation in the joys of God's redeemed, save by the cross of our Lord Jesus Christ; and that cross sweeps away all pretensions, levels all distinctions, and unites all in one holy congregation of blood-washed worshippers. The cross forms a boundary so lofty, and a defence so impenetrable, that not a single atom of earth or of nature can cross over or pass through to mingle itself with "the new creation." "*All* things are of God, who hath reconciled us to himself" (2 Cor 5:18).

You shall not break a bone of it

But, not only was Israel's *separation* from all strangers strictly maintained, in the institution of the Passover; Israel's *unity* was also as clearly enforced. "*In one house* shall it be eaten: thou shalt not carry forth anything of the flesh abroad out of the house, neither shall ye break a bone thereof" (ver. 46). Here is as fair and beauteous a type as we could have of the "one body and one Spirit." The Church of God is *one*. God sees it as such, maintains it as such, and will manifest it as such, in the view of angels, men, and devils, notwithstanding all that has been done to interfere with that hallowed unity. Blessed be God, the unity of His Church is as much in His keeping as is her justification, acceptance, and eternal security. "He keepeth all his bones; not one of them is broken" (Ps. 34:20). And, again, "a bone of him shall not be broken" (John 19:36). Despite the rudeness and hard-heartedness of Rome's soldiery, and despite all the hostile influences which have been set to work, from age to age, the body of Christ is one and its divine unity can never be broken. "THERE IS ONE BODY AND ONE SPIRIT;" and that, moreover, down here, on this very earth. Happy are they who have got faith to recognise this precious truth, and faithfulness to carry it out, in these last days; notwithstanding the almost insuperable difficulties which attend upon their profession and their practice! I believe God will own and honour such.

The Lord deliver us from that spirit of unbelief which would lead us to judge by the sight of our eyes, instead of by the light of His changeless Word!

---

[5] There is a vast difference between the divine method of dealing with the heathen (Rom. 1) and with the rejecters of the gospel (2 Thess. 1, 2). In reference to the former, we read, "And even as they did not like to retain God in their knowledge, God gave them over to a reprobate mind:" but with respect to the latter the word is "because they received not the love of *the truth* that they might *be saved* . . . God shall send them strong delusion, that they should believe *a lie*; that they all might *be damned*." The heathen refuse the testimony of creation, and are, therefore, left to themselves. The rejecters of the gospel refuse the full blaze of light which shines from the cross, and, therefore, "a strong delusion" will, ere long, be sent from God upon them. This is deeply solemn for an age like this, in the which there is so much light and so much profession.

Chapter 13

THE CONSECRATION OF THE FIRSTBORN

In the opening verses of this chapter, we are taught, clearly and distinctly, that personal devotedness and personal holiness are fruits which redeeming love produces in those who are the happy subjects thereof. The dedication of the firstborn and the feast of unleavened bread are here set forth in their immediate connexion with the deliverance of the people out of the land of Egypt. "Sanctify unto me all the firstborn, whatsoever openeth the womb among the children of Israel, both of man and of beast: it is mine. And Moses said unto the people, Remember this day, in which ye came out from Egypt, out of the house of bondage; for by strength of hand the Lord brought you out from this place: there shall no leavened bread be eaten." And again, " Seven days thou shalt eat unleavened bread, and in the seventh day shall be a feast to the Lord. Unleavened bread shall be eaten seven days: and there shall no leavened bread be seen with thee: neither shall there be leaven seen with thee in all thy quarters."

Then we have the reason of both these significant observances laid down. "And thou shalt show thy son in that day, saying, This is done *because of that* which the Lord did unto me when I came forth out of Egypt." And, again, "It shall be, when thy son asketh thee in time to come, saying, What is this? that thou shalt say unto him, By strength of hand the Lord brought us out from Egypt, from the house of bondage. And it came to pass, when Pharaoh would hardly let us go, that the Lord slew all the firstborn in the land of Egypt, both the firstborn of man and the firstborn of beast: *therefore* I sacrifice to the Lord all that openeth the matrix, being males; but all the firstborn of my children I redeem."

The more fully we enter, by the power of the Spirit of God, into the redemption which is in Christ Jesus, the more decided will be our separation, and the more whole-hearted will be our devotedness. The effort to produce either the one or the other, until redemption is known, will prove the most hopeless labour possible. All our doings must be "because of that which the Lord hath done," and not in order to get anything from Him. Efforts after life and peace prove that we are, as yet, strangers to the power of the blood; whereas the pure fruits of an experienced redemption are to the praise of Him who has redeemed us. "For by grace are ye saved, through faith; and that not of yourselves, it is the gift of God; not of works lest any man should boast; for we are his workmanship, created in Christ Jesus unto good works, which God hath before prepared that we should walk in them" (Eph. 2:8, 10). God has already prepared a path of good works for us to walk in; and He, by grace, prepares us to walk therein. It is only as saved that we can walk in such a path. Were it otherwise, we might boast; but seeing that we ourselves are as much God's workmanship as the path in which we walk, there is no room whatever for boasting.

True Christianity is but the manifestation of the life of Christ, implanted in us by the operation of the Holy Ghost, in pursuance of God's eternal counsels of sovereign grace; and all our doings, previous to the implantation of this life, are but "dead works," from which we need to have our consciences purged just as much as from "wicked works" (Heb. 9:14). The term "dead works," comprehends all works which men do with the direct object of getting life. If a man is seeking for life, it is very evident that he has not yet gotten it. He may be very sincere in seeking it, but his very sincerity only makes it the more obvious that, as yet, he has not consciously reached it. Hence, therefore, everything done in order to get life is a dead work, inasmuch as it is done without life – the life of Christ, the only true life, the only source from whence good works can flow. And, observe, it is not a question of "wicked works;" no one would think of getting life by such. No; you will find, on the contrary, that persons continually have recourse to "dead works," in order to ease their consciences, under the sense of "wicked works," whereas divine revelation teaches us that the conscience needs to be purged from the one as well as the other.

Again, as to righteousness, we read that "all our righteousnesses are as filthy rags." It is not said that "all our wickednesses," merely, "are as filthy rags." This would, at once, be admitted. But the fact is, that the very best fruit which we can produce, in the shape of religiousness and righteousness, is represented, on the page of eternal truth, as "dead works," and "filthy rags." Our very efforts after life, do but prove us to be dead; and our very efforts after righteousness do but prove us to be enwrapped in filthy rags. It is only as the actual possessors of eternal life and divine righteousness that we can walk in the divinely-prepared path of good works. Dead works and filthy rags could never be suffered to appear in such a path. None but "the redeemed of the Lord" can walk therein. It was as a redeemed people that Israel kept the feast of unleavened bread, and dedicated their firstborn to Jehovah. The former of these observances we have already considered; as to the latter, it contains a rich mine of instruction.

The destroying angel passed through the land of Egypt to destroy all the firstborn; but Israel's firstborn escaped through the death of a divinely-provided substitute. Accordingly, these latter appear before us, in this chapter, as a living people, dedicated to God. Saved by the blood of the lamb, they are privileged to consecrate their ransomed life to Him who had ransomed it. Thus it was only as redeemed that they possessed life. The grace of God alone had made them to differ, and had given them the place of living men in His presence. In their case, assuredly, there was no room for boasting; for, as to any personal merit or worthiness, we learn from this chapter that they were put on a level with an unclean and worthless thing. "Every firstling of an ass thou shalt redeem with a lamb; and if thou wilt not redeem it, then thou shalt break his neck; and all the firstborn of man among thy children shalt thou redeem" (ver. 13). There were two classes, the clean and the unclean; and man was classed with the latter. The lamb was to answer for the unclean; and if the ass were not redeemed, his neck was to be broken; so that an unredeemed man was put upon a level with an unclean animal, and that, moreover, in a condition than which nothing could be more worthless and unsightly. What a humiliating picture of man in his natural condition! Oh! that our poor proud hearts could enter more into it. Then should we rejoice more unfeignedly in the happy privilege of being washed from our guilt in the blood of the Lamb, and having all our personal vileness left behind for ever, in the tomb where our Surety lay buried.

Christ was the Lamb – the clean, the spotless Lamb. We are unclean. But – for ever adored be His matchless name! He took our position; and, *on the cross*, was made sin, and treated as such. That which we should have endured throughout the countless ages of eternity, He endured for us on the tree. He bore *all* that was due to us, there and then, in order that we might enjoy what is due to Him, for ever. He got our deserts that we might get His. The clean took, for a time, the place of the unclean, in order that the unclean might take for ever the place of the clean. Thus, whereas, by nature, we are represented by the loathsome figure of an ass with his neck broken; by grace we are represented by a risen and glorified Christ in heaven. Amazing contrast! It lays man's glory in the dust and magnifies the riches of redeeming love. It silences man's empty boastings and puts into his mouth a hymn of praise to God and the Lamb, which shall swell throughout the courts of heaven during the everlasting ages.[6]

How forcibly is one here reminded of the apostle's memorable and weighty words to the Romans, "Now if we be dead with Christ, we believe that we shall also live with him; knowing that Christ being raised from the dead, dieth no more; death hath no more dominion over him. For in that he died, he died unto sin once; but in that he liveth he liveth unto God. Likewise reckon ye also yourselves to be dead indeed unto sin, but alive unto God through Jesus Christ our Lord. Let not sin therefore reign in your mortal body, that ye should obey it in the lusts thereof. Neither yield ye your members as instruments of unrighteousness unto sin: but yield yourselves unto God, as those that are alive from the dead, and your members as instruments of righteousness unto God. For sin shall not have dominion over you: for ye are not under the law, but under grace" (Rom. 6:8-14). We are not only ransomed from the power of death and the grave, but also united to Him who has ransomed us at the heavy cost of His own precious life, that we might, in the energy of the Holy Ghost, dedicate our new life, with all its powers, to His service, so that His worthy name may be glorified in us according to the will of God and our Father.

THE FLIGHT FROM EGYPT

We are furnished, in the last few verses of Exodus 13 with a touching and beautiful example of the Lord's tender consideration of His people's need. "He knoweth our frame; He remembereth that we are dust" (Psalm 103:14). When He redeemed Israel and took them into relationship with Himself, He, in His unfathomed and infinite grace, charged Himself with all their need and weakness. It mattered not what they were or what they needed, when I AM was with them, in all the exhaustless treasures of that name. He had to conduct them from Egypt to Canaan, and we here find Him occupying Himself in selecting a suitable path for them. "And it came to pass, when Pharaoh had let the people go, that God led them not through the way of the land of the Philistines, although that was near; for God said, Lest peradventure the people repent when they see war, and they return to Egypt: but God led the people about through the way of the wilderness of the Red Sea" (ver. 17, 18).

The Lord, in His condescending grace, so orders for His people, that they do not, at their first setting out, encounter heavy trials which might have the effect of discouraging their hearts and driving them back. "The way of the wilderness" was a much more protracted route; but God had deep and varied lessons to teach His people, which could only be learnt in the desert. They were, afterwards, reminded of this fact, in the following passage: "And thou shalt remember all the way which the Lord thy God led thee, these forty years, in the wilderness, to humble thee, and to prove thee, to know what was in thine heart, whether thou wouldest keep his commandments or no. And he humbled thee, and suffered thee to hunger, and fed thee with manna, which thou knewest not, neither did thy fathers know, that he might make thee know that man doth not live by bread only, but by every word that proceedeth out of the mouth of the Lord doth man live. Thy raiment waxed not old upon thee, neither did thy foot swell, these forty years" (Deut. 8:2-4). Such precious lessons as these could never have been learnt in "the way of the land of the Philistines." In that way, they might have learnt what *war* was, at an early stage of their career; but "in the way of the wilderness," they learnt what *flesh* was, in all its crookedness, unbelief, and rebellion. But I AM was there, in all His patient grace, unerring wisdom, and infinite power. None but Himself could have met the demand. None but He could endure the opening up of the depths of a human heart. To have my heart unlocked anywhere, save in the presence of infinite grace, would plunge me in hopeless despair. The heart of man is but a little hell. What boundless mercy, then, to be delivered from its terrible depths!

> "Oh! to grace how great a debtor
> Daily I'm constrained to be;
> Let that grace, Lord, like a fetter,
> Bind my wandering heart to thee!"

"And they took their journey from Succoth, and encamped in Etham, in the edge of the wilderness. And the Lord went before them by day in a pillar of cloud, to lead them the way; and by night in a pillar of fire, to give them light; to go by day and night: he took not away the pillar of the cloud by day, nor the pillar of fire by night, from before the people." Jehovah not only selected a path for His people, but He also came down to walk with them therein, and make Himself known to them according to their need. He not only conducted them safely outside the bounds of Egypt, but He also came down, as it were, in His travelling chariot, to be their companion through all the vicissitudes of their wilderness journey. This was divine grace. They were not merely delivered out of the furnace of Egypt and then allowed to make the best of their way to Canaan. Such was not God's manner toward them. He knew that they had a toilsome and perilous journey before them, through serpents and scorpions, snares and difficulties, drought and barrenness; and He, blessed be His name for ever, would not suffer them to go alone. He would be the companion of all their toils and dangers; yea, "He went before them." He was "a guide, a glory, a defence, to save from every fear." Alas! that they should ever have grieved that Blessed One by their hardness of heart. Had they only walked humbly, contentedly, and confidingly with Him, their march would have been a triumphant one from first to last. With Jehovah in their forefront, no power could have interrupted their onward progress from Egypt to Canaan. He would have carried them through and planted them in the mountain of His inheritance, according to His promise, and by the power of His right hand; nor should as much as a single Canaanite have been allowed to remain therein to be a thorn in their side. Thus will it be, by and by, when Jehovah shall set His hand, a second time, to deliver His people from under the power of all their oppressors. May the Lord hasten the time!

6 It is interesting to see that by nature we are ranked with an unclean animal; by grace we are associated with Christ the spotless Lamb. There can be nothing lower than the place which belongs to us by nature; nothing higher than that which belongs to us by grace. Look, for example, at an ass with his neck broken; there is what an unredeemed man is worth. Look at "the precious blood of Christ;" there is what a redeemed man is worth. "Unto you that believe is the preciousness." That is, all who are washed in the blood partake of Christ's preciousness. As He is "a living stone," they are "living stones;" as He is "a precious stone, they are "precious stones." They get life and preciousness all from Him and in Him. They are as He is. Every stone in the edifice is precious, because purchased at no less a price than "the blood of the Lamb." May the people of God know more fully their place and privileges in Christ!

Chapter 14

CROSSING THE RED SEA

An impasse

"They that go down to the sea in ships, that do business in great waters; these see the works of the Lord, and his wonders in the deep" (Ps. 107:23, 24). How true is this! and yet our coward hearts do so shrink from those "great waters!" We prefer carrying on our traffic in the shallows, and, as a result, we fail to see "the works" and "wonders" of our God; for these can only be seen and known "in the deep."

It is in the day of trial and difficulty that the soul experiences something of the deep and untold blessedness of being able to count on God. Were all to go on smoothly, this would not be so. It is not in gliding along the surface of a tranquil lake that the reality of the Master's presence is felt; but actually when the tempest roars, and the waves roll over the ship. The Lord does not hold out to us the prospect of exemption from trial and tribulation; quite the opposite: He tells us we shall have to meet both the one and the other; but He promises to be with us in them; and this is infinitely better. God's presence *in* the trial is much better than exemption *from* the trial. The sympathy of His heart *with us* is sweeter far than the power of His hand *for us*. The Master's presence with His faithful servants, while passing through the furnace, was better far than the display of His power to keep them out of it (Dan. 3). We would frequently desire to be allowed to pass on our way without trial, but this would involve serious loss. The Lord's presence is never so sweet as in moments of appalling difficulty.

Thus it was in Israel's case, as recorded in this chapter.

They are brought into an overwhelming difficulty. They are called to "do business in great waters." "They are at their wit's end." Pharaoh, repenting himself of having let them go out of his land, determines to make one desperate effort to recover them. "And he made ready his chariot, and took his people with him: and he took six hundred chosen chariots, and all the chariots of Egypt, and captains over every one of them . . . And when Pharaoh drew nigh, the children of Israel lifted up their eyes, and, behold, the Egyptians marched after them; and they were sore afraid; and the children of Israel cried out unto the Lord." Here was a deeply-trying scene – one in which human effort could avail nothing. As well might they have attempted to put back with a straw the ocean's mighty tide, as seek to extricate themselves by anything that they could do. The sea was before them, Pharaoh's hosts behind them, and the mountains around them. And all this, be it observed, permitted and ordered of God. He had marked out their position before "Pi-hahiroth, between Migdol and the sea, over against Baal-zephon." Moreover, He permitted Pharaoh to come upon them. And why? Just to display Himself in the salvation of His people, and the total overthrow of their enemies. "To him that divided the Red Sea into parts; for his mercy endureth for ever. And made Israel to pass through the midst of it; for his mercy endureth for ever: but overthrew Pharaoh and his host in the Red Sea; for his mercy endureth for ever" (Ps. 136).

The purpose of God

There is not so much as a single position in all the desert-wanderings of God's redeemed, the boundaries of which are not marked off, with studious accuracy, by the hand of unerring wisdom and infinite love. The special bearings and peculiar influences of each position are carefully arranged. The Pi-hahiroths and the Migdols are all ordered with immediate reference to the moral condition of those whom God is conducting through the windings and labyrinths of the wilderness, and also to the display of His own character. Unbelief may ofttimes suggest the enquiry, "why is it thus?" God knows why; and He will, without doubt, reveal the why, whenever the revelation would promote His glory and His people's good. How often do we feel disposed to question as to the why and the wherefore of our being placed in such and such circumstances! How often do we perplex ourselves as to the reason of our being exposed to such and such trials! How much better to bow our heads in meek subjection, and say, "it is well," and "it shall be well!" When God fixes our position for us, we may rest assured it is a wise and salutary one; and even when we foolishly and wilfully choose a position for ourselves, He most graciously overrules our folly, and causes the influences of our self-chosen circumstances to work for our spiritual benefit.

It is when the people of God are brought into the greatest straits and difficulties, that they are favoured with the finest displays of God's character and actings; and for this reason He ofttimes leads them into a trying position, in order that He may the more markedly show Himself. He could have conducted Israel through the Red Sea, and far beyond the reach of Pharaoh's hosts, before ever the latter had started from Egypt; but that would not have so fully glorified His own name, or so entirely confounded the enemy, upon whom He designed to "get him honour." We too frequently lose sight of this great truth, and the consequence is that our hearts give way in the time of trial. If we could only look upon a difficult crisis as an occasion of bringing out, on our behalf, the sufficiency of divine grace, it would enable us to preserve the balance of our souls, and to glorify God, even in the deepest waters.

The unbelief of the Israelites

We feel disposed, it may be, to marvel at Israel's language, on the occasion now before us. We may feel at a loss to account for it; but the more we know of our own evil hearts of unbelief, the more we shall see how marvellously like them we are. They would seem to have forgotten the recent display of divine power on their behalf. They had seen the gods of Egypt judged, and the power of Egypt laid prostrate beneath the stroke of Jehovah's omnipotent hand. They had seen the iron chain of Egyptian bondage riven, and the furnace quenched by the same hand. All these things they had seen, and yet the moment a dark cloud appeared upon their horizon, their confidence gave way, their hearts failed, and they gave utterance to their unbelieving murmurings in the following language: "Because there were no graves in Egypt, hast thou taken us away to die in the wilderness? Wherefore hast thou dealt thus with us, to carry us forth out of Egypt! . . . It had been better for us to serve the Egyptians than that we should die in the wilderness" (ver. 11, 12). Thus is "blind unbelief," ever, "sure to err, and scan God's ways in vain." This unbelief is the same in all ages. It led David, in an evil hour, to say, "I shall one day perish by the hand of Saul; there is nothing better for me than that I should speedily escape into the land of the Philistines." (1 Sam. 27:1) And how did it turn out? Saul fell on Mount Gilboa; and David's throne was established for ever. Again, it led Elijah the Tishbite, in a moment of deep depression, to flee for his life, from the wrathful threatenings of Jezebel. How did it turn out? Jezebel was dashed to pieces on the pavement, and Elijah was taken in a chariot of fire to heaven.

So it was with Israel in their very first moment of trial. They really thought that the Lord had taken such pains to deliver them out of Egypt merely to let them die in the wilderness. They imagined that they had been preserved by the blood of the paschal lamb, in order that they might be buried in the wilderness. Thus it is that unbelief ever reasons. It leads us to interpret God in the presence of the difficulty, instead of interpreting the difficulty in the presence of God. Faith gets behind the difficulty, and there finds God, in all His faithfulness, love, and power. It is the believer's privilege ever to be in the presence of God. He has been introduced thither by the blood of the Lord Jesus Christ, and nothing should be suffered to take him thence. The place itself he never can lose, inasmuch as his Head and Representative, Christ, occupies it on His behalf. But although he cannot lose the thing itself, he can, very easily, lose all enjoyment of it, the experience and power of it. Whenever his difficulties come between his heart and the Lord, he is, evidently, not enjoying the Lord's presence, but suffering in the presence of his difficulties. Just as when a cloud comes between us and the sun, it robs us, for the time, of the enjoyment of his beams. It does not prevent him from shining, it merely hinders our enjoyment of him. Exactly so is it when we allow trials and sorrows, difficulties and perplexities, to hide from our souls the bright beams of our Father's countenance, which ever shine, with changeless lustre, in the face of Jesus Christ. There is no difficulty too great for our God; yea, the greater the difficulty, the more room there is for Him to act in His proper character, as the God of all power and grace. No doubt, Israel's position, in the opening of our chapter, was a deeply trying one – to flesh and blood perfectly overwhelming. But, then, the Maker of heaven and earth was there, and they had but to use Him.

Yet, alas! my reader, how speedily we fail when trial arises! These sentiments sound very nicely on the ear, and look very well upon paper; and, blessed be God, they are divinely true but, then, the thing is to practise them, when opportunity offers. It is in the practice of them that their power and blessedness are really proved. "If any man will *do* his will, he shall *know* of the doctrine, whether it be of God" (John 7:17).

See the salvation of the LORD

"And Moses said unto the people, Fear ye not, stand still, and see the salvation of the Lord, which he will show to you today; for the Egyptians whom ye have seen today ye shall see them again no more for ever. The Lord shall fight for you, and ye shall hold your peace" (ver. 13, 14). Here is the first attitude which faith takes in the presence of a trial. "*Stand still.*" This is impossible to flesh and blood. All who know in any measure, the restlessness of the human heart, under anticipated trial and difficulty, will be able to form some conception of what is involved in standing still. Nature must be *doing* something. It will rush hither and thither. It would fain have some hand in the matter. And although it may attempt to justify and sanctify its worthless doings, by bestowing upon them the imposing and popular title of "a legitimate use of means," yet are they the plain and positive fruits of unbelief which always shuts out God, and sees nought save the dark cloud of its own creation. Unbelief creates or magnifies difficulties, and then sets us about removing them by our own bustling and fruitless activities, which, in reality, do but raise a dust around us, which prevents our seeing God's salvation.

Faith, on the contrary, raises the soul above the difficulty, straight to God Himself, and enables one to "stand still." We gain nothing by our restless and anxious efforts. "We cannot make one hair white or black," nor "add one cubit to our stature." What could Israel do at the Red Sea? Could they dry it up? Could they level the mountains? Could they annihilate the hosts of Egypt? Impossible. There they were, enclosed within an impenetrable wall of difficulties, in view of which nature could but tremble and feel its own perfect impotency. But this was just the time for God to act. When unbelief is driven from the scene, then God can enter; and, in order to get a proper view of His actings, we must "stand still." Every movement of nature is, so far as it goes, a positive hindrance to our perception and enjoyment of divine interference on our behalf.

Stand still

This is true of us in every single stage of our history. It is true of us as sinners when, under the uneasy sense of sin upon the conscience, we are tempted to resort to our own doings, in order to obtain relief. Then, truly, we must "stand still" in order to "see the salvation of God." For what could we do in the matter of making an atonement for sin? Could we have stood with the Son of God upon the cross? Could we have accompanied Him down into the "horrible pit and the miry clay?" Could we have forced our passage upward to that eternal rock on which, in resurrection, He has taken His stand? Every right mind will at once pronounce the thought to be a daring blasphemy. God is alone in redemption; and as for us, we have but to "stand still and see the salvation of God." The very fact of its being God's salvation proves that man has nought to do in it.

The same is true of us, from the moment we have entered upon our Christian career. In every fresh difficulty, be it great or small, our wisdom is to stand still – to cease from our own works, and find our sweet repose in God's salvation. Nor can we make any distinction as to difficulties. We cannot say that there are some trifling difficulties which we ourselves can compass; while there are others in which nought save the hand of God can avail. No; all are alike beyond us. We are as little able to change the colour of a hair as to remove a mountain – to form a blade of grass as to create a world. All are alike to us, and all are alike to God. We have only, therefore, in confiding faith, to cast ourselves on Him who "humbleth himself (alike) to behold the things that are in heaven and on earth." We sometimes find ourselves carried triumphantly through the heaviest trials, while at other times, we quail, falter, and break down under the most ordinary dispensations. Why is this? Because, in the former, we are constrained to roll our burden over on the Lord; whereas, in the latter, we foolishly attempt to carry it ourselves. The Christian is, in himself, if he only realised it, like an exhausted receiver, in which a guinea and a feather have equal momenta.

The LORD shall fight for you

"The Lord shall fight for you, and ye shall hold your peace." Precious assurance! How eminently calculated to tranquillize the spirit in view of the most appalling difficulties and dangers! The Lord not only places Himself between us and our sins, but also between us and our circumstances. By doing the former, He gives us peace of conscience; by doing the latter, He gives us peace of heart. That the two things are perfectly distinct, every experienced Christian knows. Very many have peace of conscience, who have not peace of heart. They have, through grace and by faith, found Christ, in the divine efficacy of His blood, between them and all their sins; but they are not able, in the same simple way, to realise Him as standing, in His divine wisdom, love, and power, between them and their circumstances. This makes a material difference in the practical condition of the soul, as well as in the character of one's testimony. Nothing tends more to glorify the name of Jesus than that quiet repose of spirit which results from having Him between us and everything that could be a matter of anxiety to our hearts. "Thou wilt keep him in perfect peace whose mind is stayed on thee, because he trusteth in thee."

But some feel disposed to ask the question, "Are we not to do anything?" This may be answered by asking another, namely, what can we do? All who really know themselves must answer, nothing. If, therefore, we can do nothing, had we not better "stand still?" If the Lord is acting for us, had we not better stand back? Shall we run before Him? Shall we busily intrude ourselves upon His sphere of action! Shall we come in His way? There can be no possible use in two acting, when one is so perfectly competent to do all. No one would think of bringing a lighted candle to add brightness to the sun at mid-day: and yet the man who would do so might well be accounted wise, in comparison with him who attempts to assist God by his bustling officiousness.

Speak unto the children of Israel that they go forward

However, when God, in His great mercy, opens the way, faith can walk therein. It only ceases from man's way in order to walk in God's. "And the Lord said unto Moses, Wherefore criest thou unto me? Speak unto the children of Israel that they go forward." It is only when we have learnt to "stand still" that we are able effectually to go forward. To attempt the latter, until we have learnt the former, is sure to issue in the exposure of our folly and weakness. It is, therefore, true wisdom, in all times of difficulty and perplexity, to "stand still" – to wait only upon God, and He will, assuredly, open a way for us; and then we can peacefully and happily "go forward." There is no uncertainty when God makes a way for us; but every self-devised path must prove a path of doubt and hesitation. The unregenerate man may move along with great apparent firmness and decision in his own ways; but one of the most distinct elements, in the new creation, is self-distrust, and the element which answers thereto is confidence in God. It is when our eyes have seen God's salvation that we can walk therein; but this can never be distinctly seen until we have been brought to the end of our own poor doings.

There is peculiar force and beauty in the expression, "*see* the salvation of God." The very fact of our being called to "see" God's salvation, proves that the salvation is a complete one. It teaches that salvation is a thing wrought out and revealed by God, to be seen and enjoyed by us. It is not a thing made up partly of God's doing, and partly of man's. Were it so, it could not be called *God's* salvation. In order to be His, it must be wholly divested of everything pertaining to man. The only possible effect of human efforts is to raise a dust which obscures the view of God's salvation.

"Speak to the children of Israel that they go forward." Moses himself seems to have been brought to a stand, as appears from the Lord's question, "Wherefore criest thou to me?" Moses could tell the people to "stand still and see the salvation of God," while his own spirit was giving forth its exercises in an earnest cry to God. However, there is no use in crying when we ought to be acting; just as there is no use in acting when we ought to be waiting. Yet such is, ever, our way. We attempt to move forward when we ought to stand still, and we stand still when we ought to move forward. In Israel's case, the question might spring up in the heart, "whither are we to go?" To all appearance there lay an insurmountable barrier in the way of any movement forward. How were they to go through the sea? This was the point. Nature never could solve this question. But we may rest assured that God never gives a command without, at the same time, communicating the power to obey. The real condition of the heart may be tested by the command; but the soul that is, by grace, disposed to obey, receives power from above to do so. When Christ commanded the man with the withered hand to stretch it forth, the man might naturally have said, "How can I stretch forth an arm which hangs dead by my side?" But he did not raise any question whatever, for with the command, and from the same source, came the power to obey.

God makes a path for faith

Thus, too, in Israel's case, we see that with the command to go forward came the provision of grace. "But lift thou up thy rod, and stretch out thy hand over the sea, and divide it; and the children of Israel shall go on dry ground through the midst of the sea." Here was the path of faith. The hand of God opens the way for us to take the first step, and this is all that faith ever asks. God never gives guidance for two steps at a time. I must take one step, and then I get light for the next. This keeps the heart in abiding dependence upon God. "By faith they passed through the Red Sea as by dry land." It is evident that the sea was not divided throughout, at once. Had it been so, it would have been "sight" and not "faith." It does not require faith to begin a journey when I can see all the way through; but to begin when I can merely see the first step, this is faith. The sea opened as Israel moved forward, so that for every fresh step, they needed to be cast upon God. Such was the path along which the redeemed of the Lord moved, under His own conducting hand. They passed through the dark waters of death, and found these very waters to be "a wall unto them, on their right hand and on their left."

The Egyptians could not move in such a path as this. They moved on because they saw the way open before them: with them it was sight, and not faith – "Which the Egyptians assaying to do were drowned." When people *assay* to do what faith alone can accomplish, they only encounter defeat and confusion. The path along which God calls His people to walk is one which nature can never tread – "Flesh and blood cannot inherit the kingdom of God" (1 Cor. 15:50). Neither can it walk in the ways of God. Faith is the great characteristic principle of God's kingdom, and faith alone can enable us to walk in God's ways. "Without faith it is impossible to please God" (Heb. 11). It glorifies God exceedingly when we move on with Him, as it were, blindfold. It proves that we have more confidence in His eyesight than in our own. If I know that God is looking out for me, I may well close my eyes, and move on in holy calmness and stability. In human affairs we know that when there is a sentinel or watchman at his post, others can sleep quietly. How much more may we rest in perfect security, when we know that He who neither slumbers nor sleeps has His eye upon us, and His everlasting arms around us!

The LORD between the Egyptians and Israel

"And the angel of God which went before the camp of Israel, removed and went behind them; and the pillar of the cloud went from before their face, and stood behind them. And it came between the camp of the Egyptians and the camp of Israel; and it was a cloud and darkness to them, but it gave light by night to these; so that the one came not near the other all the night" (ver. 19, 20). Jehovah placed Himself right between Israel and the enemy – this was protection indeed.

Before ever Pharaoh could touch a hair of Israel's head, he should make his way through the very pavilion of the Almighty – yea, through the Almighty Himself. Thus it is that God ever places Himself between His people and every enemy, so that "no weapon formed against them can prosper." He has placed Himself between us and our sins; and it is our happy privilege to find Him between us and every one and every thing that could be against us. This is the true way in which to find both peace of heart and peace of conscience. The believer may institute a diligent and anxious search for his sins, but he cannot find them. Why? Because God is between him and them. He has cast all our sins behind His back; while, at, the same time, He sheds forth upon us the light of His reconciled countenance.

In the same manner, the believer may look for his difficulties, and not find them, because God is between him and them. If, therefore, the eye, instead of resting on our sins and sorrows, could rest only upon Christ, it would sweeten many a bitter cup, and enlighten many a gloomy hour. But one finds constantly that nine-tenths of our trials and sorrows are made up of anticipated or imaginary evils, which only exist in our own disordered, because unbelieving, minds. May my reader know the solid peace both of heart and conscience which results from having Christ, in all His fullness, between him and *all* his sins, and *all* his sorrows.

It is, at once, most solemn and interesting to note the double aspect of the "pillar," in this chapter. "It was a cloud and darkness" to the Egyptians, but "it gave light by night" to Israel. How like the cross of our Lord Jesus Christ! Truly that cross has a double aspect, likewise. It forms the foundation of the believer's peace; and, at the same time, seals the condemnation of a guilty world. The self-same blood which purges the believer's conscience and gives him perfect peace, stains this earth and consummates its guilt. The very mission of the Son of God which strips the world of its cloak, and leaves it wholly without excuse, clothes the Church with a fair mantle of righteousness, and fills her month with ceaseless praise. The very same Lamb who will terrify, by His unmitigated wrath, all tribes and classes of earth, will lead, by His gentle hand, His blood-bought flock, through the green pastures, and beside the still waters for ever (compare Rev. 6:15-17, with Rev. 7:13-17).

Pharaoh's armies are drowned

The close of our chapter shows us Israel triumphant on the shore of the Red Sea, and Pharaoh's hosts submerged beneath its waves. The fears of the former and the boastings of the latter had both alike been proved utterly groundless. Jehovah's glorious work had annihilated both the one and the other. The same waters which formed a wall for God's redeemed, formed a grave for Pharaoh. Thus it is ever: those who walk by faith, find a path to walk in, while all who assay to do so find a grave. This is a solemn truth which is not, in any wise, weakened by the fact that Pharaoh was acting in avowed and positive hostility to God, when he "assayed" to pass through the Red Sea. It will ever be found true that all who attempt to imitate faith's actings will be confounded. Happy are they who are enabled, however feebly, to walk by faith. They are moving along a path of unspeakable blessedness – a path which, though it may be marked by failure and infirmity, is, nevertheless, "begun, continued, and ended in God." Oh! that we may all enter more fully into the divine reality, the calm elevation, and the holy independence of this path.

The typical meaning

We ought not to turn from this fruitful section of our book without a reference to 1 Cor. 10 in which we have an allusion to "the cloud and the sea." "Moreover, brethren, I would not that ye should be ignorant, how that all our fathers were *under the cloud*, and all passed *through the sea*; and were all baptised unto Moses in the cloud and in the sea" (ver. 1, 2). There is much deep and precious instruction for the Christian in this passage. The apostle goes on to say, "now these things were our types," thus furnishing us with a divine warrant for interpreting Israel's baptism "in the sea and in the cloud," in a typical way; and, assuredly, nothing could be more deeply significant or practical. It was as a people thus baptised that they entered upon their wilderness journey, for which provision was made in "the spiritual meat" and "spiritual drink," provided by the hand of love. In other words, they were, typically, a people dead to Egypt and all pertaining thereto. The cloud and the sea were to them what the cross and grave of Christ are to us. The cloud secured them from their enemies; the sea separated them from Egypt: the cross, in like manner, shields us from all that could be against us, and we stand at heaven's side of the empty tomb of Jesus. Here we commence our wilderness journey. Here we begin to taste the heavenly manna and to drink of the streams which emanate from "that spiritual Rock," while, as a pilgrim people, we make our way onward to that land of rest of the which God has spoken to us.

I would further add here, that my reader should seek to understand the difference between the Red Sea and Jordan. They both have their antitype in the death of Christ. But, in the former, we see separation from Egypt; in the latter, introduction into the land of Canaan. The believer is not merely separated from this present evil world, by the cross of Christ; but he is quickened out of the grave of Christ, "raised up together, and made to sit together with Christ, in the heavenlies" (Eph. 2:5, 6). Hence, though surrounded by the things of Egypt, he is, as to his actual experience, in the wilderness; while, at the same time, he is borne upward, by the energy of faith, to that place where Jesus sits, at the right hand of God. Thus, the believer is not merely "forgiven all trespasses;" but actually associated *with* a risen Christ in heaven. He is not merely saved *by* Christ, but linked *with* Him, for ever. Nothing short of this could either satisfy God's affections or actualize His purposes, in reference to the Church.

Reader, do we understand these things? Do we believe them? Are we realizing them? Do we manifest the power of them? Blessed be the grace that has made them unalterably true with respect to every member of the body of Christ, whether it be an eye or an eye-lash, a hand or a foot. Their truth, therefore, does not depend upon our manifestation, our realization, or our understanding, but upon "THE PRECIOUS BLOOD OF CHRIST," which has cancelled all our guilt and laid the foundation of all God's counsels respecting us. Here is true rest for every broken heart and every burdened conscience.

Chapter 15

THE SONG OF DELIVERANCE

I will sing unto the Lord

This chapter opens with Israel's magnificent song of triumph on the shore of the Red Sea, when they had seen "that great work which the Lord did upon the Egyptians." They had seen God's salvation, and they, therefore, sing His praise and recount His mighty acts. "*Then* sang Moses and the children of Israel this song unto the Lord." Up to this moment, we have not heard so much as a single note of praise. We have heard their cry of deep sorrow, as they toiled amid the brick-kilns of Egypt; we have hearkened to their cry of unbelief, when surrounded by what they deemed insuperable difficulties; but, until now, we have heard no song of praise. It was not until, as a saved people, they found themselves surrounded by the fruits of God's salvation, that the triumphal hymn burst forth from the whole redeemed assembly. It was when they emerged from their significant baptism "in the cloud and in the sea," and were able to gaze upon the rich spoils of victory, which lay scattered around them, that six hundred thousand voices were heard chanting the song of victory. The waters of the Red Sea rolled between them and Egypt, and they stood on the shore as a fully delivered people, and, therefore, they were able to praise Jehovah.

In this, as in everything else, they were our types. We, too, must know ourselves as saved, in the power of death and resurrection, before ever we can present clear and intelligent worship. There will always be reserve and hesitancy in the soul, proceeding, no doubt, from positive inability to enter into the accomplished redemption which is in Christ Jesus. There may be the acknowledgement of the fact that there is salvation in Christ, and in none other; but this is a very different thing from apprehending, by faith, the true character and ground of that salvation, and realising it as *ours*. The Spirit of God reveals, with unmistakable clearness, in the Word, that the Church is united to Christ in death and resurrection; and, moreover, that a risen Christ, at God's right hand, is the measure and pledge of the Church's acceptance. When this is believed, it conducts the soul entirely beyond the region of doubt and uncertainty. How can the Christian doubt when he knows that he is continually represented before the throne of God by an Advocate, even "Jesus Christ the righteous?" It is the privilege of the very feeblest member of the Church of God to know that he was represented by Christ on the cross; that *all* his sins were confessed, borne, judged, and atoned for there. This is a divine reality, and, when laid hold of by faith, must give peace. But nothing short of it ever can give peace. There may be earnest, anxious, and most sincere desires after God. There may be the most pious and devout attendance upon all the ordinances, offices, and forms of religion. But there is no other possible way in which to get the sense of sin entirely removed from the conscience, but seeing it judged in the Person of Christ, as a sin-offering on the cursed tree. If it was judged there, once for all, it is now by the believer to be regarded as a divinely and, therefore, eternally-settled question. And that it was so judged is proved by the resurrection of the Surety. "I know that whatsoever God doeth it shall be for ever: nothing can be put to it nor anything taken from it: and God doeth it that men should fear before him" (Eccl. 3:14).

However, while it is generally admitted that all this is true in reference to the Church collectively, many find considerable difficulty in making a personal application thereof. They are ready to say, with the psalmist, "Truly, God is good to Israel, even to such as are of a clean heart. *But as for me,*" &c. (Ps. 73:1, 2). They are looking at themselves instead of at Christ, in death, and Christ, in resurrection. They are occupied rather with their appropriation of Christ than with Christ Himself. They are thinking of their capacity rather than their title. Thus they are kept in a state of the most distressing uncertainty; and, as a consequence, they are never able to take the place of happy, intelligent worshippers. They are praying for salvation instead of rejoicing in the conscious possession of it. They are looking at their imperfect fruits instead of Christ's perfect atonement.

God glorified

Now, in looking through the various notes of this song, in Exodus 15, we do not find a single note about *self*, its doings, its sayings, its feelings, or its fruits. It is all about Jehovah from beginning to end. It begins with, "I will sing unto the Lord, for *he* hath triumphed gloriously: the horse and his rider hath *he* thrown into the sea." This is a specimen of the entire song. It is a simple record of the attributes and actings of Jehovah. In chapter 14 the hearts of the people had, as it were, been pent up, by the excessive pressure of their circumstances: but in chapter 15 the pressure is removed, and their hearts find full vent in a sweet song of praise. Self is forgotten. Circumstances are lost sight of. One object, and but one, fills their vision, and that object is the Lord Himself in His character and ways. They were able to say, "Thou, Lord, hast made me glad through thy work; I will triumph in the works of thy hands" (Ps. 92:4). This is true worship. It is when poor worthless self, with all its belongings, is lost sight of, and Christ alone fills the heart, that we present proper worship. There is no need for the efforts of a fleshly pietism to awaken in the soul feelings of devotion. Nor is there any demand whatever for the adventitious appliances of religion, so called, to kindle in the soul the flame of acceptable worship. Oh! no; let but the heart be occupied with the Person of Christ, and "songs of praise" will be the natural result. It is impossible for the eye to rest on Him and the spirit not be bowed in holy worship. If we contemplate the worship of the hosts which surround the throne of God and the Lamb, we shall find that it is ever evoked by the presentation of some special feature of divine excellence or divine acting. Thus should it be with the Church on earth; and when it is not so, it is because we allow things to intrude upon us which have no place in the regions of unclouded light and unalloyed blessedness. In all true worship, God Himself is at once the object of worship, the subject of worship, and the power of worship.

Hence Exodus 15 is a fine specimen of a song of praise. It is the language of a redeemed people celebrating the worthy praise of Him who had redeemed them. "The Lord is my strength and song, and he is become my salvation: He is my God, and I will prepare him an habitation; my father's God, and I will exalt him. The Lord is a man of war, the Lord is his name, . . . thy right hand, O Lord is become glorious in power: thy right hand, O Lord, hath dashed in pieces the enemy . . . who is like unto thee, O Lord, among the gods? Who is like thee, glorious in holiness, fearful in praises, doing wonders? . . . Thou, in thy mercy, hast led forth the people which thou hast redeemed: thou hast guided them in thy strength unto thy holy habitation. . . . The Lord shall reign for ever and ever." How comprehensive is the range of this song. It begins with redemption and ends with the glory. It begins with the cross, and ends with the kingdom. It is like a beauteous rainbow, of which one end dips in "the sufferings," and the other in "the glory which should follow." It is all about Jehovah. It is an outpouring of soul produced by a view of God and His gracious and glorious actings.

Moreover, it does not stop short of the actual accomplishment of the divine purpose; as we read, "Thou *hast guided* them in thy strength unto thy holy habitation." The people were able to say this, though they had but just planted their foot on the margin of the desert. It was not the expression of a vague hope. It was not feeding upon poor blind chance. Oh! no; when the soul is wholly occupied with God, it is enabled to launch out into all the fullness of His grace, to bask in the sunshine of His countenance, and delight itself in the rich abundance of His mercy and loving-kindness. There is not a cloud upon the prospect, when the believing soul, taking its stand upon the eternal rock on which redeeming love has set it in association with a risen Christ, looks up into the spacious vault of God's infinite plans and purposes, and dwells upon the effulgence of that glory which God has prepared for all those who have washed their robes and made them white in the blood of the Lamb.

This will account for the peculiarly brilliant, elevated, and unqualified character of all those bursts of praise which we find throughout sacred Scripture, The creature is set aside; God is the object. He fills the entire sphere of the soul's vision. There is nothing of man, his feelings, or his experiences, and, therefore, the stream of praise flows copiously and uninterruptedly forth. How different is this from some of the hymns which we so often hear sung in Christian assemblies, so full of our failings, our feebleness, our shortcomings. The fact is, we can never sing with real, spiritual intelligence and power when we are looking at ourselves. We shall ever be discovering something within which will act as a drawback to our worship. Indeed, with many, it seems to be accounted a Christian grace to be in a continual state of doubt and hesitation; and, as a consequence, their hymns are quite in character with their condition. Such persons, however sincere and pious, have never yet, in the actual experience of their souls, entered upon the proper ground of worship. They have not yet got done with themselves. They have not passed through the sea; and, as a spiritually baptised people, taken their stand on the shore, in the power of resurrection. They are still, in some way or another, occupied with self. They do not regard self as a crucified thing, with which God is for ever done.

May the Holy Ghost lead all God's people into fuller, clearer, and worthier apprehensions of their place and privilege as those who, being washed from their sins in the blood of Christ, are presented before God in all that infinite and unclouded acceptance in which He stands, as the risen and glorified Head of His Church. Doubts and fears do not become them, for their divine Surety has not left a shadow of a foundation on which to build a doubt or a fear. Their place is within the veil. They "have boldness to enter into the holiest by the blood of Jesus" (Heb. 10:19). Are there any doubts or fears in the holiest? Is it not evident that a doubting spirit virtually calls in question the perfectness of Christ's work – a work which has been attested, in the view of all created intelligence, by the resurrection of Christ from the dead? That blessed one could not have left the tomb unless all ground of doubting and fearing had been perfectly removed on behalf of His people. Wherefore, it is the Christian's sweet privilege ever to triumph in a full salvation. The Lord Himself has become his salvation; and he has only to enjoy the fruits of that which God has wrought for him, and to walk to His praise while waiting for that time, when "Jehovah shall reign for ever and ever."

The habitation of God is with men

But there is one note in this song, to which I shall just invite my reader's attention. "He is my God and I will prepare him an habitation." It is worthy of note that when the heart was full to overflowing with the joy of redemption, it gives expression to its devoted purpose in reference to "a habitation for God." Let the Christian reader ponder this. God dwelling with man is a grand thought pervading Scripture from Exodus 15 to Revelation. Hearken to the following utterance of a devoted heart: "Surely I will not come into the tabernacle of my house nor go up into my bed; I will not give sleep to mine eyes or slumber to mine eyelids, until I find out a place for the Lord, *an habitation* for the mighty God of Jacob" (Ps. 132:3-5). Again, "For the zeal of thine house hath eaten me up" (Ps. 69:9; John 2:17). I do not attempt to pursue this subject here; but I would fain awaken such an interest concerning it in the breast of my reader, as shall lead him to pursue it, prayerfully, for himself, from the earliest notice of it in the Word until he arrives at that soul-stirring announcement, "Behold the tabernacle of God is with men, and he will dwell with them, and they shall be his people, and God himself shall be with them and be their God. And God shall wipe away all tears from their eyes" (Rev. 21:3, 4).

DEPARTURE FOR THE WILDERNESS

"So Moses brought Israel from the Red Sea; and they went out into the wilderness of Shur: and they went three days in the wilderness and found no water" (ver. 22). It is when we get into wilderness experience, that we are put to the test as to the real measure of our acquaintance with God and with our own hearts. There is a freshness and an exuberance of joy connected with the opening of our Christian career, which very soon receives a check from the keen blast of the desert; and then, unless there is a deep sense of what God is to us, above and beyond everything else, we are apt to break down, and, "in our hearts, turn back again into Egypt." The discipline of the wilderness is needful, not to furnish us with a title to Canaan, but to make us acquainted with God and with our own hearts; to enable us to enter into the power of our relationship, and to enlarge our capacity for the enjoyment of Canaan when we actually get there (see Deut. 8:2-5).

The greenness, freshness, and luxuriance of spring have peculiar charms, which will pass away before the scorching heat of summer; but then, with proper care, that very heat which removes the fair traces of spring, produces the mellowed and matured fruits of autumn. Thus it is also in the Christian life; for there is, as we know, a striking and deeply instructive analogy between the principles which obtain in the kingdom of nature and those which characterise the kingdom of grace, seeing it is the same God whose handiwork meets our view in both.

There are three distinct positions in which we may contemplate Israel, namely, in Egypt, in the wilderness, and in the land of Canaan. In all these, they are "our types;" but we are in all three together. This may seem paradoxical, but it is true. As a matter of actual fact, we are in Egypt, surrounded by natural things, which are entirely adapted to the natural heart. But, inasmuch as we have been called by God's grace into fellowship with His Son Jesus Christ, we, according to the affections and desires of the new nature, necessarily find our place outside of all that which belongs to Egypt[7], (i.e., the world in its natural state), and this causes us to taste of wilderness experience, or, in other words, it places us, as a matter of experience, in the wilderness. The divine nature earnestly breathes after a different order of things – after a purer atmosphere than that with which we find ourselves surrounded, and thus it causes us to feel Egypt to be a moral desert.

But then, inasmuch as we are, in God's view, eternally associated with Him who is passed right through into the heavenlies, and taken His seat there in triumph and majesty, it is our happy privilege to know ourselves, by faith, as "sitting together with him" there (Eph. 2). So that although we are, as to our bodies, in Egypt, we are, as to our experience, in the wilderness, while at the same time, faith conducts us, in spirit, into Canaan, and enables us to feed upon "the old corn of the land," i.e., upon Christ, not as One come down to earth merely, but as One gone back to heaven and seated there in glory.

Mara – the bitter waters

The concluding verses of this 15th chapter show us Israel in the wilderness. Up to this point it seemed to them to be all fair sailing. Heavy judgments poured upon Egypt, but Israel perfectly exempt – the army of Egypt dead upon the sea shore, but Israel in triumph. All this was well enough; but alas! the aspect of things speedily changed. The notes of praise were soon exchanged for the accents of discontent. "When they came to Marah they could not drink of the waters of Marah, for they were bitter: therefore the name of it was called Marah. And the people murmured against Moses, saying, What shall we drink?" Again, "the whole congregation of the children of Israel murmured against Moses and Aaron in the wilderness: and the children of Israel said unto them, Would to God we had died by the hand of the Lord in the land of Egypt, when we sat by the flesh pots, and when we did eat bread to the full! for ye have brought us forth into this wilderness to kill this whole assembly with hunger."

Here were the trials of the wilderness. "What shall we eat?" and "what shall we drink?" The waters of Marah tested the heart of Israel and developed their murmuring spirit; but the Lord showed them that there was no bitterness which He could not sweeten with the provision of His own grace. "And the Lord showed them a tree, which when he had cast into the waters, the waters were made sweet; there he made for them a statute and an ordinance, and there he proved them." Beauteous figure this of Him who was, in infinite grace, cast into the bitter waters of death, in order that those waters might yield nought but sweetness to us for ever. We can truly say, "the bitterness of death is past," and nothing remains for us but the eternal sweets of resurrection.

Verse 26 sets before us the momentous character of this first stage of God's redeemed in the wilderness. We are in great danger, at this point, of falling into a fretful, impatient, murmuring spirit. The only remedy for this is to keep the eye steadily fixed on Jesus – "looking unto Jesus." He, blessed be His name, ever unfolds himself according to the need of His people; and they, instead of complaining of their circumstances, should only make their circumstances an occasion of drawing afresh upon Him. Thus it is that the wilderness ministers to our experience of what God is. It is a school in which we learn His patient grace and ample resources. "Forty years suffered he their manners in the wilderness" (Acts 13:18). The spiritual mind will ever own that it is worth having bitter waters for God to sweeten. "We glory in tribulations also: knowing that tribulation worketh patience; and patience, experience; and experience, hope; and hope maketh not ashamed; because the love of God is shed abroad in our hearts by the Holy Ghost which is given unto us" (Rom. 5:3-5).

Elim – the wells and the palms

However, the wilderness has its Elims as well as its Marahs; its wells and palm trees, as well as its bitter waters. "And they came to Elim, where were twelve wells of water, and threescore and ten palm trees: and they encamped there by the waters" (Ver. 27). The Lord graciously and tenderly provides green spots in the desert for His journeying people; and though they are, at best, but oases, yet are they refreshing to the spirit and encouraging to the heart. The sojourn at Elim was eminently calculated to soothe the hearts of the people, and hush their murmurings. The grateful shade of its palm trees, and the refreshing of its wells, came in, sweetly and seasonably, after the trial of Marah, and significantly set forth, in our view, the precious virtues of that spiritual ministry which God provides for his people down here. "The twelve and "the seventy " are numbers intimately associated with ministry.

But Elim was not Canaan. Its wells and palm trees were but foretastes of that happy land which lay beyond the bounds of the sterile desert on which the redeemed had just entered. It furnished refreshment, no doubt, but it was wilderness refreshment. It was but for passing moment, designed, in grace, to encourage their depressed spirits, and nerve them for their onward march to Canaan. Thus it is, as we know, with ministry in the Church. It is a gracious provision for our need, designed to refresh, strengthen, and encourage our hearts, "until we all come to the fullness of the measure of the stature of Christ" (Eph. 4).

---

[7] There is a wide moral difference between Egypt and Babylon, which it is important to understand. Egypt was that out of which Israel came; Babylon was that into which they were afterwards carried (comp. Amos 5:25-27 with Acts 7:42, 43). Egypt expresses what man has made of the world; Babylon

expresses what Satan has made, is making, or will make, of the professing Church. Hence, we are not only surrounded with the *circumstances* of Egypt, but also by the moral *principles* of Babylon.

This renders our "days" what the Holy Ghost has termed "perilous." (*chalepoi* – "difficult"). It demands a special energy of the Spirit of God, and complete subjection to the authority of the Word, to enable one to meet the combined influence of the realities of Egypt and the spirit and principles of Babylon. The former meet the natural desires of the heart; while the latter connect themselves with, and address themselves to, the *religiousness* of nature, which gives them a peculiar hold upon the heart. Man is a religious being, and peculiarly susceptible of the influences which arise from music, sculpture, painting, and pompous rites and ceremonies. When these things stand connected with the full supply of all his natural wants – yes, with all the ease and luxury of life, nothing but the mighty power of God's Word and Spirit can keep one true to Christ.

We should also remark that there is a vast difference between the destinies of Egypt and those of Babylon. The 19th of Isaiah sets before us the blessings that are in store for Egypt. It concludes thus: "And the Lord shall smite Egypt; he shall smite and heal it: and they shall return even unto the Lord, and he shall be entreated of them, and shall heal them. . . . in that day shall Israel be the third with Egypt and with Assyria, even a blessing in the midst of the land, whom the Lord of Hosts shall bless, saying, Blessed be Egypt my people, and Assyria the work of my hands, and Israel mine inheritance" (ver. 22-25).

Very different is the close of Babylon's history, whether viewed as a literal city or a spiritual system. "I will also make it a possession for the bittern, and pools of water; and I will sweep it with the besom of destruction, saith the Lord of hosts" (Isaiah 14:23). "It shall never be inhabited, neither shall it be dwelt in from generation to generation" (Isaiah 13:20). So much for Babylon literally; and looking at it from a mystic or spiritual point of view, we read its destiny in Revelation 18. The entire chapter is a description of Babylon, and it concludes thus: "A strong angel took up a stone, like a great millstone, and cast it into the sea, saying, "Thus, with violence shall that great city Babylon be thrown down, and shall be found no more at all" (Verse 21).

With what immense solemnity should those words fall upon the ears of all who are in any wise connected with Babylon – that is to say, with the false, professing church. "Come out of her, my people, that ye be not partakers of her sins, and that ye receive not of her plagues!" (Rev. 18:5). The "power" of the Holy Ghost will necessarily produce, or express itself in a certain "form," and the enemy's aim has ever been to rob the professing church of the power, while he leads her to cling to, and perpetuate the form – to stereotype the form when all the spirit and life has passed away. Thus he builds the spiritual Babylon. The stones of which this city is built are lifeless professors; and the slime or mortar which binds these stones together is "a form of godliness without the power."

Oh! my beloved reader, let us see to it that we fully, clearly and influentially understand these things.

Chapter 16

THE MANNA

The people's murmurings

"And they took their journey from Elim, and all the congregation of the children of Israel came unto the wilderness of Sin, which is between Elim and Sinai, on the fifteenth day of the second month after their departure out of the land of Egypt" (Chap. 16:1). Here we find Israel in a very marked and interesting position. It is still the wilderness, no doubt, but it is a most important and significant stage thereof, namely, "between Elim and Sinai." The former was the place where they had so recently experienced the refreshing springs of divine ministry; the latter was the place where they entirely got off the ground of free and sovereign grace, and placed themselves under a covenant of works. These facts render "the wilderness of Sin" a singularly interesting portion of Israel's journey. Its features and influences are as strongly marked as those of any point in their whole career. They are here seen as the subjects of the same grace which had brought them up out of the land of Egypt, and, therefore, all their murmurings are instantly met by divine supplies. When God acts in the display of His grace, there is no hindrance. The streams of blessing which emanate from Him, flow onward without interruption. It is only when man puts himself under law that he forfeits everything; for then God must allow him to prove how much he can claim on the ground of his own works.

When God visited and redeemed His people, and brought them forth out of the land of Egypt, it assuredly was not for the purpose of suffering them to die of hunger and thirst in the wilderness. They should have known this. They ought to have trusted Him, and walked in the confidence of that love which had so gloriously delivered them from the horrors of Egyptian bondage. They should have remembered that it was infinitely better to be in the desert with God, than in the brick-kilns with Pharaoh. But no; the human heart finds it immensely difficult to give God credit for pure and perfect love. It has far more confidence in Satan than God. Look, for a moment, at all the sorrow and suffering, the misery and degradation which man has endured by reason of his having hearkened to the voice of Satan, and yet he never gives utterance to a word of complaint of his service, or of desire to escape from under his hand. He is not discontented with Satan, or weary of serving him. Again and again, he reaps bitter fruits in those fields which Satan has thrown open to him; and yet, again and again, he may be seen sowing the self-same seed, and undergoing the self-same labours.

How different it is in reference to God! When we have set out to walk in His ways, we are ready, at the earliest appearance of pressure or trial, to murmur and rebel. Indeed, there is nothing in which we so signally fail as in the cultivation of a confiding and thankful spirit. Ten thousand mercies are forgotten in the presence of one single trying privation. We have been frankly forgiven all our sins, "accepted in the Beloved," made heirs of God and joint-heirs with Christ, the expectants of eternal glory; and, in addition to all, our path through the desert is strewed with countless mercies; and yet let but a cloud, the size of a man's hand, appear on the horizon, and we at once forget the rich mercies of the past in view of this single cloud, which, after all, may only "break in blessings on our head." The thought of this should humble us deeply in the presence of God. How unlike we are in this, as in every other respect, to our blessed Exemplar! Look at Him – the true Israel in the wilderness – surrounded by wild beasts, and fasting for forty days. How did He carry Himself? Did He murmur? Did He complain of His lot? Did He wish Himself in other circumstances? Ah! no. God was the portion of His cup and the lot of His inheritance (Ps. 16). And, therefore, when the tempter approached and offered Him the necessaries, the glories, the distinctions, and the honours of this life, He refused them all, and tenaciously held fast the position of absolute dependence upon God and implicit obedience to His word. He would only take bread from God and glory from Him likewise.

Very different was it with Israel after the flesh! No sooner did they feel the pressure of hunger than "they murmured against Moses and Aaron in the wilderness." They seemed to have actually lost the sense of having been delivered by the hand of Jehovah, for they said, "*Ye* have brought us forth into this wilderness." And, again, in chapter 17, "the people murmured against Moses and said, Wherefore is this that *thou* hast brought us up out of Egypt to kill us, and our children, and our cattle with thirst?" Thus did they, on every occasion, evince a fretful, murmuring spirit, and prove how little they realised the presence and the hand of their Almighty and infinitely gracious Deliverer.

Now, nothing is more dishonouring to God than the manifestation of a complaining spirit on the part of those that belong to Him. The apostle gives it as a special mark of Gentile corruption that, "when they knew God, they glorified him not as God, *neither were thankful."* Then follows the practical result of this unthankful spirit. "They became vain in their imaginations, and their foolish heart was darkened" (Rom. 1:21). The heart that ceases to retain a thankful sense of God's goodness will speedily become "dark." Thus Israel lost the sense of being in God's hands; and this led, as might be expected, to still thicker darkness, for we find them, further on in their history, saying, "Wherefore hath the Lord brought us into this land, *to fall by the sword,* that our wives and our children shall be a prey?" (Num. 14:3). Such is the line along which a soul out of communion will travel. It first loses the sense of being in God's hands for good, and, finally, begins to deem itself in His hands for evil. Melancholy progress this!

The bread from heaven

However, the people being so far the subjects of grace, are provided for; and our chapter furnishes the marvellous account of this provision. "Then said the Lord unto Moses, Behold, I will rain bread from heaven for you." They, when enveloped in the chilling cloud of their unbelief, had said, "Would to God we had died by the hand of the Lord in the land of Egypt, when we sat by the flesh-pots, and when we did eat bread to the full." But now the word is, "bread from heaven." Blessed contrast! How amazing the difference between the flesh-pots, the leeks, onions, and garlick of Egypt, and this heavenly manna – "angels' food!" The former belonged to earth, the latter to heaven.

But, then, this heavenly food was, of necessity, a test of Israel's condition, as we read, "That I may prove them, whether they will walk in my law or no." It needed a heart weaned from Egypt's influences, to be satisfied with, or enjoy "bread from heaven." In point of fact, we know that the people were not satisfied with it, but despised it, pronounced it "light food," and lusted for flesh. Thus they proved how little their hearts were delivered from Egypt, or disposed to walk in God's law. "In their hearts they turned back again into Egypt" (Acts 7:39). But, instead of getting back thither, they were, ultimately, carried away beyond Babylon (Acts 7:43). This is a solemn and salutary lesson for Christians. If those who are redeemed from this present world, do not walk with God in thankfulness of heart, satisfied with His provision for the redeemed in the wilderness, they are in danger of falling into the snare of Babylonish influence. This is a serious consideration. It demands a heavenly taste to feed on bread from heaven. Nature cannot relish such food. It will ever yearn after Egypt, and, therefore, it must be kept down.

Christ, the bread of life which came down from heaven

It is our privilege, as those who have been baptised into

Christ's death, and "risen again through the faith of the operation of God," to feed upon Christ as "the bread of life which came down from heaven." This is our wilderness food – Christ as ministered by the Holy Ghost, through the written word; while, for our spiritual refreshment, the Holy Ghost has come down, as the precious fruit of the smitten Rock – Christ, as smitten for us. Such is our rare portion, in this desert world.

Now, it is obvious that, in order to enjoy such a portion as this, our hearts must be weaned from everything in this present evil world – from all that would address itself to us as natural men – as men alive in the flesh. A worldly heart – a carnal mind, would neither find Christ in the Word, nor enjoy Him if found. The manna was so pure and delicate that it could not bear contact with earth. It fell upon the dew, (see Numb. 11:9) and had to be gathered ere the sun was up. Each one, therefore, had to rise early and seek his daily portion. So it is with the people of God now. The heavenly manna must be gathered fresh every morning. Yesterday's manna will not do for today, nor today's for tomorrow. We must feed upon Christ every-day, with fresh energy of the Spirit, else we shall cease to grow. Moreover, we must make Christ our primary object. We must seek Him *"early,"* before "other things" have had time to take possession of our poor susceptible hearts. Many of us, alas! fail in this. We give Christ a secondary place, and the consequence is, we are left feeble and barren. The enemy, ever watchful, takes advantage of our excessive spiritual indolence to rob us of the blessedness and strength which flow from feeding upon Christ. The new life in the believer can *only* be nourished and sustained by Christ. "As the living Father hath sent me, and I live by the Father; so he that eateth me, even he shall live by me" (John 6:57).

The grace of the Lord Jesus Christ, as the One who came down from heaven, to be His people's food is ineffably precious to the renewed soul; but, in order to enjoy Him thus, we need to realise ourselves, as in the wilderness, separated to God, in the power of accomplished redemption. If I am walking with God through the desert, I shall be satisfied with the food which He provides, and that is, Christ as come down from heaven. "The old corn of the land of Canaan" has its antitype in *Christ ascended up* on high, and seated in the glory. As such, He is the proper food of those who by faith, know themselves as raised up together and seated together with Him in the heavenlies. But the manna, that is, *Christ as come down* from heaven, is for the people of God, in their wilderness life and experience. As a people journeying down here, we need a Christ who also journeyed down here; as a people seated in spirit up there, we have a Christ who is seated up there. This may help to explain the difference between the manna and the old corn of the land. It is not a question of redemption; that we have in the blood of the cross, and there alone. It is simply the provision which God has made for His people, according to their varied attitudes, whether as actually toiling in the desert, or in spirit taking possession of the heavenly inheritance.

The glory of the Lord in the cloud

What a striking picture is presented by Israel in the wilderness! Egypt was behind them, Canaan before them, and the sand of the desert around them; while they themselves were called to look up to heaven for their daily supply. The wilderness afforded not one blade of grass nor one drop of water for the Israel of God. In Jehovah alone was their portion. Most touching illustration of God's pilgrim people in this wilderness world! They have nothing here. Their life, being heavenly, can only be sustained by heavenly things. Though *in* the world, they are not *of* it, for Christ has chosen them out of it. As a heaven-born people, they are on their way to their birth-place, and sustained by food sent from thence. Theirs is an upward and an onward course. The glory leads *only* thus. It is utterly vain to cast the eye backward in the direction of Egypt; not a ray of the glory can there be discerned. "They looked *toward the wilderness,* and behold the glory of the

Lord appeared in the clouds." Jehovah's chariot was in the wilderness, and all who desired companionship with Him should be there likewise; and, if there, the heavenly manna should be their food, and that alone.

The Christian's nourishment

True, this manna was strange sustenance, such as an Egyptian could never understand, appreciate, or live upon; but those who had been "baptised in the cloud and in the sea," could, if walking in consistency with that significant baptism, enjoy and be nourished by it. Thus is it now in the case of the true believer. The worldling cannot understand how he lives. Both his life and that which sustains it lie entirely beyond the range of nature's keenest vision. Christ is his life, and on Christ he lives. He feeds, by faith, upon the powerful attractions of one who, though being "God over all, blessed for ever," "took upon him the form of a servant, and was made in the likeness of men" (Phil. 2:7). He traces Him from the bosom of the Father to the cross, and from the cross to the throne, and finds Him, in every stage of His journey, and in every attitude of His life, to be most precious food for his new man. All around, though, in fact, Egypt, is morally a waste howling wilderness, affording nothing for the renewed mind; and, just in proportion as the Christian finds any material to feed upon, must his spiritual man be hindered in his progress. The only provision which God has made is the heavenly manna, and on this the true believer should ever feed.

It is truly deplorable to find Christians seeking after the things of this world. It proves, very distinctly, that they are "loathing" the heavenly manna, and esteeming it "light food." They are ministering to that which they ought to mortify. The activities of the new life will ever show themselves in connexion with the subjugation of "the old man with his deeds;" and the more that is accomplished, the more will we desire to feed upon the "bread which strengthens man's heart." As in nature, the more we exercise, the better the appetite, so in grace, the more our renewed faculties are called into play, the more we feel the need of feeding, each day, upon Christ. It is one thing to know that we have life in Christ, together with full forgiveness and acceptance before God, and it is quite another to be in habitual communion with Him – feeding upon Him by faith – making Him the exclusive food of our souls. Very many profess to have found pardon and peace in Jesus, who, in reality, are feeding upon a variety of things which have no connexion with Him. They feed their minds with the newspapers and the varied frivolous and vapid literature of the day. Will they find Christ there? Is it by such instrumentality that the Holy Ghost ministers Christ to the soul? Are these the pure dew-drops on which the heavenly manna descends for the sustenance of God's redeemed in the desert? Alas! no; they are the gross materials in which the carnal mind delights. How then can a true Christian live upon such? We know, by the teaching of God's word, that he carries about with him two natures; and it may be asked, Which of the two is it that feeds upon the world's news and the world's literature? Is it the old or the new? There can be but the one reply. Well, then, which of the two am I desirous of cherishing? Assuredly my conduct will afford the truest answer to this enquiry. If I sincerely desire to grow in the divine life – if my one grand object is to be assimilated and devoted to Christ – if I am earnestly breathing after an extension of God's kingdom *within*, I shall, without doubt, seek continually that character of nourishment which is designed of God to promote my spiritual growth. This is plain. A man's acts are always the truest index of his desires and purposes. Hence, if I find a professing Christian neglecting his Bible, yet finding abundance of time – yea, some of his choicest hours – for the newspaper, I can be at no loss to decide as to the true condition of his soul. I am sure he cannot be spiritual – cannot be feeding upon, living for, or witnessing to, Christ.

 If an Israelite neglected to gather, in the freshness of the morning hour, his daily portion of the divinely appointed food, he would speedily have become lacking in strength for his journey. Thus is it with us. We must make Christ the paramount object of our souls' pursuit, else our spiritual life will inevitably decline. We cannot even feed upon feelings and experiences connected with Christ, for they, inasmuch as they are fluctuating, cannot form our spiritual nourishment. It was Christ yesterday, and it must be Christ today, and Christ for ever. Moreover, it will not do to feed partly on Christ and partly on other things. As, in the matter of *life*, it is Christ *alone*; so, in the matter of *living*, it must be Christ *alone*. As we cannot mingle anything with that which *imparts* life; so neither can we mingle anything with that which *sustains* it.

The omer of manna as a witness

It is quite true that, in spirit, and by faith, we can, even now, feed upon a risen and glorified Christ, ascended up to heaven in virtue of accomplished redemption, as prefigured by "the old corn of the land" (see Joshua 5). And not only so, but we know that when God's redeemed shall have entered upon those fields of glory, rest, and immortality, which lie beyond the Jordan, they shall, in actual fact, be done with wilderness food; but they will not be done with Christ nor with the remembrance of that which constitutes the specific nourishment of their desert life.

Israel were never to forget, amid the milk and honey of the land of Canaan, that which had sustained them during their forty years' sojourn in the wilderness. "This is the thing which the Lord commandeth, Fill an omer of it to be kept for your generations; that they may see the bread wherewith I have fed you in the wilderness, when I brought you forth from the land of Egypt . . . As the Lord commanded Moses, so Aaron laid it up before the testimony, to be kept" (ver. 32-34). Most precious memorial of the faithfulness of God! He did not suffer them to die of hunger, as their foolish hearts had unbelievingly anticipated. He rained bread from heaven for them, fed them with angels' food, watched over them with all the tenderness of a nurse, bore with them, carried them on eagles' wings; and, had they only continued on the proper ground of grace, He would have put them in eternal possession of all the promises made to their fathers. The pot of manna, therefore, containing, as it did, a man's daily portion, and laid up before the Lord, furnishes a volume of truth. There was no worm therein nor anything of taint. It was the record of Jehovah's faithfulness, in providing for those whom He had redeemed out of the hand of the enemy.

Assimilating the truth and putting the Word into practice

Not so, however, when man hoarded it up for himself. Then the symptoms of corruptibility soon made their appearance. We cannot, if entering into the truth and reality of our position, hoard up. It is our privilege, day by day, to enter into the preciousness of Christ, as the One who came down from heaven to give life unto the world. But if any, in forgetfulness of this, should be found hoarding up for tomorrow, that is, laying up truth beyond his present need, instead of turning it to profit in the way of renewing strength it will surely become corrupt. This is a salutary lesson for us. It is a deeply solemn thing to learn truth; for there is not a principle which we profess to have learnt which we shall not have to prove practically. God will not have us theorists. One often trembles to hear persons make high professions and use expressions of intense devotedness, whether, in prayer or otherwise, lest when the hour of trial comes, there may not be the needed spiritual power to carry out what the lips have uttered.

There is a great danger of the intellect's outstripping the conscience and the affections. Hence it is that so many seem, at first, to make such rapid progress up to a certain point; but there they stop short and appear to retrograde. Like an Israelite gathering up more manna than he required for one day's food. He might appear to be accumulating the heavenly food far more diligently than others; yet every particle beyond the day's supply was not only useless, but far worse than useless, inasmuch as it "bred worms." Thus is it with the Christian. He must *use* what he gets. He must feed upon Christ as a matter of actual need, and the need is brought out in actual service. The character and ways of God, the preciousness and beauty of Christ, and the living depths of the Word are only unfolded to faith and need. It is as we use what we receive that more will be given. The path of the believer is to be a practical one; and here it is that so many of us come short. It will often be found that those who get on most rapidly in theory are the slowest in the practical and experimental elements, because it is more a work of intellect than of heart and conscience. We should ever remember that Christianity is not a set of opinions, a system of dogmas, or a number of views. It is pre-eminently a living reality – a personal, practical, powerful thing, telling itself out in all the scenes and circumstances of daily life, shedding its hallowed influence over the entire character and course, and imparting its heavenly tone to every relationship which one may be called of God to fill. In a word, it is that which flows from being associated and occupied with Christ. This is Christianity. There may be clear views, correct notions, sound principles, without any fellowship with Jesus; but an orthodox creed without Christ will prove a cold, barren, dead thing.

Christian reader, see carefully to it that you are not only saved by Christ, but also living on Him. Make Him the daily portion of your soul. Seek Him "*early*," seek Him "*only*." When anything solicits your attention, ask the question, "Will this bring Christ to my heart! Will it unfold Him to my affections or draw me near to His Person?" If not, reject it at once: yes, reject it, though it present itself under the most specious appearance and with the most commanding authority. If your honest purpose be to get on in the divine life, to progress in spirituality, to cultivate personal acquaintance with Christ, then challenge your heart solemnly and faithfully as to this. Make Christ your habitual food. Go, gather the manna that falls on the dew-drops, and feed upon it with an appetite sharpened by a diligent walk with God through the desert.

May the rich grace of God the Holy Ghost abundantly strengthen you in all this![8]

The Sabbath

There is one point more in our chapter which we shall notice, namely the institution of the Sabbath, in its connexion with the manna and Israel's position, as here set forth. From the 2nd chapter of Genesis down to the chapter now before us, we find no mention made of this institution. This is remarkable. Abel's sacrifice, Enoch's walk with God, Noah's preaching, Abraham's call, together with the detailed history of Isaac, Jacob, and Joseph, are all presented; but there is no allusion to the Sabbath until we find Israel recognised as a people in relationship and consequent responsibility to Jehovah. The Sabbath was interrupted in Eden; and here we find it again instituted for Israel in the wilderness. But alas! man has no heart for God's rest. And it came to pass that "There went out some of the people on the seventh day for to gather, and they found none. And the Lord said unto Moses, How long refuse ye to keep my commandments and my laws? See, for that the Lord hath given you the Sabbath, therefore he giveth you on the sixth day the bread of two days: abide ye every man in his place; let no man go out of his place on the seventh day" (ver. 27-29). God would have His people enjoying sweet repose with Himself. He would give them rest, food, and refreshment, even in the wilderness. But man's heart is not disposed to rest with God. The people could remember and speak of the time when they "*sat* by the flesh pots" in Egypt; but they could not appreciate the blessedness of sitting in their tents, enjoying with God "the rest of the holy Sabbath," feeding upon the heavenly manna.

And, be it remarked, that the Sabbath is here presented as a matter of gift. "The Lord hath *given* you the Sabbath." Further on, in this book, we shall find it put in the form of a law, with a curse and a judgment attached to it, in the case of disobedience; but whether fallen man gets a privilege or a law, a blessing or a curse, it is all alike. His *nature* is bad. He can neither rest with, nor work for, God, If God works and makes a rest for him, he will not keep it; and if God tells him to work, he will not do it. Such is man. He has no heart for God. He can make use of the name of the Sabbath as a something to exalt himself, or as the badge of his own religiousness; but when we turn to Exodus 16 we find that he cannot prize *God's* Sabbath as a *gift*; and when we turn to Numbers 15:32-36, we find he cannot keep it as a *law.*

Now, we know that the Sabbath, as well as the manna, was a type. In itself, it was a real blessing – a sweet mercy from the hand of a loving and gracious God, who would relieve the toil and travail of a sin-stricken earth by the refreshment of one day of rest out of the seven. Whatever way we look at the institution of the Sabbath, we must see it to be pregnant with richest mercy, whether we view it in reference to man or to the animal creation. And, albeit, that Christians observe the first day of the week – the Lord's day, and attach to it its proper principles, yet is the gracious providence equally observable, nor would any mind at all governed by right feelings, seek, for a moment, to interfere with such a signal mercy. "The Sabbath was made for man;" and although man never has kept it, according to the divine thought about it, that does not detract from the grace which shines in the appointment of it, nor divest it of its deep significancy as a type of that eternal rest which remains for the people of God, or as a shadow of that substance which faith now enjoys in the Person and work of a risen Christ.

Let not the reader, therefore, suppose that in anything which has been, or may be, stated, in these pages, the object is to touch, in the slightest degree, the merciful provision of one day's rest for man and the animal creation, much less to interfere with the distinct place which the Lord's day occupies in the New Testament. Nothing is further from the writer's thoughts. As a man he values the former, and as a Christian he rejoices in the latter, far too deeply to admit of his penning or uttering a single syllable which would interfere with either the one or the other. He would only ask the reader to weigh, with a dispassionate mind, in the balance of Holy Scripture, every line and every statement, and not form any harsh judgment beforehand.

This subject will come before us again, in our further meditations, if the Lord will. May we learn to value more the rest which our God has provided for us in Christ, and while enjoying Him as our rest, may we feed upon Him as the "hidden manna," laid up, in the power of resurrection, in the inner sanctuary – the record of what God has accomplished, on our behalf, by coming down into this world, in His infinite grace, in order that we might be before Him, according to the perfectness of Christ, and feed on His unsearchable riches for ever.

---

[8] My reader will find it profitable to turn to the 6th of John, and prayerfully meditate upon it, in connexion with the subject of the manna. The Passover being near, Jesus feeds the multitude, and then takes His departure to a mountain, there to be alone. From thence He comes to the relief of His distressed people, tossed upon the troubled waters. After this He unfolds the doctrine of His Person and work, and declares how He was to give His flesh for the life of the world, and that none could have life save by eating His flesh and drinking His blood. Finally, He speaks of Himself as ascending up where He was before and of the quickening power of the Holy Ghost. It is, indeed, a rich and copious chapter, in which the spiritual reader will find a vast fund of truth for the comfort and edification of his soul.

Chapter 17

REPHIDIM

The struck rock

"And all the congregation of the children of Israel journeyed from the wilderness of Sin, after their journeys, according to the commandment of the Lord, and pitched in Rephidim: and there was no water for the people to drink. Wherefore the people did chide with Moses, and said, Give us water that we may drink. And Moses said unto them, Why chide ye with me? Wherefore do ye tempt the Lord?"(chap. 17:1, 2). Did we not know something of the humiliating evil of our own hearts, we should be quite at a loss to account for Israel's marvellous insensibility to all the Lord's goodness, faithfulness, and mighty acts. They had just seen bread descending from heaven to feed six hundred thousand people in the wilderness: and now they are "ready to stone" Moses for bringing them out into the wilderness to kill them with thirst. Nothing can exceed the desperate unbelief and wickedness of the human heart, save the superabounding grace of God. In that grace alone can any one find relief under the growing sense of his evil nature which circumstances tend to make manifest. Had Israel been transported directly from Egypt to Canaan, they would not have made such sad exhibitions of what the human heart is; and, as a consequence, they would not have proved such admirable ensamples or types for us; but their forty years' wandering in the desert furnishes us with a volume of warning, admonition, and instruction, fruitful beyond conception. From it we learn, amongst many other things, the unvarying tendency of the heart to distrust God. Anything, in short, for it but God. It would rather lean upon a cobweb of human resources than upon the arm of an Omnipotent, All-wise, and infinitely gracious God; and the smallest cloud is more than sufficient to hide from its view the light of His blessed countenance. Well, therefore, may it be termed "an evil heart of unbelief" which will ever show itself ready to "depart from the living God."

It is interesting to note the two great questions raised by unbelief, in this and the preceding chapter. They are precisely similar to those which spring up, within and around us, every day, namely, "what shall we eat? and what shall we drink?" We do not find the people raising the third question in the category, "wherewithal shall we be clothed?" But here are the questions of the wilderness, "*What!*" "*Where!*" "*How?*" Faith has a brief but comprehensive answer to all the three, namely, GOD! Precious, perfect, answer! Oh! that the writer and the reader were more thoroughly acquainted with its force and fullness! We assuredly need to remember, when placed in a position of trial, that "there hath no temptation taken us but such as is common to man: but God is faithful, who will not suffer you to be tempted above that ye are able; but will with the temptation also make a way to escape, (or an "issue" *ekbasin*,) that ye may be able to bear it" (1 Cor. 10:13). Whenever we get into trial, we may feel confident that, with the trial, there is an issue, and all we need is a broken will and a single eye to see it.

"And Moses cried unto the Lord, saying; What shall I do unto this people? they be almost ready to stone me. And the Lord said unto Moses, Go on before the people, and take with thee of the elders of Israel; and thy rod, wherewith thou smotest the river, take in thine hand, and go. Behold, I will stand before thee there upon the rock in Horeb, and thou shalt smite the rock, and there shall come water out of it, that the people may drink. And Moses did so in the sight of the elders of Israel" (ver. 4-6). Thus all is met by the most perfect grace. Every murmur brings out a fresh display. Here we have the refreshing stream gushing from the smitten rock – beauteous type of the Spirit given as the fruit of Christ's accomplished sacrifice. In chapter 16 we have a type of Christ coming down from heaven to give life to the world. In chapter 17 we have a type of the Holy Ghost "shed forth," in virtue of Christ's finished work. "They drank of that spiritual Rock that followed them, and that Rock was Christ" (1 Cor. 10:4). But who could drink till the Rock was smitten? Israel might have gazed on that rock and died of thirst while gazing; but, until smitten by the rod of God, it could yield no refreshment. This is plain enough. The Lord Jesus Christ was the centre and foundation of all God's counsels of love and mercy. Through Him all blessing was to flow to man. The streams of grace were designed to gush forth from "the Lamb of God;" but then it was needful that the Lamb should be slain – that the work of the cross should be an accomplished fact, ere any of these things could be actualized. It was when the Rock of ages was cleft by the hand of Jehovah, that the flood-gates of eternal love were thrown wide open, and perishing sinners invited by the testimony of the Holy Ghost to "drink abundantly," drink deeply, drink freely. "The gift of the Holy Ghost" is the result of the Son's accomplished work upon the cross. "The promise of the Father" could not be fulfilled until Christ had taken His seat at the right hand of the majesty in the heavens, having wrought out perfect righteousness, answered all the claims of holiness, magnified the law and made it honourable, borne the unmitigated wrath of God against sin, exhausted the power of death, and deprived the grave of its victory. He, having done all this, "ascended up on high, led captivity captive, and gave gifts unto men. Now that He ascended, what is it but that he also descended first into the lower parts of the earth? He that descended is the same also that ascended up far above all heavens, that he might fill all things" (Eph. 4:8-10).

This is the true foundation of the Church's peace, blessedness, and glory, for ever. Until the rock was smitten, the stream was pent up, and man could do nothing. What human hand could bring forth water from a flinty rock? And so, we may ask, what human righteousness could afford a warrant for opening the flood-gates of divine love? This is the true way in which to test man's competency. He could not, by his doings, his sayings, or his feelings, furnish a ground for the mission of the Holy Ghost. Let him be or do what he may, he could not do this. But thank God, it is done; Christ has finished the work; the true Rock has been smitten, and the refreshing stream has issued forth, so that thirsty souls may drink. "The water that I shall give him," says Christ, "shall be in him a well of water, springing up into everlasting life" (John 4:14). Again; "In the last day, that great day of the feast, Jesus stood and cried, saying, If any man thirst, let him come unto me and drink. He that believeth on me, as the scripture hath said, out of his belly shall flow rivers of living water. But this spake he of the Spirit which they that believe on him should receive: for the Holy Ghost was not yet given, because that Jesus was not yet glorified (John 7:37-39; compare, also, Acts 19:2).

Thus, as in the manna, we have a type of Christ, so in the stream gushing from the rock we have a type of the Holy Ghost. "If thou knewest the gift of God, (i.e., Christ) . . . thou wouldst have asked of him, and he would have given thee living water," – i.e., the Spirit.

Such, then, is the teaching conveyed to the spiritual mind by the smitten rock; but the name of the place in which this significant type was presented is a standing memorial of man's unbelief. "He called the name of the place Massah (i.e., temptation,) and Meribah, (i.e., chiding,) because of the chiding of the children of Israel, and because they tempted the Lord, saying, Is the Lord among us or not?" (ver. 7). After such repeated assurances and evidences of Jehovah's presence, to raise such an enquiry proves the deep-seated unbelief of the human heart. It was, in point of fact, tempting Him. Thus did the Jews, in the day of Christ's presence amongst them, seek of Him a sign from heaven, tempting Him. Faith never acts thus; it believes in, and enjoys, the divine presence, not by a sign, but by the knowledge of Himself. It knows He is there to be enjoyed, and it enjoys Him. Lord, grant us a more artless spirit of confidence!

The battle against Amalek

The next point suggested by our chapter is one of special interest to us. "Then came Amalek and fought with Israel in Rephidim. And Moses said unto Joshua, Choose us out men, and go out, fight with Amalek: tomorrow I will stand on the top of the hill, with the rod of God in mine hand" (ver. 8, 9). The gift of the Holy Ghost leads to conflict. The light rebukes and conflicts with the darkness. Where all is dark there is no struggle; but the very feeblest struggle bespeaks the presence of light. "The flesh lusteth against the Spirit, and the Spirit against the flesh; and these are contrary the one to the other, so that ye should not do the things that ye would" (Gal. 5:17). Thus it is in the chapter before us; we have the rock smitten and the water flowing forth, and immediately we read, "then came Amalek and fought with Israel."

This is the first time that Israel are seen in conflict with an external foe. Up to this point, the Lord had fought for them, as we read in chap. 14. "The Lord shall fight for you, and ye shall hold your peace." But now the word is, "choose us out *men*." True, God must now fight *in* Israel, as, before, He had fought *for* them. This marks the difference, as to the type; and as to the antitype, we know that there is an immense difference between Christ's battles *for* us, and the Holy Ghost's battles *in* us. The former, blessed be God, are all over, the victory gained, and a glorious and an everlasting peace secured. The latter, on the contrary, are still going on.

Pharaoh and Amalek represent two different powers or influences; Pharaoh represents the hindrance to Israel's deliverance from Egypt; Amalek represents the hindrance to their walk with God through the wilderness. Pharaoh used the things of Egypt to keep Israel from serving the Lord; he, therefore, prefigures Satan, who uses "this present evil world" against the people of God. Amalek, on the other hand, stands before us as the type of the flesh. He was the grandson of Esau, who preferred a mess of pottage to the birthright (see Gen. 36:12). He was the first who opposed Israel, after their baptism "in the cloud and in the sea." These facts serve to fix his character with great distinctness; and, in addition to these, we know that Saul was set aside from the kingdom of Israel, in consequence of his failing to destroy Amalek (1 Sam. 15). And, further, we find that Haman is the last of the Amalekites of whom we find any notice in scripture. He was hanged on a gallows, in consequence of his wicked attempt against the seed of Israel (see Esther). No Amalekite could obtain entrance into the congregation of the Lord. And, finally, in the chapter now before us, the Lord declares perpetual war with Amalek.

All these circumstances may be regarded as furnishing conclusive evidence of the fact that Amalek is a type of the flesh. The connexion between his conflict with Israel and the water flowing out of the rock is most marked and instructive, and in full keeping with the believer's conflict with his evil nature, which conflict is, as we know, consequent upon his having the new nature, and the Holy Ghost dwelling therein. Israel's conflict began when they stood in the full power of redemption, and had tasted "that spiritual meat and drunk of that spiritual Rock." Until they met Amalek, they had nothing to do. They did not cope with Pharaoh. They did not break the power of Egypt nor snap asunder the chains of its thraldom. They did not divide the sea or submerge Pharaoh's hosts beneath its waves. They did not bring down bread from heaven, or draw forth water out of the flinty rock. They neither had done, nor could they do, any of these things; but now they are called to fight with Amalek. All the previous conflict had been between Jehovah and the enemy. They had but to "stand still" and gaze upon the mighty triumphs of Jehovah's outstretched arm and enjoy the fruits of victory. The Lord had fought *for* them; but now He fights *in* or *by* them.

Thus is it also with the Church of God. The victories on which her eternal peace and blessedness are founded were gained, single-handed, by Christ *for* her. He was alone on the cross, alone in the tomb. The Church had to stand aside, for how could she be there? How could she vanquish Satan, endure the wrath of God, or rob death of its sting? Impossible. These things lay far beyond the reach of sinners, but not beyond the reach of Him who came to save them, and who alone was able to bear upon his shoulder the ponderous weight of all their sins, and roll the burden away for ever, by His infinite sacrifice, so that God the Holy Ghost, proceeding from God the Father, in virtue of the perfect atonement of God the Son, can take up His abode in the Church collectively, and in each member thereof individually.

Now it is when the Holy Ghost thus takes up His abode in us, consequent upon Christ's death and resurrection, that our conflict begins. Christ has fought *for* us; the Holy Ghost fights *in* us. The very fact of our enjoying this first rich spoil of victory, puts us into direct conflict with the foe. But the comfort is that we are victors ere we enter upon the field of conflict at all. The believer approaches to the battle singing, "Thanks be to God which giveth us the victory through our Lord Jesus Christ" (1 Cor. 15:57). We do not, therefore, fight uncertainly or as those that beat the air, while we seek to keep under the body and bring it into subjection (1 Cor. 9:26, 27). "We are more than conquerors through Him that loved us (Rom. 8:37). The grace in which we stand renders the flesh utterly void of power to lord it over us (see Rom. 6 passim). If the law is "the strength of sin," grace is the weakness thereof. The former gives sin power over us; the latter gives us power over sin.

"And Moses said unto Joshua, Choose us out men, and go out, fight with Amalek: tomorrow I will stand on the top of the hill, with the rod of God in mine hand. So Joshua did as Moses had said unto him, and fought with Amalek: and Moses, Aaron, and Hur went up to the top of the hill. And it came to pass, when Moses held up his hand, that Israel prevailed: and when he let down his hand, Amalek prevailed. But Moses' hands were heavy; and they took a stone and put it under him, and he sat thereon; and Aaron and Hur stayed up his hands, the one on the one side and the other on the other side; and his hands were steady until the going down of the sun. And Joshua discomfited Amalek and his people with the edge of the sword" (verses 9-13).

We have, here, two distinct things, namely, conflict and intercession. Christ is on high *for* us, while the Holy Ghost carries on the mighty struggle *in* us. The two things go together. It is as we enter, by faith, into the prevalency of Christ's intercession on our behalf, that we make head against our evil nature.

The Christian's struggle with the flesh

Some there are who seek to overlook the fact of the Christian's conflict with the flesh. They look upon regeneration as a total change or renewal of the old nature. Upon this principle, it would, necessarily, follow that the believer has nothing to struggle with. If my nature is renewed, what have I to contend with? Nothing. There is nothing within, inasmuch as my old nature is made new; and nothing without can affect me, inasmuch as there is no response from within. The world has no charms for one whose flesh is entirely changed; and Satan has nothing by or on which to act. To all who maintain such a theory, it may be said that they seem to forget the place which Amalek occupies in the history of the people of God. Had Israel conceived the idea that, when Pharaoh's hosts were gone, their conflict was at an end, they would have been sadly put about when Amalek came upon them. The fact is, *theirs* only then began. Thus it is with the believer, for "all these things happened unto Israel for ensamples, and they are written for our admonition" (1 Cor. 10:11). But there could be no "type," no "ensample," no "admonition" in "these things," for one whose old nature is made new. Indeed, such an one can have but little need of any of those gracious provisions which God has made in His kingdom for those who are the subjects thereof.

We are distinctly taught in the Word that the believer carries about with him that which answers to Amalek, that is, "the flesh" – "the old man" – "the carnal mind" (Rom. 6:6; 8:7;

Gal. 5:17). Now, if the Christian, upon perceiving the stirrings of his evil nature, begins to doubt his being a Christian, he will not only render himself exceedingly unhappy, but also deprive himself of his vantage ground against the enemy. The flesh exists in the believer and will be there to the end of the chapter. The Holy Ghost fully recognises it as existing, as we may easily see, from various parts of the New Testament. In Romans 6 we read, "Let not sin therefore *reign* in your mortal bodies." Such a precept would be entirely uncalled for if the flesh were not existing in the believer. It would be out of character to tell us not to let sin reign, if it were not actually dwelling in us. There is a great difference between dwelling and reigning. It dwells in a believer, but it reigns in an unbeliever.

However, though it dwells in us, we have, thank God, a principle of power over it. "Sin shall not have dominion over you, for ye are not under the law, but under grace." The grace which, by the blood of the cross, has put away sin, insures us the victory, and gives us present power over its indwelling principle.

We have died to sin, and hence it has no claim over us. "He that has died is justified from sin." "Knowing this, that our old man has been crucified together, that the body of sin might be destroyed, that henceforth we should not serve sin" (Rom. 6:6). "And Joshua discomfited Amalek and his people with the edge of the sword." All was victory; and Jehovah's banner floated over the triumphant host, bearing the sweet and heart-sustaining inscription, "Jehovah-nissi" (the Lord my banner). The assurance of victory should be as complete as the sense of forgiveness, seeing both alike are founded upon the great fact that Jesus died and rose again. It is in the power of this that the believer enjoys a purged conscience and subdues indwelling sin. The death of Christ having answered all the claims of God in reference to our sins, His resurrection becomes the spring of power, in all the details of conflict, afterwards. He died *for* us, and now He lives *in* us. The former gives us peace, the latter gives us power.

Christ, our intercessor

It is edifying to remark the contrast between Moses on the hill and Christ on the throne. The hands of our great Intercessor can never hang down. His intercession never fluctuates. "He *ever* liveth to make intercession for us" (Heb. 7). His intercession is never-ceasing and all-prevailing. Having taken His place on high, in the power of divine righteousness, He acts for us, according to what He is, and according to the infinite perfectness of what He has done. His hands can never hang down, nor can He need any one to hold them up. His perfect advocacy is founded upon His perfect sacrifice. He presents us before God, clothed in His own perfections, so that though we may ever have to keep our faces in the dust, in the sense of what we are, yet the Spirit can only testify to us of what He is before God for us, and of what we are in Him. "We are not in the flesh but in the Spirit" (Rom. 8). We are in *the body,* as to the fact of our condition; but we are not in *the flesh,* as to the principle of our standing. Moreover, the flesh is in us, though we are dead to it; but we are not in the flesh, because we are alive with Christ.

We may further remark, on this chapter, that Moses had the rod of God with him on the hill – the rod with which he had smitten the rock. This rod was the expression or symbol of the power of God, which is seen alike in atonement and intercession. When the work of atonement was accomplished, Christ took His seat in heaven, and sent down the Holy Ghost to take up His abode in the Church; so that there is an inseparable connexion between the work of Christ and the work of the Spirit. There is the application of the power of God in each.

Chapter 18

THE VISIT OF JETHRO

Israel, the Gentiles and the Church

We here arrive at the close of a very marked division of the book of Exodus. We have seen God, in the exercise of His perfect grace, visiting and redeeming His people; bringing them forth out of the land of Egypt; delivering them, first, from the hand of Pharaoh and then from the hand of Amalek. Furthermore, we have seen, in the manna, a type of Christ come down from heaven; in the rock, a type of Christ smitten for His people; and in the gushing stream, a type of the Spirit given. Then follows, in striking and beautiful order, a picture of the future glory, divided into its three grand departments, namely, "the Jew, the Gentile, and the Church of God."

During the period of Moses' rejection by his brethren he was taken apart and presented with a bride – the companion of his rejection. We were led to see, at the opening of this book, the character of Moses' relationship with this bride. He was "a husband by blood" to her. This is precisely what Christ is to the Church. Her connexion with Him is founded upon death and resurrection; and she is called to fellowship with His sufferings. It is, as we know, during the period of Israel's unbelief, and of Christ's rejection, that the Church is called out; and when the Church is complete, according to the divine counsels, when the "fullness of the Gentiles is come in," Israel shall again be brought into notice.

Thus it was with Zipporah and Israel of old. Moses had sent her back, during the period of his mission to Israel; and when the latter were brought forth as a fully delivered people, we read that "Jethro, Moses' father-in-law, took Zipporah, Moses' wife, after he had sent her back, and her two sons, of which the name of the one was Gershom; for he said, I have been an alien in a strange land; and the name of the other was Eliezer; for the God of my fathers, said he, was mine help, and delivered me from the sword of Pharaoh. And Jethro, Moses' father-in-law, came with his sons and his wife unto Moses into the wilderness, where he encamped at the mount of God. And he said unto Moses, I thy father-in-law, Jethro, am come unto thee, and thy wife and her two sons with her. And Moses went out to meet his father-in-law, and did obeisance, and kissed him; and they asked each other of their welfare; and they came into the tent. And Moses told his father-in-law all that the Lord had done unto Pharaoh, and to the Egyptians, for Israel's sake, and all the travail that had come upon them by the way, and how the Lord delivered them. And Jethro rejoiced for all the goodness which the Lord had done to Israel, whom he had delivered from the hand of the Egyptians. And Jethro said, Blessed be the Lord, who hath delivered you out of the hand of the Egyptians, and out of the hand of Pharaoh; who hath delivered the people from under the hand of the Egyptians. Now I know that the Lord is greater than all gods; for in the thing wherein they dealt proudly he was above them. And Jethro Moses' father-in-law, took a burnt-offering and sacrifices for God: and Aaron came, and all the elders of Israel, to eat bread with Moses' father-in-law before God" (chap 18:2-12).

This is a deeply interesting scene. The whole congregation assembled, in triumph before the Lord – the Gentile presenting sacrifice – and in addition, to complete the picture, the bride of the deliverer, together with the children whom God had given him, are all introduced. It is, in short, a singularly striking foreshadowing of the coming kingdom. "The Lord will give grace and glory." We have already seen, in what we have travelled over of this book, very much of the actings of "grace;" and here we have, from the pencil of the Holy Ghost, a beauteous picture of "glory," – a picture which must be regarded as peculiarly important, as exhibiting the varied fields in which that glory shall be manifested.

"The Jew, the Gentile, and the Church of God" are scriptural distinctions which can never be overlooked without marring that perfect range of truth which God has revealed in His holy Word. They have existed ever since the mystery of the Church was fully developed by the ministry of the Apostle Paul, and they shall exist throughout the millennial age. Hence, every spiritual student of Scripture will give them their due place in his mind.

The apostle expressly teaches us, in his Epistle to the Ephesians, that the mystery of the Church had not been made known, in other ages, to the sons of men, as it was revealed to him. But, though not directly revealed, it had been shadowed forth in one way or another; as, for example, in Joseph's marriage with an Egyptian, and in Moses' marriage with an Ethiopian. The type or shadow of a truth is a very different thing from a direct and positive revelation of it. The great mystery of the Church was not revealed until Christ, in heavenly glory, revealed it to Saul of Tarsus. Hence, all who look for the full unfolding of this mystery in the law, the prophets, or the psalms, will find themselves engaged in unintelligent labour. When, however, they find it distinctly revealed in the Epistle to the Ephesians, they will be able, with interest and profit, to trace its foreshadowing in Old Testament Scripture.

Thus we have, in the opening of our chapter, a millennial scene. All the fields of glory lie open in vision before us. "*The Jew*" stands forth as the great earthly witness of Jehovah's faithfulness, His mercy, and His power. This is what the Jew has been in bygone ages, it is what he is now, and what he will be, world without end. "The Gentile" reads, in the book of God's dealings with the Jew, his deepest lessons. He traces the marvellous history of that peculiar and elect people – "a people terrible from their beginning hitherto." He sees thrones and empires overturned – nations shaken to their centre – every one and everything compelled to give way, in order to establish the supremacy of that people on whom

Jehovah has set His love. "Now I know," he says, "that the Lord is greater than all gods: for in the thing wherein they dealt proudly he was above them" (ver. 11). Such is the confession of "the Gentile," when the wondrous page of Jewish history lies open before him.

Lastly, *"The Church of God"* collectively, as prefigured by Zipporah, and the members thereof individually, as seen in Zipporah's sons, are presented as occupying the most intimate relationship with the deliverer. All this is perfect in its way. We may be asked for our proofs. The answer is, "I speak as unto wise men; judge ye what I say." We can never build a doctrine upon a type; but when a doctrine is revealed a type thereof may be discerned with accuracy and studied with profit. In every case, a spiritual mind is essentially necessary, either to understand the doctrine or discern the type. "The natural man receiveth not the things of the Spirit of God: for they are foolishness unto him: neither can he know them, because they are spiritually discerned" (1 Cor. 2:14).

The rulers who assisted Moses

From verse 13 to the end of our chapter, we have the appointment of rulers, who were to assist Moses in the management of the affairs of the congregation. This was the suggestion of Jethro, who feared that Moses would "wear away" in consequence of his labours. In connexion with this, it may be profitable to look at the appointment of the seventy elders in Numbers 11. Here we find the spirit of Moses crushed beneath the ponderous responsibility which devolved upon him, and he gives utterance to the anguish of his heart in the following accents. "And Moses said unto the Lord, Wherefore hast thou afflicted thy servant? And wherefore have I not found favour in thy sight, that thou layest the burden of all this people upon me? Have I conceived all this people? have I begotten them that thou shouldst say unto me, Carry them in thy bosom, as a nursing father beareth the sucking child, unto the land which thou swarest unto their fathers. . . . I am not able to bear all this people alone because it is too heavy for me. And if thou deal thus with me, kill me, I pray thee, out of hand, if I have found favour in thy sight; and let me not see my wretchedness" (Num. 11:11-15).

In all this we see Moses evidently retiring from a post of honour. If God were pleased to make him the sole instrument in managing the assembly, it was only so much the more dignity and privilege conferred upon him. True, the responsibility was immense; but faith would own that God was amply sufficient for that. Here, however, the heart of Moses failed him (blessed servant as he was), and he says, "I am not able to bear all this people *alone*, because it is too heavy for *me.*" But he was not asked to bear them alone; for God was with him. They were not too heavy for God. It was He that was bearing them; Moses was but the instrument. He might just as well have spoken of his rod as bearing the people; for what was he but a mere instrument in God's hand, as the rod was in his? It is here the servants of Christ constantly fail; and the failure is all the more dangerous because it wears the appearance of humility. It seems like distrust of oneself and deep lowliness of spirit, to shrink from heavy responsibility; but all we need to inquire is, has God imposed that responsibility? If so, He will assuredly be with me in sustaining it; and having Him with me, I can sustain anything. With Him, the weight of a mountain is nothing; without Him, the weight of a feather is overwhelming. It is a totally different thing if a man, in the vanity of his mind, thrust himself forward and take a burden upon his shoulder which God never intended him to bear, and, therefore, never fitted him to bear it; we may then, surely, expect to see him crushed beneath the weight; but if God lays it upon him, He will qualify and strengthen him to carry it.

It is never the fruit of humility to depart from a divinely-appointed post. On the contrary, the deepest humility will express itself by remaining there in simple dependence upon God. It is a sure evidence of being occupied about *self* when we shrink from service on the ground of inability. God does not call us unto service on the ground of our ability, but of His own; hence, unless I am filled with thoughts about myself, or with positive distrust of Him, I need not relinquish any position of service or testimony because of the heavy responsibilities attaching thereto. All power belongs to God, and it is quite the same whether that power acts through one agent or through seventy; the power is still the same: but if one agent refuse the dignity, it is only so much the worse for him. God will not force people to abide in a place of honour, if they cannot trust Him to sustain them there. The way lies always open to them to step down from their dignity, and sink into the place where base unbelief is sure to put us.

Thus it was with Moses. He complained of the burden, and the burden was speedily removed; but with it the high honour of being allowed to carry it. "And the Lord said unto Moses, Gather unto me seventy men of the elders of Israel whom thou knowest to be the elders of the people, and officers over them; and bring them unto the tabernacle of the congregation, that they may stand there with thee. And I will come down and talk with thee there; and I will take of the spirit which is upon thee, and will put it upon them; and they shall bear the burden of the people with thee, that thou bear it not thyself alone" (Num. 11:16, 17). There was no fresh power introduced. It was the same Spirit, whether in one or in seventy. There was no more value or virtue in the flesh of seventy men than in the flesh of one man. "It is the Spirit that quickeneth; the flesh profiteth nothing" (John 6:63). There was nothing, in the way of power, gained; but a great deal, in the way of dignity, lost by this movement on the part of Moses.

In the after part of Numbers 11 we find Moses giving utterance to accents of unbelief, which called forth from the Lord a sharp rebuke. "Is the Lord's hand waxed short? Thou shalt see now whether my word shall come to pass unto thee or not." If my reader will compare ver. 11-15 with 21, 22, he will see a marked and solemn connexion. The man who shrinks from responsibility, on the ground of his own feebleness, is in great danger of calling in question the fullness and sufficiency of God's resources. This entire scene teaches a most valuable lesson to every servant of Christ who may be tempted to feel himself alone or overburdened in his work. Let such an one bear in mind that, where the Holy Ghost is working, one instrument is as good and as efficient as seventy; and where He is not working seventy are of no more value than one. It all depends upon the energy of the Holy Ghost. With Him, one man can do all, endure all, sustain all. Without Him, seventy men can do nothing. Let the lonely servant remember, for the comfort and encouragement of his sinking heart, that, provided he has the presence and power of the Holy Ghost with him, he need not complain of his burden, nor sigh for a division of labour. If God honour a man by giving him a great deal of work to do, let him rejoice therein and not murmur; for if he murmur, he can very speedily lose his honour. God is at no loss for instruments. He could, from the stones, raise up children unto Abraham; and He can raise up, from the same, the needed agents to carry on His glorious work.

Oh! for a heart to serve Him! A patient, humble, self-emptied, devoted heart! A heart ready to serve in company, ready to serve alone, a heart so filled with love to Christ that it will find its joy – its chief joy – in serving Him, let the sphere or character of service be what it may. This assuredly is the special need of the day in which our lot is cast. May the Holy Ghost stir up our hearts to a deeper sense of the exceeding preciousness of the name of Jesus, and enable us to yield a fuller, clearer, more unequivocal response to the changeless love of His heart!

ISRAEL AT THE FOOT OF MOUNT SINAI

The covenant of grace

We have now arrived at a most momentous point in Israel's history. We are called to behold them standing at the foot of "the mount that might be touched, and that burned with fire." The fair millennial scene which opened before us in the preceding chapter has passed away. It was but a brief moment of sunshine in which a very vivid picture of the kingdom was afforded; but the sunshine was speedily followed by the heavy clouds which gathered around that "palpable mount," where Israel, in a spirit of dark and senseless legality, abandoned Jehovah's covenant of pure grace for man's covenant of works. Disastrous movement! A movement fraught with the most dismal results. Hitherto, as we have seen, no enemy could stand before Israel – no obstacle was suffered to interrupt their onward and victorious march. Pharaoh's hosts were overthrown – Amalek and his people were discomfited with the edge of the sword – all was victory, because God was acting on behalf of His people, in pursuance of His promise to Abraham, Isaac, and Jacob.

In the opening verses of the chapter now before us, the Lord recapitulates His actings toward Israel in the following touching and beautiful language: "Thus shalt thou say to the house of Jacob, and tell the children of Israel: Ye have seen what I did unto the Egyptians, and how I bare you on eagles' wings, and brought you unto myself. Now therefore, if ye will obey my voice indeed, and keep my covenant, then ye shall be a peculiar treasure unto me above all people: for all the earth is mine. And ye shall be unto me a kingdom of priests and an holy nation" (ver. 3-6). Observe, it is *"my voice"* and *"my covenant."* What was the utterance of that "voice?" and what did that "covenant" involve? Had Jehovah's voice made itself heard for the purpose of laying down the rules and regulations of a severe and unbending law-giver? By no means. It had spoken to demand freedom for the captive – to provide a refuge from the sword of the destroyer – to make a way for the ransomed to pass over – to bring down bread from heaven, to draw forth water out of the flinty rock. Such had been the gracious and intelligible utterances of Jehovah's "voice," up to the moment at which "Israel camped before the mount."

And as to His "covenant," it was one of unmingled grace. It proposed no condition – it made no demands – it put no yoke on the neck – no burden on the shoulder. When "the God of glory appeared unto Abraham," in Ur of the Chaldees, He certainly did not address him in such words as, "thou shalt do this," and "thou shalt not do that." Ah! no; such language was not according to the heart of God. It suits Him far better to place "a fair mitre" upon a sinner's head, than to "put a yoke upon his neck." His word to Abraham was, "I WILL GIVE." The land of Canaan was not to be purchased by man's doings, but to be given by God's grace. Thus it stood; and, in the opening of the book of Exodus, we see God coming down in grace to make good His promise to Abraham's seed. The condition in which He found that seed made no difference, inasmuch as the blood of the lamb furnished Him with a perfectly righteous ground on which to make good His promise. He evidently had not promised the land of Canaan to Abraham's seed on the ground of anything that He foresaw in them, for this would have totally destroyed the real nature of a promise. It would have made it a compact and not a promise; "but God gave it to Abraham by promise," and not by compact (read Galatians 3).

Hence, in the opening of this 19th chapter, the people are

reminded of the grace in which Jehovah had hitherto dealt with them; and they are also assured of what they should yet be, provided they continued to hearken to mercy's heavenly "voice," and to abide in the "covenant" of free and absolute grace. "Ye shall be a peculiar treasure unto me above all people." How could they be this? Was it by stumbling up the ladder of self-righteousness and legalism? Would they be "a peculiar treasure" when blasted by the curses of a broken law – a law which they had broken before ever they received it? Surely not. How then were they to be this "peculiar treasure?" By standing in that position in which Jehovah surveyed them when He compelled the covetous prophet to exclaim, "How goodly are thy tents, O Jacob, and thy tabernacles, O Israel! As the valleys are they spread forth, as gardens by the river's side, as the trees of lign aloes which the Lord hath planted, and as cedar trees beside the waters. He shall pour the water out of his buckets, and his seed shall be in many waters, and his king shall be higher than Agag, and his kingdom shall be exalted. God brought him forth out of Egypt; he hath as it were the strength of an unicorn" (Num. 24:5-8).

A presumptuous commitment

However, Israel was not disposed to occupy this blessed position. Instead of rejoicing in God's "holy promise," they undertook to make the most presumptuous vow that mortal lips could utter. "All the people answered together, and said, *"All that the Lord hath spoken we will do"* (chap. 19:8). This was bold language. They did not even say, "we hope to do" or "we will endeavour to do." This would have expressed a measure of self-distrust. But no; they took the most absolute ground. "We will do." Nor was this the language of a few vain, self-confident spirits who presumed to single themselves out from the whole congregation. No; *all* the people answered *together*." They were unanimous in the abandonment of the "holy promise" – the "holy covenant."

And now, observe the result. The moment Israel uttered

their "singular vow," the moment they undertook to "do," there was a total alteration in the aspect of things. "And the Lord said unto Moses, Lo, I come unto thee *in a thick cloud* . . . And thou shalt set bounds unto the people, round about, saying, Take heed to yourselves, that ye go not up into the mount, or touch the border of it: whosoever toucheth the mount, shall be surely put to death." This was a very marked change; the One who had just said, "I bare you on eagles' wings, and brought you unto myself," now envelopes Himself "in a thick cloud," and says, "set bounds unto the people round about." The sweet accents of grace and mercy are exchanged for the "thunderings and lightnings" of the fiery mount. Man had presumed to talk of his miserable doings in the presence of God's magnificent grace. Israel had said, "we will do," and they must be put at a distance in order that it may be fully seen what they are able to do. God takes the place of moral distance; and the people are but too well disposed to have it so, for they are filled with fear and trembling; and no marvel, for the sight was "terrible," – "so terrible that Moses said, I exceedingly fear and quake." Who could endure the sight of that "devouring fire," which was the apt expression of divine holiness? "The Lord came from Sinai, and rose up from Seir unto them; he shined forth from Paran, and he came with ten thousands of saints; from his right hand went a fiery law for them" (Deut. 33:2). The term "fiery," as applied to the law, is expressive of its holiness: "Our God is a consuming fire," – perfectly intolerant of evil, in thought, word, and deed.

Thus, then, Israel made a fatal mistake in saying, "we will do." It was taking upon themselves a vow which they were not able, even were they willing, to pay; and we know who has said, "better that thou shouldest not vow, than that thou shouldest vow and not pay." It is of the very essence of a vow that it assumes the competency to fulfil; and where is man's competency? As well might a bankrupt draw a cheque on the bank, as a helpless sinner make a vow. A man who makes a vow, denies the truth, as to his nature and condition. He is ruined, what can he do? He is utterly without strength, and can neither will nor do anything good. Did Israel keep their vow? Did they do "all that the Lord commanded?" Witness the golden calf, the broken tables, the desecrated Sabbath, the despised and neglected ordinances, the stoned messengers, the rejected and crucified Christ, the resisted Spirit. Such are the overwhelming evidences of man's dishonoured vows. Thus must it ever be when fallen humanity undertakes to vow.

Christian reader, do you not rejoice in the fact that your eternal salvation rests not on your poor shadowy vows and resolutions, but on "the one offering of Jesus Christ once?" Oh, yes, "this is our joy, which ne'er can fail." Christ has taken all our vows upon Himself, and gloriously discharged them for ever. His resurrection-life flows through His members and produces in them results which legal vows and legal claims never could effect. He is our life, and He is our righteousness. May his name be precious to our hearts. May His cause ever command our energies. May it be our meat and our drink to spend and be spent in His dear service.

I cannot close this chapter without noticing, in connexion, a passage in the Book of Deuteronomy, which may present a difficulty to some minds. It has direct reference to the subject on which we have been dwelling. "And the Lord heard the voice of your words, when ye spake unto me; and the Lord said unto me, I have heard the voice of the words of this people, which they have spoken unto thee: *they have well said all that they have spoken* (Deut. 5:28). From this passage it might seem as though the Lord approved of their making a vow; but if my reader will take the trouble of reading the entire context, from ver. 24-27, he will see at once that it has nothing whatever to say to the vow, but that it contains the expression of their terror at the consequences of their vow. They were not able to endure that which was commanded. "If," said they, "we hear the voice of the Lord our God any more, then we shall die. For who is there of all flesh that hath heard the voice of the living God speaking out of the midst of the fire, as we have, and lived! Go thou near, and hear all that the Lord our God shall say; and speak thou unto us all that the Lord our God shall speak unto thee; and we will hear it and do it." It was the confession of their own inability to encounter Jehovah in that awful aspect which their proud legality had led Him to assume. It is impossible that the Lord could ever commend an abandonment of free and changeless grace for a sandy foundation of "works of law."

Chapter 20

THE LAW

Law and grace

It is of the utmost importance to understand the true character and object of the moral law, as set forth in this chapter. There is a tendency in the mind to confound the principles of law and grace, so that neither the one nor the other can be rightly understood. Law is shorn of its stern and unbending majesty; and grace is robbed of all its divine attractions. God's holy claims remain unanswered, and the sinner's deep and manifold necessities remain unreached by the anomalous system framed by those who attempt to mingle law and grace. In point of fact, they can never be made to coalesce, for they are as distinct as any two things can be. Law sets forth what man ought to be; grace exhibits what God is. How can these ever be wrought up into one system? How can the sinner ever be saved by a system made up of half law, half grace? Impossible. It must be either the one or the other.

The law has sometimes been termed "the transcript of the mind of God." This definition is entirely defective. Were we to term it a transcript of the mind of God as to what man ought to be, we should be nearer the truth. If I am to regard the ten commandments as the transcript of the mind of God, then, I ask, is there nothing in the mind of God save "thou shalt" and "thou shalt not?" Is there no grace? No mercy? No loving kindness? Is God not to manifest what He is? Is He not to tell out the deep secrets of that love which dwells in His bosom? Is there nought in the divine character but stern requirement and prohibition? Were this so, we should have to say, "God is law " instead of "God is love." But, blessed be His name, there is more in His heart than could ever be wrapped up in the "ten words" uttered on the fiery mount. If I want to see what God is, I must look at Christ; "for in Him dwelleth all the fullness of the godhead bodily" (Col. 2:9). "The law was given by Moses, but grace and truth came by Jesus Christ" (John 1:17). Assuredly there was a measure of truth in the law. It contained the truth as to what man ought to be. Like everything else emanating from God, it was perfect so far as it went – perfect for the object for which it was administered; but that object was not, by any means, to unfold, in the view of guilty sinners, the nature and character of God. There was no grace – no mercy. "He that despised Moses' law died without mercy" (Heb. 10.28). "The man that doeth these things shall live by them" (Lev. 18:5; Rom. 10:5). "Cursed is every one that continueth not in all things that are written in the book of the law to do them" (Deut. 27:26; Gal 3:10). This was not grace. Indeed, mount Sinai was not the place to look for any such thing. There Jehovah revealed Himself in awful majesty, amid blackness, darkness, tempest, thunderings, and lightnings. These were not the attendant circumstances of an economy of grace and mercy; but they were well suited to one of truth and righteousness; and the law was that and nothing else.

In the law God sets forth what a man ought to be, and pronounces a curse upon him if he is not that. But then a man finds, when he looks at himself in the light of the law, that he actually *is* the very thing which the law condemns. How then is he to get life by it? It proposes life and righteousness as the ends to be attained, by keeping it; but it proves, at the very outset, that we are in a state of death and unrighteousness. We want the very things at the beginning which the law proposes to be gained at the end. How, therefore, are we to gain them? In order to *do* what the law requires, I must have life; and in order to be what the law requires, I must have righteousness; and if I have not both the one and the other, I am "cursed." But the fact is, I have neither. What am I to do? This is the question. Let those who "desire to be teachers of the law" furnish an answer. Let them furnish a satisfactory reply to an upright conscience, bowed down under the double sense of the spirituality and inflexibility of the law and its own hopeless carnality.

The purpose of the law

The truth is, as the apostle teaches us, "the law entered that the offence might abound" (Rom. 5:20). This shows us, very distinctly, the real object of the law. It came in by the way in order to set forth the exceeding sinfulness of sin (Rom. 7:13). It was, in a certain sense, like a perfect mirror let down from heaven to reveal to man his moral derangement. If I present myself, with deranged habit, before a mirror, it shows me the derangement, but does not set it right. If I measure a crooked wall, with a perfect plumb-line, it reveals the crookedness, but does not remove it. If I take out a lamp on a dark night, it reveals to me all the hindrances and disagreeables in the way, but it does not remove them. Moreover, the mirror, the plumb-line, and the lamp, do not *create* the evils which they severally point out; they neither *create* nor *remove*, but simply *reveal*. Thus is it with the law; it does not create the evil in man's heart, neither does it remove it; but, with unerring accuracy, it reveals it.

"What shall we say then? Is the law sin? God forbid. Yea, I had not known sin but by the law; for I had not known lust except the law had said, Thou shalt not covet" (Rom. 7:7). He does not say that he would not have had "lust." No; but merely that "he had not known it." The "lust" was there; but he was in the dark about it until the law, as "the candle of the Almighty," shone in upon the dark chambers of his heart and revealed the evil that was there. Like a man in a dark room, who may be surrounded with dust and confusion, but he cannot see anything thereof by reason of the darkness. Let the beams of the sun dart in upon him, and he quickly perceives all. Do the sunbeams create the dust? Surely not. The dust is there, and they only detect and reveal it. This is a simple illustration of the effect of the law. It judges man's character and condition. It proves him to be a sinner and shuts him up under the curse. It comes to judge what he is, and curses him if he is not what it tells him he ought to be.

It is, therefore, a manifest impossibility that any one can get life and righteousness by that which can only curse him; and unless the condition of the sinner, and the character of the law are totally changed, it can do nought else but curse him. It makes no allowance for infirmities, and knows nothing of sincere, though imperfect, obedience. Were it to do so, it would not be what it is, "holy, just, and good." It is just because the law is what it is, that the sinner cannot get life by it. If he could get life by it, it would not be perfect, or else he would not be a sinner. It is impossible that a sinner can get life by a perfect law, for inasmuch as it is perfect, it must needs condemn him. Its absolute perfectness makes manifest and seals man's absolute ruin and condemnation. "Therefore by deeds of law shall no flesh living be justified in his sight; for by the law is the knowledge of sin" (Rom. 3:20). He does not say, "by the law is sin," but only "the knowledge of sin." "For until the law, sin was in the world; but sin is not imputed when there is no law" (Rom. 5:13). Sin was there, and it only needed law to develop it in the form of "transgression." It is as if I say to my child, "you must not touch that knife." My very prohibition reveals the tendency in his heart to do his own will. It does not create the tendency, but only reveals it.

The apostle John says that "sin is lawlessness" (1 John 3:4). The word "transgression" does not develop the true idea of the Spirit in this passage. In order to have "transgression" I must have a definite rule or line laid down. Transgression means a passing across a prohibited line; such a line I have in the law. I take any one of its prohibitions, such as, "thou shalt not kill," "thou shalt not commit adultery," "thou shalt not steal." Here, I have a rule or line set before me; but I find I have within me the very principles against which these prohibitions are expressly directed. Yea, the very fact of my being told not to commit murder, shows that I have murder in my nature. There would be no necessity to tell me not to do a thing which I had no tendency to do; but the exhibition of God's will, as to what I ought to be, makes manifest the tendency of my will to be what I ought not. This is plain enough, and is in full keeping with the whole of the apostolic reasoning on the point.

The curse of the law

Many, however, will admit that we cannot get life by the law; but they maintain, at the same time, that the law is our rule of life. Now, the apostle declares that "as many as are of works of law are under the curse" (Gal 3:10). It matters not who they are, if they occupy the ground of law, they are, of necessity, under the curse. A man may say, "I am regenerate, and, therefore, not exposed to the curse." This will not do. If regeneration does not take one off the ground of law, it cannot take him beyond the range of the curse of the law. If the Christian be under the former, he is, of necessity, exposed to the latter. But what has the law to do with regeneration? Where do we find anything about it in Exodus 20? The law has but one question to put to a man – a brief, solemn, pointed question, namely, "Are you what you ought to be?" If he answer in the negative, it can but hurl its terrible anathema at him and slay him. And who will so readily and emphatically admit that, in himself, he is anything but what he ought to be, as the really regenerate man? Wherefore, if he is under the law, he must, inevitably, be under the curse. The law cannot possibly lower its standard: nor yet amalgamate with grace. Men do constantly seek to lower its standard; they feel that they cannot get up to it, and they, therefore, seek to bring it down to them; but the effort is in vain: it stands forth in all its purity, majesty, and stern inflexibility, and will not accept a single hair's breadth short of perfect obedience; and where is the man, regenerate or unregenerate, that can undertake to produce that? It will be said, "We have perfection in Christ." True; but that is not by the law, but by grace; and we cannot possibly confound the two economies. Scripture largely and distinctly teaches that we are not justified by the law; nor is the law our rule of life. That which can only curse can never justify; and that which can only kill can never be a rule of life. As well might a man attempt to make a fortune by a deed of bankruptcy filed against him.

A yoke impossible to carry

If my reader will turn to Acts 15, he will see how the attempt to put Gentile believers under the law, as a rule of life, was met by the Holy Ghost. "There rose up certain of the sect of the Pharisees which believed, saying, that it was needful to circumcise them, and to command them to keep the law of Moses." This was nothing else than the hiss of the old serpent, making itself heard in the dark and depressing suggestion of those early legalists. But let us see how it was met by the mighty energy of the Holy Ghost, and the unanimous voice of the twelve apostles and the whole Church. "And when there had been much disputing, Peter rose up, and said unto them, Men and brethren, ye know how that a good while ago, God made choice among us, that the Gentiles by my mouth should hear," – what? Was it the requirements and the curses of *the law* of Moses? No: blessed be God, these are not what He would have falling on the ears of helpless sinners. Hear what then? "SHOULD HEAR THE WORD OF THE GOSPEL AND BELIEVE." This was what suited the nature and character of God. He never would have troubled men with the dismal accents of requirement and prohibition. These Pharisees were not His messengers; far from it. They were not the bearers of glad tidings, nor the publishers of peace, and therefore, their "feet" were anything but "beautiful" in the eyes of One who only delights in mercy.

"Now, therefore," continues the apostle, "why tempt ye God, to put a yoke upon the neck of the disciples, which neither our fathers nor we were able to bear?" This was strong, earnest language. God did not want "to put a yoke upon the neck" of those whose hearts had been set free by the gospel of peace. He would rather exhort them to stand fast in the liberty of Christ, and not be "entangled again with the yoke of bondage." He would not send those whom He had received to His bosom of love, to be terrified by the "blackness, and darkness, and tempest," of "the mount that might be touched." How could we ever admit the thought that those whom God had received in grace He would rule by law? Impossible. "We believe," says Peter, "that through the GRACE OF THE LORD JESUS CHRIST we shall be saved even as they." Both the Jews, who had received the law, and the Gentiles, who never had, were now to be "*saved* through *grace*." And not only were they to be "saved" by grace, but they were to "stand" in grace (Rom 5:2), and to "grow in grace" (2 Peter 3:18). To teach anything else was to "tempt God." Those Pharisees were subverting the very foundations of the Christian faith; and so are all those who seek to put believers under the law. There is no evil or error more abominable in the sight of the Lord than legalism. Hearken to the strong language – the accents of righteous indignation – which fell from the Holy Ghost, in reference to those teachers of the law: "I would they were even cut off which trouble you" (Gal, 5:12).

And, let me ask, are the thoughts of the Holy Ghost changed, in reference to this question? Has it ceased to be a tempting of God to place the yoke of legality upon a sinner's neck? Is it now in accordance with His gracious will that the law should be read out in the ears of sinners? Let my reader reply to these enquiries in the light of the fifteenth of Acts and the Epistle to the Galatians. These scriptures, were there no other, are amply sufficient to prove that God never intended that the "Gentiles should hear the word" of the law. Had He so intended, He would, assuredly, have "made choice" of some one to proclaim it in their ears. But no; when He sent forth His "fiery law," He spoke only in *one* tongue; but when He proclaimed the glad tidings of salvation, through the blood of the Lamb, He spoke in the language "of *every nation under heaven*." He spoke in such a way as that "*every man in his own tongue wherein he was born,"* might hear the sweet story of grace (Acts 2:1-11).

Further, when He was giving forth, from mount Sinai, the stern requirements of the covenant of works, He addressed Himself exclusively to *one* people. His voice was only heard within the narrow enclosures of the Jewish nation; but when, on the plains of Bethlehem, "the angel of the Lord" declared "good tidings of great joy," he added those characteristic words, "which shall be *to all people."* And, again, when the risen Christ was sending forth His heralds of salvation, His commission ran thus, "Go ye into *all the world* and preach the gospel to *every creature"* (Mark 16:15; Luke 2:10). The mighty tide of grace which had its source in the bosom of God, and its channel in the blood of the Lamb, was designed to rise, in the resistless energy of the Holy Ghost, far above the narrow enclosures of Israel, and roll through the length and breadth of a sin-stained world. "Every creature" must hear, "in his own tongue," the message of peace, the word of the gospel, the record of salvation, through the blood of the cross.

Finally, that nothing might be lacking to prove to our poor legal hearts that mount Sinai was not, by any means, the spot where the deep secrets of the bosom of God were told out, the Holy Ghost has said, both by the mouth of a prophet and an apostle, "How beautiful are the feet of them that preach the gospel of peace and bring glad tidings of good things!" (Isa. 3:7; Rom. 10:15). But of those who sought to be teachers of the law the same Holy Ghost has said, "I would they were even cut off that trouble you."

The law and the gospel

Thus, then, it is obvious that the law is neither the ground of life to the sinner nor the rule of life to the Christian. Christ is both the one and the other. He is our life and He is our rule of life. The law can only curse and slay. Christ is our life and righteousness. He became a curse for us by hanging on a tree. He went down into the place where the sinner lay – into the place of death and judgment – and having, by His death, entirely discharged all that was or could be against us, He became, in resurrection, the source of life and the ground of righteousness to all who believe in His name. Having thus life and righteousness in Him, we are called to walk, not merely as the law directs, but to "walk even as he walked." It will hardly be deemed needful to assert that it is directly contrary to Christian ethics to kill, commit adultery, or steal. But were a Christian to shape his way according to these commands, or according to the entire Decalogue, would he yield the rare and delicate fruits which the Epistle to the Ephesians sets forth? Would the ten commandments ever cause a thief to give up stealing, and go to work that he might have to give? Would they ever transform a thief into a laborious and liberal man? Assuredly not. The law says, "thou shalt not steal;" but does it say, "go and give to him that needeth" – "go feed, clothe, and bless your enemy" – "go gladden by your benevolent feelings and your beneficent acts the heart of him who only and always seeks your hurt?" By no means; and yet, were I under the law, as a rule, it could only curse me and slay me. How is this, when the standard in the New Testament is so much higher? Because I am weak, and the law gives me no strength and shows me no mercy. The law *demands* strength from one that has none, and *curses* him if he cannot display it. The gospel *gives* strength to one that has none, and *blesses* him in the exhibition of it. The law proposes life as the *end* of obedience. The gospel gives life as the only proper *ground* of obedience.

But that I may not weary the reader with arguments, let me ask if the law be, indeed, the rule of a believer's life, where are we to find it so presented in the New Testament? The inspired apostle evidently had no thought of its being the rule when he penned the following words: "For in Christ Jesus neither circumcision availeth anything nor uncircumcision, but a new creation. And as many as walk according to *this rule,* peace be on them, and mercy, and upon the Israel of God" (Gal. 6:15, 16). What "rule?" The law? No, but the "new creation." Where shall we find this in Exodus 20? It speaks not a word about "new creation." On the contrary, it addresses itself to man as he is, in his natural or old-creation state, and puts him to the test as to what he is really able to do. Now if the law were the rule by which believers are to walk, why does the apostle pronounce his benediction on those who walk by another rule altogether? Why does he not say, "as many as walk according to the rule of the ten commandments?" Is it not evident, from this one passage, that the Church of God has a higher rule by which to walk? Unquestionably. The ten commandments, though forming, as all true Christians admit, a part of the canon of inspiration, could never be the rule of life to one who has, through infinite grace, been introduced into the new creation – one who has received new life, in Christ.

But some may ask, "Is not the law perfect? And, if perfect, what more would you have?" The law is divinely perfect. Yea, it is the very perfection of the law which causes it to curse and slay those who are not perfect if they attempt to stand before it. "The law is spiritual, but I am carnal." It is utterly impossible to form an adequate idea of the infinite perfectness and spirituality of the law. But then this perfect law coming in contact with fallen humanity – this spiritual law coming in contact with "the carnal mind," could only "work wrath" and "enmity" (Rom. 4:15; Rom. 8:7). Why? Is it because the law is not perfect? No, but because it is, and man is a sinner. If man were perfect, he would carry out the law in all its spiritual perfectness; and even in the case of true believers, though they still carry about with them an evil nature, the apostle teaches us "that the righteousness of the law is fulfilled in us who walk not after the flesh, but after the Spirit" (Rom. 8:4). "He that loveth another hath fulfilled the law" – "love worketh no ill to his neighbour: therefore love is the fulfilling of the law" (Rom, 13:8-10). If I love a man, I shall not steal his property – nay, I shall seek to do him all the good I can. All this is plain and easily understood by the spiritual mind; but is leaves entirely untouched the question of the law, whether as the ground of life to a sinner or the rule of life to the believer.

The two great commandments

If we look at the law, in its two grand divisions, it tells a man to love God with all his heart, and with all his soul, and with all his mind; and to love his neighbour as himself. This is the sum of the law. This, and not a tittle less, is what the law demands. But where has this demand ever been responded to by any member of Adam's fallen posterity? Where is the man who could say he loves God after such a fashion? "The carnal mind (i.e., the mind which we have by nature) is enmity against God." Man hates God and His ways. God came, in the Person of Christ, and showed Himself to man – showed Himself, not in the overwhelming brightness of His majesty, but in all the charm and sweetness of perfect grace and condescension. What was the result? Man hated God. "Now have they both seen and hated both me and my Father" (John 15:24). But, it must be said, " Man ought to love God." No doubt, and he deserves death and eternal perdition if he does not. But can the law produce this love in man's heart? Was that its design? By no means, "for the law worketh wrath." The law finds man in a state of enmity against God; and without ever altering that state – for that was not its province – it commands him to love God with all his heart, and curses him if he does not. It was not the province of the law to alter or improve man's nature; nor yet could is impart any power to carry out its righteous demands. It said "This do, and thou shalt live." It commanded man to love God. It did not reveal what God was to man, even in his guilt and ruin; but it told man what he ought to be toward God. This was dismal work. It was not the unfolding of the powerful attractions of the divine character, producing in man true repentance toward God, melting his icy heart, and elevating his soul in genuine affection and worship. No: it was an inflexible command to love God; and, instead of producing love, it "worked wrath;"

not because God ought not to be loved, but because man was a sinner.

Again, "Thou shalt love thy neighbour as thyself." Can "the natural man" do this? Does he love his neighbour as himself? Is this the principle which obtains in the chambers of commerce, the exchanges, the banks, the marts, the fairs, and the markets of this world? Alas! no. Man does not love his neighbour as he loves himself. No doubt he ought: and if he were right, he would. But, then, he is all wrong – totally wrong – and unless he is "born again" of the word and the Spirit of God, he cannot "see nor enter the kingdom of God." The law cannot produce this new birth. It kills "the old man," but does not, and cannot, create "the new." As an actual fact we know that the Lord Jesus Christ embodied, in His glorious Person, both God and our neighbour, inasmuch as He was, according to the foundation-truth of the Christian religion, "God manifest in the flesh." How did man treat Him? Did he love Him with all his heart, or as himself? The very reverse. He crucified Him between two thieves, having previously preferred a murderer and a robber to that blessed One who had gone about doing good – who had come forth from the eternal dwelling-place of light and love – Himself the very living personification of that light and love – whose bosom had ever heaved with purest sympathy with human need – whose hand had ever been ready to dry the sinner's tears and alleviate his sorrows. Thus we stand and gaze upon the cross of Christ, and behold in it an unanswerable demonstration of the fact that it is not within the range of man's nature or capacity to keep the law.[9]

Thou shalt make me an altar of earth

It is peculiarly interesting to the spiritual mind, after all that has passed before us, to observe the relative position of God and the sinner at the close of this memorable chapter. "And the Lord said unto Moses, Thus thou shalt say unto the children of Israel . . . an altar of earth thou shalt make unto me, and shalt sacrifice thereon thy burnt-offerings, and thy peace offerings, thy sheep and thine oxen: in all places where I record my name, I WILL COME UNTO THEE, and I WILL BLESS THEE. And if thou wilt make an altar of stone, thou shalt not build it of hewn stone: for if thou lift up thy tool upon it, thou hast polluted it. Neither shalt thou go up by steps unto mine altar, that thy nakedness be not discovered thereon" (ver. 22, 26).

Here we find man not in the position of *a doer*, but of *a worshipper*; and this, too, at the close of Exodus 20. How plainly this teaches us that the atmosphere of Mount Sinai is not that which God would have the sinner breathing; that it is not the proper meeting place between God and man. "In all places where I record *my name, I will come unto thee, and I will bless thee.*" How unlike the terrors of the fiery mount is that spot where Jehovah records *His name,* whither He "comes" to "bless" His worshipping people!

But, further, God will meet the sinner at an altar without a hewn stone or a step – a place of worship which requires no human workmanship to erect, or human effort to approach. The former could only pollute, and the latter could only display human "nakedness." Admirable type of the meeting-place where God meets the sinner now, even the Person and work of His Son, Jesus Christ, where all the claims of law, of justice, and of conscience, are perfectly answered! Man has, in every age, and in every clime, been prone, in one way or another, to "lift up his tool" in the erection of his altar, or to approach thereto by steps of his own making. But the issue of all such attempts has been "pollution" and "nakedness." "We all do fade as a leaf, and all our righteousnesses are as filthy rags?" Who will presume to approach God clad in a garment of "filthy rags?" or who will stand to worship with a revealed "nakedness?" What can be more preposterous than to think of approaching God in a way which necessarily involves either pollution or nakedness? And yet thus it is in every case in which human effort is put forth to open the sinner's way to God. Not only is there no need of such effort, but defilement and nakedness are stamped upon it. God has come down so very near to the sinner, even in the very depths of his ruin, that there is no need for his lifting up the tool of legality, or ascending the steps of self-righteousness – yea, to do so, is but to expose his uncleanness and his nakedness.

Such are the principles with which the Holy Ghost closes this most remarkable section of inspiration. May they be indelibly written upon our hearts, that so we may more clearly and fully understand the essential difference between LAW and GRACE.

---

[9] For further exposition of the law, and also of the doctrine of the Sabbath, the reader is referred to a tract, entitled "A Scriptural Inquiry into the True Nature of the Sabbath, the Law, and the Christian Ministry."

Chapters 21-23

THE ORDINANCES

The justice of God and the corruption of man

The study of this section of our book is eminently calculated to impress the heart with a sense of God's unsearchable wisdom and infinite goodness. It enables one to form some idea of the character of a kingdom governed by laws of divine appointment. Here, too, we may see the amazing condescension of Him who, though He is the great God of heaven and earth, can, nevertheless, stoop to adjudicate between man and man in reference to the death of an ox, the loan of a garment, or the loss of a servant's tooth. "Who is like unto the Lord our God, who humbleth himself to behold the things that are in heaven and on earth?" He governs the universe, and yet He can occupy Himself with the provision of a covering for one of His creatures. He guides the angel's flight and takes notice of a crawling worm. He humbles Himself to regulate the movements of those countless orbs that roll through infinite space and to record the fall of a sparrow.

As to the character of the judgment set forth in the chapters before us, we may learn a double lesson. These judgments and ordinances bear a twofold witness: they convey to the ear a twofold message, and present to the eye two sides of a picture. They tell of God and they tell of man.

In the first place, on God's part, we find Him enacting laws which exhibit strict, even-handed, perfect justice. "Eye for eye, tooth for tooth, hand for hand, foot for foot, burning for burning, wound for wound, stripe for stripe." Such was the character of the laws, the statutes, and the judgments by which God governed His earthly kingdom of Israel. Everything was provided for, every interest was maintained, and every claim was met. There was no partiality – no distinction made between the rich and the poor. The balance in which each man's claim was weighed was adjusted with divine accuracy, so that no one could justly complain of a decision. The pure robe of justice was not to be tarnished with the foul stains of bribery, corruption and partiality. The eye and the hand of a divine Legislator provided for everything; and a divine Executive inflexibly dealt with every defaulter. The stroke of justice fell only on the head of the guilty, while every obedient soul was protected in the enjoyment of all his rights and privileges.

Then, as regards man, it is impossible to read over these laws and not be struck with the disclosure which they indirectly, but really, make of his desperate depravity. The fact of Jehovah's having to enact laws against certain crimes, proves the capability, on man's part, of committing those crimes. Were the capability and the tendency not there, there would be no need of the enactments. Now, there are many who, if the gross abominations forbidden in these chapters were named to them, might feel disposed to adopt the language of Hazael and say, "Is thy servant a dog that he should do this thing?" Such persons have not yet travelled down into the deep abyss of their own hearts. For albeit there are crimes here forbidden which would seem to place man, as regards his habits and tendencies, below the level of a "dog," yet do those very statutes prove, beyond all question, that the most refined and cultivated member of the human family carries about, in his bosom, the seeds of the very darkest and most horrifying abominations. For whom were those statutes enacted? For man. Were they needful? Unquestionably. But they would have been quite superfluous if man were incapable of committing the sins referred to. But man *is* capable; and hence we see that man is sunk to the very lowest possible level – that his nature is wholly corrupt – that, from the crown of his head to the sole of his foot, there is not so much as a speck of moral soundness.

How can such a being ever stand, without an emotion of fear, in the full blaze of the throne of God? How can he stand within the holiest? How can he stand on the sea of glass? How can he enter in by the pearly gates and tread the golden streets? The reply to these inquiries unfolds the amazing depths of redeeming love and the eternal efficacy of the blood of the Lamb. Deep as is man's ruin, the love of God is deeper still. Black as is his guilt, the blood of Jesus can wash it all away. Wide as is the chasm separating man from God, the cross has bridged it. God has come down to the very lowest point of the sinner's condition, in order that He might lift him up into a position of infinite favour, in eternal association with His own Son. Well may we exclaim, "Behold what manner of love the Father hath bestowed on us, that we should be called the sons of God" (1 John 3:1). Nothing could fathom man's ruin but God's love, and nothing could equal man's guilt but the blood of Christ. But now the very depth of the ruin only magnifies the love that has fathomed it, and the intensity of the guilt only celebrates the efficacy of the blood that can cleanse it. The very vilest sinner who believes in Jesus can rejoice in the assurance that God sees him and pronounces him *"clean every whit."*

The Hebrew servant

Such, then, is the double character of instruction to be gleaned from the laws and ordinances in this section, looked at as a whole; and the more minutely we look at them, in detail, the more impressed we shall be with a sense of their fullness and beauty. Take, for instance, the very first ordinance that presents itself, namely, that of the Hebrew servant.

"Now these are the judgments which thou shalt set before them. If thou buy an Hebrew servant, six years he shall serve: and in the seventh he shall go out free for nothing. If he came in by himself, he shall go out by himself: if he were married, then his wife shall go out with him. If his master have given him a wife, and she have borne him sons or daughters, the wife and her children shall he her master's, and he shall go out by himself. And if the servant shall plainly say, I love my master, my wife, and my children; I will not go out free; then his master shall bring him unto the judges: he shall also bring him to the door, or unto the door post; and his master shall bore his ear through with an awl; and he shall serve him for ever" (chap. 21:1-6). The servant was perfectly free to go out, so far as he was personally concerned. He had discharged every claim, and could, therefore, walk abroad in unquestioned freedom; but because of his love to his master, his wife, and his children, he voluntarily bound himself to perpetual servitude; and not only so, but he was also willing to bear, in his own person, the marks of that servitude.

The application of this to the Lord Jesus Christ will be obvious to the intelligent reader. In Him we behold the One who dwelt in the bosom of the Father before all worlds – the object of His eternal delight – who might have occupied, throughout eternity, this His personal and entirely peculiar place, inasmuch as there lay upon Him no obligation (save that which ineffable love created and ineffable love incurred) to abandon that place. Such, however, was His love to the Father whose counsels were involved, and for the Church collectively, and each individual member thereof, whose salvation was involved, that He, voluntarily, came down to earth, emptied Himself, and made Himself of no reputation, took upon Him the form of a servant and the marks of perpetual service. To these marks we probably have a striking allusion in the Psalms. "Mine ears hast thou digged" (Ps. 40:6, marg). This psalm is the expression of Christ's devotedness to God. "Then said I, Lo, I come: in the volume of the book it is written of me, I delight to do thy will, O my God: yea thy law is within my heart." He came to do the will of God, whatever that will might be. He never once did His own will, not even in the reception and salvation of sinners, though surely His loving heart, with all its affections, was most fully in that glorious work. Still He receives and saves only as the servant of the Father's counsels. "All that the Father giveth me shall come to me; and him that cometh to me I will in no wise cast out. For I came down from heaven, not to do mine own will, but the will of him that sent me. And this is the Father's will which hath sent me, that of all which he hath given me I should lose nothing, but should raise it up again at the last day" (John 6:37-39).

Here we have a most interesting view of the servant-character of the Lord Jesus Christ. He, in perfect grace, holds Himself responsible to receive all who come within the range of the divine counsels; and not only to receive them, but to preserve them through all the difficulties and trials of their devious path down here, yea, in the article of death itself, should it come, and to raise them all up in the last day. Oh! how secure is the very feeblest member of the Church of God! He is the subject of God's eternal counsels, which counsels the Lord Jesus Christ is pledged to carry out. Jesus loves the Father, and, in proportion to the intensity of that love, is the security of each member of the redeemed family. The salvation of any sinner who believes on the name of the Son of God is, in one aspect of it, but the expression of Christ's love to the Father. If one such could perish, through any cause whatsoever, it would argue that the Lord Jesus Christ was unable to carry out the will of God, which were nothing short of positive blasphemy against His sacred name, to whom be all honour and majesty throughout the everlasting ages.

Thus we have, in the Hebrew servant, a type of Christ in His pure devotedness to the Father. But there is more than this: "I love my wife and my children." "Christ loved the church and gave himself for it, that he might sanctify and cleanse it with the washing of water by the word, that he might present it to himself a glorious church, not having spot, or wrinkle, or any such thing; but that it should be holy and without blemish" (Eph. 5:25-27). There are various other passages of Scripture presenting Christ as the antitype of the Hebrew servant, both in His love for the Church, as a body, and for all believers personally. In Matthew 13, John 10 and

13, and Hebrews 2, my reader will find special teaching on the point.

The apprehension of this love of the heart of Jesus cannot fail to produce a spirit of fervent devotedness to the One who could exhibit such pure, such perfect, such disinterested love. How could the wife and children of the Hebrew servant fail to love one who had voluntarily surrendered his liberty in order that he and they might be together? And what is the love presented in the type, when compared with that which shines in the antitype? It is as nothing. "The love of Christ passeth knowledge." It led Him to think of us before all worlds – to visit us in the fullness of time – to walk deliberately to the door post – to suffer for us on the cross, in order that He might raise us to companionship with himself, in His everlasting kingdom and glory.

Were I to enter into a full exposition of the remaining statutes and judgments of this portion of the Book of Exodus, it would carry me much further than I feel, at present, led to go.[10] I will merely observe, in conclusion, that it is impossible to read the section and not have the heart drawn out in adoration of the profound wisdom, well-balanced justice, and yet tender considerateness which breathe throughout the whole. We rise up from the study of it with this conviction deeply wrought into the soul, that the One who speaks here is "the only true," "the only wise," and the infinitely gracious God.

May all our meditations on His eternal word have the effect of prostrating our souls in worship before Him whose perfect ways and glorious attributes shine there, in all their blessedness and brightness, for the refreshment, the delight, and the edification of His blood-bought people.

---

[10] I would here observe, once for all, that the feasts referred to in Ex. 23:14-19 and the offerings in Ex. 29 being brought out in all their fullness and detail, in the book of Leviticus, I shall reserve them until we come to dwell upon the contents of that singularly rich and interesting book.

Chapter 24

THE BLOOD OF THE COVENANT

This chapter opens with an expression remarkably characteristic of the entire Mosaic economy. "And he said unto Moses, Come up unto the Lord, thou and Aaron, Nadab, and Abihu, and seventy of the elders of Israel; and worship ye *afar off . . . they shall not come nigh,* neither shall the people *go up* with him." We may search from end to end of the legal ritual, and not find those two precious words, *"draw nigh."* Ah! no; such words could never be heard from the top of Sinai, nor from amid the shadows of the law. They could only be uttered at heaven's side of the empty tomb of Jesus, where the blood of the cross has opened a perfectly cloudless prospect to the vision of faith. The words, "afar off," are as characteristic of the law, as "draw nigh" are of the gospel. Under the law, the work was never done, which could entitle a sinner to draw nigh. Man had not fulfilled his promised obedience; and the "blood of calves and goats" could not atone for the failure, or give his guilty conscience peace. Hence, therefore, he had to stand "afar off." Man's vows were broken and his sin unpurged; how, then, could he draw nigh? The blood of ten thousand bullocks could not wipe away one stain from the conscience, or give the peaceful sense of nearness to God.

However, the "first covenant" is here dedicated with blood. An altar is erected at the foot of the hill, with "twelve pillars, according to the twelve tribes of Israel." "And he sent young men of the children of Israel, which offered burnt-offerings, and sacrificed peace offerings of oxen unto the Lord. And Moses took half of the blood, and put it in basins; and half of the blood he sprinkled on the altar . . . And Moses took the blood, and sprinkled it on the people, and said, Behold the blood of the covenant, which the Lord hath made with you concerning all these words." Although, as the apostle teaches us, it was "impossible that the blood of bulls and goats could take away sin," yet did it "sanctify to the purifying of the flesh," and, as "a shadow of good things to come," it availed to maintain the people in relationship with Jehovah.

"Then went up Moses, and Aaron, Nadab, and Abihu, and seventy of the elders of Israel; and they saw the God of Israel: and there was under his feet as it were a paved work of a sapphire stone, and as it were the body of heaven in clearness. And upon the nobles of the children of Israel he laid not his hand: also they saw God and did eat and drink." This was the manifestation of "the God of Israel," in light and purity, majesty and holiness. It was not the unfolding of the affections of a Father's bosom, or the sweet accents of a Father's voice, breathing peace and inspiring confidence into the heart. No; the "paved work of a sapphire stone" told out that unapproachable purity and light which could only tell a sinner to keep off. Still, "they saw God and did eat and drink." Touching proof of divine forbearance and mercy, as also of the power of the blood!

Looking at this entire scene as a mere illustration, there is much to interest the heart. There is the defiled camp *below* and the sapphire pavement *above*; but the altar, at the foot of the hill, tells us of that way by which the sinner can make his escape from the defilement of his own condition, and mount up to the presence of God, there to feast and worship in perfect peace. The blood which flowed around the altar furnished man's only title to stand in the presence of that glory which "was like a devouring fire on the top of the mount in the eyes of the children of Israel."

"And Moses went into the midst of the cloud, and gat him up into the mount; and Moses was in the mount forty days and forty nights." This was truly a high and holy position for Moses. He was called away from earth and earthly things. Abstracted from natural influences, he is shut in with God, to hear from his mouth the deep mysteries of the Person and work of Christ; for such, in point of fact, we have unfolded in the tabernacle and all its significant furniture – "the patterns of things in the heavens." The blessed One knew full well what was about to be the end of man's covenant of works; but He unfolds to Moses, in types and shadows, His own precious thoughts of love and counsels of grace, manifested in, and secured by, Christ.

Blessed, for evermore, be the grace which has not left us under a covenant of works. Blessed be He who has "hushed the law's loud thunders and quenched mount Sinai's flame" by "the blood of the everlasting covenant," and given us a peace which no power of earth or hell can shake. "Unto him that loved us, and washed us from our sins in his own blood, and hath made us kings and priests unto God and his Father; to him be glory and dominion for ever and ever. Amen."

Chapter 25

THE TABERNACLE

Introduction

This chapter forms the commencement of one of the richest veins in Inspiration's exhaustless mine – a vein in which every stroke of the mattock brings to light untold wealth. We know the mattock with which alone we can work in such a mine, namely, the distinct ministry of the Holy Ghost. Nature can do nothing here. Reason is blind – imagination utterly vain – the most gigantic intellect, instead of being able to interpret the sacred symbols, appears like a bat in the sunshine, blindly dashing itself against the objects which it is utterly unable to discern. We must compel reason and imagination to stand without, while, with a chastened heart, a single eye, and a spiritual mind, we enter the hallowed precincts and gaze upon the deeply significant furniture. God the Holy Ghost is the only One who can conduct us through the courts of the Lord's house, and expound to our souls the true meaning of all that there meets our view. To attempt the exposition, by the aid of intellect's unsanctified powers, would be infinitely more absurd than to set about the repairs of a watch with a blacksmith's tongs and hammer. "The patterns of things in the heavens" cannot be interpreted by the natural mind, in its most cultivated form. They must all be read in the light of heaven. Earth has no light which could at all develop their beauties. The One who furnished the patterns can alone explain what the patterns mean. The One who furnished the beauteous symbols can alone interpret them.

To the human eye there would seem to be a desultoriness

in the mode in which the Holy Ghost has presented the furniture of the tabernacle; but, in reality, as might be expected, there is the most perfect order, the most remarkable precision, the most studious accuracy. From chapter 25 to chapter 30, inclusive, we have a distinct section of the Book of Exodus. This section is divided into two parts, the first terminating at chapter 27:19, and the second at the close of chapter 30. The former begins with the ark of the covenant, inside the vail, and ends with the brazen altar and the court in which that altar stood. That is, it gives us, in the first place, Jehovah's throne of judgment, whereon He sat as Lord of all the earth; and it conducts us to that place where He met the sinner, in the credit and virtue of accomplished atonement. Then, in the latter, we have the mode of man's approach to God – the privileges, dignities, and responsibilities of those who, as priests, were permitted to draw nigh to the Divine Presence and enjoy worship and communion there. Thus the arrangement is perfect and beautiful. How could it be otherwise, seeing that it is divine? The ark and the brazen altar present, as it were, two extremes. The former was the throne of God established in "justice and judgment." (Ps. 89:14). The latter was the place of approach for the sinner where "mercy and truth" went before Jehovah's face. Man, in himself, dared not to approach the ark to meet God, for "the way into the holiest of all was not yet made manifest" (Heb. 9:8). But God could approach the altar of brass, to meet man as a sinner. "Justice and judgment" could not admit the sinner in; but "mercy and truth" could bring God out; not, indeed, in that overwhelming brightness and majesty in which He was wont to shine forth from between those mystic supporters of His throne – "the cherubim of glory" – but in that gracious ministry which is symbolically presented to us in the furniture and ordinances of the tabernacle.

All this may well remind us of the path trodden by that blessed One, who is the antitype of all these types – the substance of all these shadows. He travelled from the eternal throne of God in heaven, down to the depths of Calvary's cross. He came from all the glory of the former down into all the shame of the latter, in order that He might conduct His redeemed, forgiven, and accepted people back with Himself, and present them faultless before that very throne which He had left on their account. The Lord Jesus fills up, in His own person and work, every point between the throne of God and the dust of death, and every point between the dust of death and the throne of God. In Him God has come down, in perfect grace, to the sinner; in Him the sinner is brought up, in perfect righteousness, to God. All the way, from the ark to the brazen altar, was marked with the footprints of love; and all the way from the brazen altar to the ark of God was sprinkled with the blood of atonement; and as the ransomed worshipper passes along that wondrous path, he beholds the name of Jesus stamped on all that meets his view. May that name be dearer to our hearts! Let us now proceed to examine the chapters consecutively.

It is most interesting to note here, that the first thing which the Lord communicates to Moses is His gracious purpose to have a sanctuary or holy dwelling-place in the midst of His people – a sanctuary composed of materials, which directly point to Christ, His Person, His work, and the precious fruit of that work, as seen in the light, the power, and the varied graces of the Holy Ghost. Moreover, these materials were the fragrant fruit of the grace of God – the voluntary offerings of devoted hearts. Jehovah, whose majesty, "the heaven of heavens could not contain," was graciously pleased to dwell in a boarded and curtained tent, erected for Him by those who cherished the fond desire to hail His presence amongst them. This tabernacle may be viewed in two ways: first, as furnishing "a pattern of things in the heavens;" and, secondly, as presenting a deeply significant type of the body of Christ. The various materials of which the tabernacle was composed will come before us, as we pass along; we shall, therefore, consider the three comprehensive subjects put before us in this chapter, namely, the ark; the table; and the candlestick.

The ark and its contents

The ark of the covenant occupies the leading place in the divine communications to Moses. Its position, too, in the tabernacle was most marked. Shut in within the vail, in the holiest of all, it formed the base of Jehovah's throne. Its very name conveys to the mind its import. An ark, so far as the word instructs us, is designed to preserve *intact* whatever is put therein. An ark carried Noah and his family, together with all the orders of creation, in safety over the billows of judgment which covered the earth. An ark, at the opening of this book, was faith's vessel for preserving "a proper child" from the waters of death. When, therefore, we read of "the ark of the covenant," we are led to believe that it was designed of God to preserve His covenant unbroken, in the midst of an erring people. In it, as we know, the second set of tables were deposited. As to the first set, they were broken in pieces, beneath the mount, showing that man's covenant was wholly abolished – that his work could never, by any possibility, form the basis of Jehovah's throne of government. "Justice and judgment are the habitation of that throne," whether in its earthly or heavenly aspect. The ark could not contain within its hallowed inclosure, broken tables. Man might fail to fulfil his self-chosen vow; but God's law must be preserved in its divine integrity and perfectness. If God was to set up His throne in the midst of His people, He could only do so in a way worthy of Himself. His standard of judgment and government must be perfect.

"And thou shalt make staves of shittim wood, and overlay them with gold. And thou shalt put the staves into the rings by the sides of the ark, that the ark may be borne with them." The ark of the covenant was to accompany the people in all their wanderings. It never rested while they were a travelling or a conflicting host. It moved from place to place in the wilderness. It went before them into the midst of Jordan; it was their grand rallying point in all the wars of Canaan; it was the sure and certain earnest of power wherever it went.

No power of the enemy could stand before that which was the well-known expression of the divine presence and power. The ark was to be Israel's companion in travel, in the desert; and "the staves" and "the rings" were the apt expression of its travelling character.

However, it was not always to be a traveller. "The afflictions of David," as well as the wars of Israel, were to have an end. The prayer was yet to be breathed and answered, "Arise, O Lord, into *thy rest:* thou and *the ark of thy strength"* (Ps. 132:8). This most sublime petition had its partial accomplishment in the palmy days of Solomon, when "the priests brought in the ark of the covenant of the Lord unto his place, into the oracle of the house, to the most holy place, even under the wings of the cherubims. For the cherubims spread forth their two wings over the place of the ark, and the cherubims covered the ark, and the staves thereof above. *And they drew out the staves,* that the ends of the staves were seen out in the holy place before the oracle, and they were not seen without: and there they are unto this day" (1 Kings 8:6-8). The sand of the desert was to be exchanged for the golden floor of the temple. (1 Kings 6:30). The wanderings of the ark were to have an end; there was "neither enemy nor evil occurrent," and therefore, "the staves were drawn out."

Nor was this the only difference between the ark in the tabernacle and in the temple. The apostle, speaking of the ark in its wilderness habitation, describes it as "the ark of the covenant, overlaid round about with gold, wherein was the golden pot that had manna, and Aaron's rod that budded, and the tables of the covenant" (Heb. 9:4). Such were the contents of the ark in its wilderness journeyings – the pot of manna, the record of Jehovah's faithfulness, in providing for His redeemed in the desert, and Aaron's rod, "a token against the rebels," to "take away their murmurings" (compare Exod. 16:32-39; and Num. 17:10). But when the moment arrived in which "the staves" were to be "drawn out," when the wanderings and wars of Israel were over, the "exceeding magnifical" house was completed, when the sun of Israel's glory had reached, in type, its meridian, as marked by the wealth and splendour of Solomon's reign, then the records of wilderness need and wilderness failure were unnoticed, and nothing remained save that which constituted the eternal foundation of the throne of the God of Israel, and of all the earth. *"There was nothing in the ark, save the two tables of stone,* which Moses put there at Horeb" (1 Kings 8:9).

But all this brightness was soon to be overcast by the heavy clouds of human failure and divine displeasure. The rude foot of the uncircumcised was yet to walk across the ruins of that beautiful house, and its faded light and departed glory were yet to elicit the contemptuous "hiss" of the stranger. This would not be the place to follow out these things in detail; I shall only refer my reader to the last notice which the Word of God affords us of "the ark of the covenant," – a notice which carries us forward to a time when human folly and sin shall no more disturb the resting-place of that ark, and when neither a curtained tent, nor yet a temple made with hands, shall contain it. "And the seventh angel sounded; and there were great voices in heaven, saying, The kingdoms of this world are become the kingdoms of our Lord, and of his Christ: and he shall reign for ever and ever. And the four and twenty elders, which sat before God on their seats, fell upon their faces, and worshipped God, saying, We give thee thanks, O Lord God almighty, which art, and wast, and art to come; because thou has taken to thee thy great power and hast reigned. And the nations were angry, and thy wrath is come, and the time of the dead, that they should be judged, and that thou shouldest give reward unto thy servants the prophets, and to the saints, and them that fear thy name, small and great; and shouldst destroy them which destroy the earth. And the temple of God was opened in heaven, and there was seen in his temple *the ark of his covenant*: and there were lightnings, and voices, and thunderings, and an earthquake, and great hail" (Rev. 11:15-19).

The mercy-seat

The mercy-seat comes next in order. "And thou shalt make a mercy-seat of pure gold; two cubits and a half shall be the length thereof, and a cubit and a half the breadth thereof. And thou shalt make two cherubims of gold, of beaten work shalt thou make them, in the two ends of the mercy-seat. And make one cherub on the one end, and the other cherub on the other end; even of the mercy-seat shall ye make the cherubims on the two ends thereof. And the cherubims shall stretch forth their wings on high, covering the mercy-seat with their wings, and their faces shall look one to another; toward the mercy-seat shall the faces of the cherubims be. And thou shalt put the mercy seat above upon the ark; and in the ark shalt thou put the testimony that I shall give thee. And there I will meet with thee, and I will commune with thee from above the mercy-seat, from between the two cherubims which are upon the ark of the testimony, of all things which I will give thee in commandment unto the children of Israel."

Here Jehovah gives utterance to His gracious intention of coming down from the fiery mount to take His place upon the mercy seat. This He could do, inasmuch as the tables of testimony were preserved unbroken beneath, and the symbols of his power, whether in creation or providence, rose on the right hand and on the left – the inseparable adjuncts of that throne on which Jehovah had seated himself – a throne of grace founded upon divine righteousness and supported by justice and judgment. Here the glory of the God of Israel shone forth. From hence He issued His commands, softened and sweetened by the gracious source from whence they emanated, and the medium through which they came – like the beams of the mid-day sun, passing through a cloud, we can enjoy their genial and enlivening influence without being dazzled by their brightness. "His commandments are not grievous," when received from off the mercy-seat, because they come in connexion with grace, which gives the ears to hear and the power to obey.

Looking at the ark and mercy-seat together, we may see in them a striking figure of Christ, in His Person and work. He having, in His life, magnified the law and made it honourable, became, through death, a propitiation or mercy-seat for every one that believeth. God's mercy could only repose on a pedestal of perfect righteousness. "Grace reigns through righteousness unto eternal life by Jesus Christ our Lord" (Rom. 5:21). The only proper meeting place between God and man is the point where grace and righteousness meet and perfectly harmonise. Nothing but perfect righteousness could suit God; and nothing but perfect grace could suit the sinner. But where could these attributes meet in one point? Only in the cross. There it is that "mercy and truth are met together; righteousness and peace have kissed each other" (Ps. 85:10). Thus it is that the soul of the believing sinner finds peace. He sees that God's righteousness and his justification rest upon precisely the same basis, namely, Christ's accomplished work. When man, under the powerful action of *the truth* of God, takes his place as a sinner, God can, in the exercise of *grace*, take His place as a Saviour, and then every question is settled, for the cross having answered all the claims of divine justice, mercy's copious streams can flow unhindered. When a righteous God and a ruined sinner meet, on a blood-sprinkled platform, all is settled for ever – settled in such a way as perfectly glorifies God, and eternally saves the sinner. God must be true, though every man be proved a liar; and when man is so thoroughly brought down to the lowest point of his own moral condition before God as to be willing to take the place which God's truth assigns him, he then learns that God has revealed Himself as the righteous Justifier of such an one. This must give settled peace to the conscience; and not only so, but impart a capacity to commune with God, and hearken to His holy precepts in the intelligence of that relationship into which divine grace has introduced us.

Hence, therefore, "the holiest of all" unfolds a truly wondrous scene. The ark, the mercy seat, the cherubim, the glory! What a sight for the high-priest of Israel to behold as, once a year, he went in within the vail! May the Spirit of God open the eyes of our understandings, that we may understand more fully the deep meaning of those precious types.

The table of showbread

Moses is next instructed about *"the table of showbread,"* or bread of presentation. On this table stood the food of the priests of God. For seven days those twelve loaves of "fine flour with frankincense" were presented before the Lord, after which, being replaced by others, they became the food of the priests who fed upon them in the holy place (see Lev. 24:5-9). It is needless to say that those twelve loaves typify "the man Christ Jesus." The "fine flour," of which they were composed, mark His perfect manhood, while the "frankincense" points out the entire devotion of that manhood to God. If God has His priests ministering in the holy place, He will assuredly have a table for them, and a well-furnished table too. Christ is the table and Christ is the bread thereon. The pure table and the twelve loaves shadow forth Christ, as presented before God unceasingly, in all the excellency of His spotless humanity, and administered as food to the priestly family. The "seven days" set forth the perfection of the divine enjoyment of Christ; and the "twelve loaves" the administration of that enjoyment in and by man. There is also, I should venture to suggest, the idea, of Christ's connexion with the twelve tribes of Israel, and the twelve apostles of the Lamb.

The candlestick of pure gold

The candlestick of pure gold comes next in order, for God's priests need *light* as well as *food*: and they have both the one and the other in Christ. In this candlestick there is no mention of anything but pure gold. "All of it shall be one *beaten* work of pure gold." "The seven lamps" which "gave light over against the candlestick," express the perfection of the light and energy of the Spirit, founded upon and connected with the perfect efficacy of the work of Christ. The work of the Holy Ghost can never be separated from the work of Christ. This is set forth, in a double way, in this beautiful figure of the golden candlestick. "The seven lamps" being connected with "the shaft" of "beaten gold," points us to Christ's finished work as the sole basis of the manifestation of the Spirit in the Church. The Holy Ghost was not given until Jesus was glorified (comp. John 7:39 with Acts 19:2-6). In the third chapter of Revelation, Christ is presented to the Church of Sardis as "having the seven spirits." It was as "exalted to the right hand of God" that the Lord Jesus "shed forth" the Holy Ghost upon His church, in order that she might shine according to the power and perfection of her position, in the holy place, her proper sphere of being, of action, and of worship.

Then, again, we find it was one of Aaron's specific functions to light and trim those seven lamps. "And the Lord spake unto Moses, saying, Command the children of Israel that they bring unto thee pure oil olive, beaten for the light, to cause the lamps to burn continually. Without the vail of the testimony, in the tabernacle of the congregation, shall Aaron order it, from the evening unto the morning, before the Lord continually: it shall be a statute for ever in your generations. He shall order the lamps upon the pure candlestick before the Lord continually" (Lev. 24:1-4). Thus we may see how the work of the Holy Ghost in the Church is linked with Christ's work on earth and His work in heaven. "The seven lamps" were there, no doubt; but priestly energy and diligence were needed in order to keep them trimmed and lighted. The priest would continually need "the tongs and snuff-dishes" for the purpose of removing anything that would not be a fit vehicle for the "pure beaten oil." Those tongs and snuff-dishes were of "beaten gold" likewise, for the whole matter was the direct result of divine operation. If the Church shine, it is only by the energy of the Spirit, and that energy is founded upon Christ, who, in pursuance of God's eternal counsel, became in His sacrifice and Priesthood, the spring and power of everything to His Church. All is of God. Whether we look within that mysterious vail, and behold the ark with its cover, and the two significant figures attached thereto; or if we gaze on that which lay without the vail, the pure table and the pure candlestick, with their distinctive vessels and instruments – all speak to us of God, whether as revealed to us in connexion with the Son or the Holy Ghost.

Christian reader, your high calling places you in the very midst of all these precious realities. Your place is not merely amid "the patterns of things in the heavens," but amid "the heavenly things themselves." You have "boldness to enter into the holiest by the blood of Jesus." You are a priest unto God. "The showbread" is yours. Your place is at "the pure table," to feed on the priestly food, in the light of the Holy Ghost. Nothing can ever deprive you of those divine privileges. They are yours for ever. Let it be your care to watch against everything that might rob you of the *enjoyment* of them. Beware of all unhallowed tempers, lusts, feelings, and imaginations. Keep nature down – keep the world out – keep Satan off. May the Holy Ghost fill your whole soul with Christ. Then you will be practically holy and abidingly happy. You will bear fruit, and the Father will be glorified, and your joy shall be full.

Chapter 26

THE CURTAINS, COVERINGS AND BOARDS

The materials of the first covering

The section of our book which now opens before us contains the instructive description of the curtains and coverings of the tabernacle, wherein the spiritual eye discerns the shadows of the various features and phases of Christ's manifested character. "Moreover, thou shalt make the tabernacle with ten curtains of fine twined linen, and blue, and purple, and scarlet: with cherubims of cunning work shalt thou make them." Here we have the different aspects of "the man Christ Jesus." The "fine twined linen" prefigures the spotless purity of His walk and character; while the "blue, the purple, and the scarlet" present Him to us as "the Lord from *heaven*," who is to *reign* according to the divine counsels, but whose royalty is to be the result of His *sufferings*. Thus we have a spotless man, a heavenly man, a royal man, a suffering man. These materials were not confined to the " curtains" of the tabernacle, but were also used in making "the vail" (ver. 31), "the hanging for the door of the tent" (ver. 36), "the hanging for the gate of the court" (chap. 27:16), "the cloths of service and the holy garments of Aaron" (chap. 39:1). In a word, it was Christ everywhere, Christ in all, Christ alone.[11]

The fine twined linen

"The fine twined linen," as expressive of Christ's spotless manhood, opens a most precious and copious spring of thought to the spiritual mind; it furnishes a theme on which we cannot meditate too profoundly. The truth respecting Christ's humanity must be received with scriptural accuracy, held with spiritual energy, guarded with holy jealousy, and confessed with heavenly power. If we are wrong as to this, we cannot be right as to anything. It is a grand, vital, fundamental truth, and if it be not received, held, guarded, and confessed, as God has revealed it in His holy word, the entire superstructure must be unsound. Nothing can be more deplorable than the looseness of thought and expression which seems to prevail in reference to this all-important doctrine. Were there more reverence for the word of God, there would be more accurate acquaintance with it; and, in this way, we should happily avoid all those erroneous and unguarded statements which surely must grieve the Holy Spirit of God, whose province it is to testify of Jesus.

When the angel had announced to Mary the glad tidings of the Saviour's birth, she said unto him, "How shall this be, seeing I know not a man?" Her feeble mind was utterly incompetent to enter into, much less to fathom, the stupendous mystery of "God manifest in the flesh." But mark carefully the angelic reply – a reply, not to a sceptic mind, but to a pious, though ignorant, heart. "The Holy Ghost shall come upon thee, and the power of the Highest shall overshadow thee; wherefore, also, that holy thing which shall be born of thee shall be called the Son of God" (Luke 1:34, 35). Mary, doubtless, imagined that this birth was to be according to the principles of ordinary generation. But the angel corrects her mistake, and, in correcting it, enunciates one of the grandest truths of revelation. He declares to her that divine power was about to form A REAL MAN – "the second man – the Lord from heaven" – one whose nature was divinely pure, utterly incapable of receiving or communicating any taint. This Holy One was made "*in the likeness* of sinful flesh," without sin in the flesh. He partook of real *bona fide* flesh and blood without a particle or shadow of the evil thereto attaching.

This is a cardinal truth which cannot be too accurately laid hold of or too tenaciously held. The incarnation of the Son – His mysterious entrance into pure and spotless flesh, formed, by the power of the Highest, in the virgin's womb, is the foundation of the "great mystery of godliness" of which the topstone is a glorified God-man in heaven, the Head, Representative, and Model of the redeemed Church of God. The essential purity of His manhood perfectly met the claims of God; the reality thereof met the necessities of man. He was a man, for none else would do to meet man's ruin. But He was such a man as could satisfy all the claims of the throne of God. He was a spotless, real man, in whom God could perfectly delight, and on whom man could unreservedly lean.

I need not remind the enlightened reader that all this, if taken apart from death and resurrection, is perfectly unavailable to us. We needed not only an incarnate, but a crucified and risen Christ. True, He should be incarnate to be crucified; but it is death and resurrection which render incarnation available to us. It is nothing short of a deadly error to suppose that, in incarnation, Christ was taking man into union with Himself. This could not be. He Himself expressly teaches the contrary. "Verily, verily, I say unto you, except a corn of wheat fall into the ground and *die*, it abideth *alone*: but if it die, it bringeth forth much fruit" (John 12:24). There could be no union between sinful and holy flesh, pure and impure, corruptible and incorruptible, mortal and immortal. Accomplished death is the only base of a unity between Christ and His elect members. It is in beautiful connexion with the words, "Rise, let us go hence," that He says, "I am the vine, ye are the branches." "We have been planted together in the likeness of his death." "Our old man is crucified with him, that the body of sin might be destroyed." "In whom also are ye circumcised with the circumcision made without hands, in putting off the body of the sins of the flesh, by the circumcision of Christ; buried with him in baptism, wherein also ye are risen with him through the faith of the operation of God, who hath raised him from the dead." I would refer my reader to Romans 6 and Colossians 2 as a full and comprehensive statement of the truth on this important subject. It was only as dead and risen that Christ and His people could become one. The true corn of wheat had to fall into the ground and die ere a full ear could spring up and be gathered into the heavenly garner.

But while this is a plainly revealed truth of Scripture, it is equally plain that incarnation formed, as it were, the first layer of the glorious superstructure; and the curtains of "fine twined linen" prefigure the moral purity of "the man Christ Jesus." We have already seen the manner of His conception; and, as we pass along the current of His life here below, we meet with instance after instance of the same spotless purity. He was forty days in the wilderness, tempted of the devil, but there was no response in His pure nature to the tempter's foul suggestions. He could touch the leper and receive no taint. He could touch the bier and not contract the smell of death. He could pass unscathed through the most polluted atmosphere. He was, as to His manhood, like a sunbeam emanating from the fountain of light, which can pass, without a soil, through the most defiling medium. He was perfectly unique in nature, constitution, and character. None but He could say, "Thou wilt not suffer thine holy One to see corruption." This was in reference to His humanity, which, as being perfectly holy and perfectly pure, was capable of being a sin-bearer. "His own self bare our sins in his own body on the tree." Not *to* the tree, as some would teach us; but "*on* the tree." It was on the cross that Christ was our sin-bearer, and only there. "He hath made him to be sin for us who knew no sin, that we might be made the righteousness of God in him" (2 Cor. 5:21).

The blue, purple and scarlet

"*Blue*" is the ethereal colour, and marks the heavenly character of Christ, who, though He had come down into all the circumstances of actual and true humanity – sin excepted – yet was He "the Lord from heaven." Though He was "very man," yet He ever walked in the uninterrupted consciousness of His proper dignity, as a heavenly stranger. He never once forgot whence He had come, where He was, or whither He was going. The spring of all His joys was on high. Earth could neither make Him richer nor poorer. He found this world to be "a dry and thirsty land, where no water is;" and, hence, His spirit could only find its refreshment above. It was entirely heavenly. "No man hath ascended up to heaven, but he that came down from heaven, even the son of man *who is in heaven*" (John 3:13).

"*Purple*" denotes royalty, and points us to Him who "was born King of the Jews;" who offered Himself as such to the Jewish nation, and was rejected; who before Pontius Pilate witnessed a good confession, avowing Himself a king, when, to mortal vision, there was not so much as a single trace of royalty. "Thou sayest that I am a king." And "hereafter ye shall see the Son of man sitting at the right hand of power, and coming in the clouds of heaven." And, finally, the inscription upon His cross, "in letters of Hebrew, and Greek, and Latin" – the language of religion, of science, and of government declared Him, to the whole known world, to be "Jesus of Nazareth, the King of the Jews." Earth disowned His claims – so much the worse for it – but not so heaven; there His claim was fully recognised. He was received as a conqueror into the eternal mansions of light, crowned with glory and honour, and seated, amid the acclamations of angelic hosts, on the throne of the majesty in the heavens, there to wait until His enemies be made His footstool. "Why do the heathen rage, and the people imagine a vain thing? The kings of the earth set themselves, and the rulers take counsel together, against the Lord and against his anointed, saying, Let us break their bands asunder, and cast away their cords from us. He that sitteth in the heavens shall laugh; the Lord shall have them in derision. Then shall he speak unto them in his wrath, and vex them in his sore displeasure. Yet have I set *my king* upon my holy hill of Zion. I will declare the decree: the Lord hath said unto me, Thou art my Son; this day have I begotten thee. Ask of me, and I shall give thee the heathen for thine inheritance, and the uttermost parts of the earth for thy possession. Thou shalt break them with a rod of iron; thou shalt dash them in pieces like a potter's vessel. Be wise, now, therefore, O ye kings; be instructed, ye judges of the earth. Serve the Lord with fear, and rejoice with trembling. Kiss the Son, lest he be angry, and ye perish from the way, when his wrath is kindled but a little. BLESSED ARE ALL THEY THAT PUT THEIR TRUST IN HIM" (Ps. 2).

"*Scarlet,*" when genuine, is produced by death; and this makes its application to a suffering Christ safe and appropriate. "Christ hath suffered for us in the flesh." Without death, all would have been unavailing. We can admire "the blue" and "the purple" but without "the scarlet" the tabernacle would have lacked an all-important feature. It was by death that Christ destroyed him that had the power of death. The Holy Ghost, in setting before us a striking figure of Christ – the true tabernacle – could not possibly omit that phase of His character which constitutes the groundwork of His connexion with His body the Church, of His claim to the throne of David, and the headship of all creation. In a word, He not only unfolds the Lord Jesus to our view, in these significant curtains, as a spotless man, a royal man, but also a suffering man; one who, *by death*, should make good His claims to all that to which, as man, He was entitled, in the divine counsels.

But we have much more in the curtains of the tabernacle than the varied and perfect phases of the character of Christ. We have also the unity and consistency of that character. Each phase is displayed in its own proper perfectness; and one never interferes with, or mars the exquisite beauty of, another. All was in perfect harmony beneath the eye of God, and was so displayed in "the pattern which was showed to Moses on the mount," and in the copy which was exhibited below. "Every one of the curtains shall have one measure. The five curtains shall be coupled together one to another; and other five curtains shall be coupled one to another." Such was the fair proportion and consistency in all the ways of Christ, as a perfect man, walking on the earth, in whatever aspect or relationship we view Him. When acting in one character, we never find anything that is, in the very least degree, inconsistent with the divine integrity of another. He was, at all times, in all places, under all circumstances, the perfect man. There was nothing out of that fair and lovely proportion which belonged to Him, in all His ways. "Every one of the curtains shall have one measure."

The two sets of five curtains each may symbolise the two grand aspects of Christ's character, as acting toward God and toward man. We have the same two aspects in the law, namely, what was due to God, and what was due to man; so that, as to Christ, if we look in, we find "thy law is within my heart;" and if we look at His outward character and walk, we see those two elements adjusted with perfect accuracy, and not only adjusted, but inseparably linked together by the heavenly grace and divine energy which dwelt in His most glorious Person.

"And thou shalt make *loops of blue* upon the edge of the one curtain, from the selvedge in the coupling; and likewise shalt thou make in the uttermost edge of another curtain, in the coupling of the second . . . And thou shalt make fifty *taches of gold,* and couple the curtains together with the taches; and *it shall be one tabernacle.*" We have here displayed to us, in the "loops of *blue,*" and "taches of *gold,*" that *heavenly* grace and *divine* energy in Christ which enabled Him to combine and perfectly adjust the claims of God and man; so that in responding to both the one and the other, He never, for a moment, marred the unity of His character. When crafty and hypocritical men tempted Him with the enquiry, "Is it lawful to give tribute to Caesar or not?" His wise reply was, "Render to Caesar the things that are Caesar's, and to God the things that are God's."

Nor was it merely Caesar, but man in every relation that had all his claims perfectly met in Christ. As He united in His perfect Person the nature of God and man, so He met in His perfect ways the claims of God and man. Most interesting would it be to trace, through the gospel narrative, the exemplification of the principle suggested by the "loops of blue," and "taches of gold;" but I must leave my reader to pursue this study under the immediate guidance of the Holy Ghost, who delights to expatiate upon every feature and every phase of that perfect One whom it is His unvarying purpose and undivided object to exalt.

The curtain of goats' hair

The curtains on which we have been dwelling were covered with other "curtains of goats' hair;" (ver. 7-14). Their beauty was hidden from those without by that which bespoke roughness and severity. This latter did not meet the view of those within. To all who were privileged to enter the hallowed enclosure nothing was visible save "the blue, the purple, the scarlet, and fine twined linen," the varied yet combined exhibition of the virtues and excellencies of that divine Tabernacle in which God dwelt within the vail – that is, of Christ, through whose flesh, the antitype of all these, the beams of the divine nature shone so delicately, that the sinner could behold without being overwhelmed by their dazzling brightness.

As the Lord Jesus passed along this earth, how few really knew Him! How few had eyes anointed with heavenly eyesalve to penetrate and appreciate the deep mystery of His character! How few saw "the blue, the purple, the scarlet, and fine twined linen!" It was only when faith brought man into His presence that He ever allowed the brightness of what He was to shine forth – ever allowed the glory to break through the cloud. To nature's eye there would seem to have been a reserve and a severity about Him which were aptly prefigured by the "covering of goats' hair." All this was the result of His profound separation and estrangement, not from sinners personally, but from the thoughts and maxims of men. He had nothing in common with man as such, nor was it within the compass of mere nature to comprehend or enjoy Him. "No man," said He, "can come to me, except the Father which hath sent me draw him;" and when one of those "drawn" ones confessed His name, He declared that "flesh and blood hath not revealed it unto thee, but my Father which is in heaven" (comp. John 6:44; Matt. 16:17). He was "a root out of a dry ground," having neither "form nor comeliness" to attract the eye or gratify the heart of man. The popular current could never flow in the direction of One who, as he passed rapidly across the stage of this vain world, wrapped Himself up in a "covering of goats' hair." Jesus was not popular. The multitude might follow Him for a moment, because His ministry stood connected, in their judgment, with "the loaves and fishes" which met their need; but they were just as ready to cry, "Away with him!" as "Hosanna to the Son of David!" Oh! let Christians remember this! Let the servants of Christ remember it! Let all preachers of the gospel remember it! Let one and all of us ever seek to bear in mind the *"covering of goats' hair!"*

The rams' skins dyed red

But if the goats' skins expressed the severity of Christ's separation from earth, "the rams' skins *dyed red*" exhibit His intense consecration and devotedness to God, which was carried out even unto *death*. He was the only perfect Servant that ever stood in God's vineyard. He had one object which He pursued, with an undeviating course, from the manger to the cross, and that was to glorify the Father and finish His work. "Wist ye not that I must be about my Father's business" was the language of His youth, and the accomplishment of that "business" was the design of His life. "His meat was to do the will of him that sent him and to finish his work." "The rams' skins dyed red" formed as distinct a part of His ordinary habit as the "goats' hair." His perfect devotion to God separated Him from the habits of men.

The badgers' skins

"*The badgers' skins*" may exhibit to us the holy vigilance with which the Lord Jesus guarded against the approach of everything hostile to the purpose which engrossed His whole soul. He took up His position for God, and held it with a tenacity which no influence of men or devils, earth or hell, could overcome. The covering of badgers' skins was "above," (ver. 14), teaching us that the most prominent feature in the character of "the man Christ Jesus" was an invincible determination to stand as a witness for God on the earth. He was the true Naboth, who gave up His life rather than surrender the truth of God, or give up that for which He had taken His place in this world.

The goat, the ram, and the badger, must be regarded as exhibiting certain natural features, and also as symbolising certain moral qualities; and we must take both into account in our application of these figures to the character of Christ. The human eye could only discern the former. It could see none of the moral grace, beauty, and dignity, which lay beneath the outward form of the despised and humble Jesus of Nazareth. When the treasures of heavenly wisdom flowed from His lips, the inquiry was, "Is not this the carpenter?" or "How knoweth this man letters, having never learned?" When He asserted His eternal Sonship and Godhead, the word was, "Thou art not yet fifty years old," or "They took up stones to cast at him." In short, the acknowledgement of the Pharisees, in John 9, was true in reference to men in general. "As for this fellow, we know not from whence he is."

It would be utterly impossible, in the compass of a volume like this, to trace the unfoldings of those precious features of Christ's character through the gospel narratives. Sufficient has been said to open up springs of spiritual thought to my reader, and to furnish some faint idea of the rich treasures which are wrapped up in the curtains and coverings of the tabernacle. Christ's hidden being, secret springs and inherent excellencies – His outward and unattractive form – what He was in Himself, what He was to Godward, and what He was to manward – what he was in the judgment of faith, and what in the judgment of nature – all is sweetly and impressively told out to the circumcised ear, in the "curtains of blue, purple, scarlet, and fine twined linen:" and the "coverings of skins."

The boards

"The boards for the tabernacle" were made of the same wood as was used in constructing "the ark of the covenant." Moreover, they were upheld by the sockets of silver formed out of the atonement; their hooks and chapiters being of the same (compare attentively chap. 30:11-16, with chap. 38:25-28). The whole framework of the tent of the tabernacle was based on that which spoke of atonement or ransom, while the "hooks and chapiters" at the top set forth the same. The sockets were buried in the sand, and the hooks and chapiters were above. It matters not how deep you penetrate, or how high you rise, that glorious and eternal truth is emblazoned before you, "I HAVE FOUND A RANSOM." Blessed be God, "we are not redeemed with corruptible things, as silver and gold, . . . But with the precious blood of Christ, as of a lamb without blemish and without spot."

Christ the door

The tabernacle was divided into three distinct parts, namely, "the holy of holies," "the holy place," and "the court of the tabernacle." The entrance into each of these was of the same materials, "blue, purple, scarlet, and fine twined linen" (compare Ex. 26:31, 36; Ex. 27:16). The interpretation of which is simply this: Christ forms the only doorway into the varied fields of glory which are yet to be displayed, whether on earth, in heaven, or in the heaven of heavens. "Every family, in heaven and earth," will be ranged under His headship, as all will be brought into everlasting felicity and glory, on the ground of His accomplished atonement. This is plain enough, and needs no stretch of the imagination to grasp it. We know it to be true: and when we know the truth which is shadowed forth, the shadow is easily understood. If only our hearts be filled with Christ, we shall not go far astray in our interpretations of the tabernacle and its furniture. It is not a head full of learned criticism that will avail us much here, but a heart full of affection for Jesus, and a conscience at rest in the blood of His cross.

May the Spirit of God enable us to study these things with more interest and intelligence! May He "open our eyes that we may behold wondrous things out of his law."

---

[11] The expression, "*white* and *clean*," gives peculiar force and beauty to the type which the Holy Ghost has presented in the "fine twined linen." Indeed, there could not be a more appropriate emblem of spotless manhood.

Chapter 27

THE BRAZEN ALTAR

The order of divine communications

We have now arrived at the brazen altar which stood at the door of the tabernacle; and I would call my reader's most particular attention to the order of the Holy Ghost in this portion of our book. We have already remarked that from chapter 25 to the nineteenth verse of chapter 27 forms a distinct division, in which we are furnished with a description of the ark and mercy-seat, the table and candlestick, the curtains and the vail; and, lastly, the brazen altar and the court in which that altar stood. If my reader will turn to chapter 35:15, chapter 37:25, chapter 40:26, he will remark that the golden altar of incense is noticed, in each of the three instances, between the candlestick and the brazen altar. Whereas, when Jehovah is giving directions to Moses, the brazen altar is introduced immediately after the candlestick and the curtains of the tabernacle. Now, inasmuch as there must be a divine reason for this difference, it is the privilege of every diligent and intelligent student of the word to inquire what that reason is.

Why, then, does the Lord, when giving directions about the furniture of the "holy place," omit the altar of incense and pass out to the brazen altar which stood at the door of the tabernacle? The reason, I believe, is simply this. He first describes the mode in which He would manifest Himself to man: and then He describes the mode of man's approach to Him. He took His seat upon the throne, as " the Lord of all the earth." The beams of His glory were hidden behind the vail – type of Christ's flesh (Heb. 10:20); but there was the manifestation of Himself, in connexion with man, as in "the pure table," and by the light and power of the Holy Ghost, as in the candlestick. Then we have the manifested character of Christ as a man down here on this earth, as seen in the curtains and coverings of the tabernacle. And, finally, we have the brazen altar as the grand exhibition of the meeting-place between a holy God and a sinner. This conducts us, as it were, to the extreme point, from which we return, in company with Aaron and his sons, back to the holy place, the ordinary priestly position, where stood the golden altar of incense. Thus the order is strikingly beautiful. The golden altar is not spoken of until there is a priest to burn incense thereon, for Jehovah showed Moses the patterns of things in the heavens according to the order in which these things are to be apprehended by faith. On the other hand, when Moses gives directions to the congregations (chap. 35), when he records the labours of "Bezaleel and Aholiab," (chap. 37 and chap. 38), and when he sets up the tabernacle (chap. 40), he follows the simple order in which the furniture was placed.

The prayerful investigation of this interesting subject, and a comparison of the passages above referred to, will amply repay my reader. We shall now examine the brazen altar.

The altar

This altar was the place where the sinner approached God, in the power and efficacy of the blood of atonement. It stood "at the door of the tabernacle of the tent of the congregation," and on it all the blood was shed. It was composed of "shittim wood and brass." The wood was the same as that of the golden altar of incense; but the metal was different, and the reason of this difference is obvious. The altar of brass was the place where sin was dealt with according to the divine judgment concerning it. The altar of gold was the place from whence the precious fragrance of Christ's acceptableness ascended to the throne of God. The "shittim wood" as the figure of Christ's humanity, must be the same in each case; but in the brazen altar we see Christ meeting the fire of divine justice; in the golden altar, we behold Him feeding the divine affections. At the former, the fire of divine wrath was quenched, at the latter, the fire of priestly worship, is kindled. The soul delights to find Christ in both; but the altar of brass is what meets the need of a guilty conscience. It is the very first thing for a poor, helpless, needy, convicted sinner. There cannot be settled peace, in reference to the question of sin, until the eye of faith rests on Christ as the antitype of the brazen altar. I must see my sin reduced to ashes in the pan of the altar, ere I can enjoy rest of conscience in the presence of God. It is when I know, by faith in the record of God, that He Himself has dealt with my sin in the Person of Christ, at the brazen altar – that He has satisfied all His own righteous claims – that He has put away my sin out of His holy presence, so that it can never come back again – it is then, but not until then, that I can enjoy divine and everlasting peace.

The gold and the brass

I would here offer a remark as to the real meaning of the "gold" and "brass" in the furniture of the tabernacle. "Gold" is the symbol of divine righteousness, or the divine nature in "the man Christ Jesus." "Brass" is the symbol of righteousness, demanding judgment of sin, as in the brazen altar; or the judgment of uncleanness, as in the brazen laver. This will account for the fact that *inside* the tent of the tabernacle, all was gold – the ark, the mercy-seat, the table, the candlestick, the altar of incense. All these were the symbols of the divine nature – the inherent personal excellence of the Lord Jesus Christ. On the other hand, *outside* the tent of the tabernacle, – all was brass – the brazen altar and its vessels, the laver and its foot.

The claims of righteousness, as to sin and uncleanness, must be divinely met ere there can be any enjoyment of the precious mysteries of Christ's Person, as unfolded in the inner sanctuary of God. It is when I see all sin and all uncleanness perfectly judged and washed away, that I can, as a priest, draw nigh and worship in the holy place, and enjoy the full display of all the beauty and excellency of the God-man, Christ Jesus.

The reader can, with much profit, follow out the application of this thought in detail, not merely in the study of the tabernacle and the temple, but also in various passages of the word; for example, in the first chapter of Revelation, Christ is seen "girt about the paps with a *golden* girdle," and having "his feet like unto fine *brass*, as if they burned in a furnace." "The golden girdle" is the symbol of His intrinsic righteousness. The "feet like unto the brass," express the unmitigated judgment of evil – He cannot tolerate evil, but must crush it beneath His feet.

Such is the Christ with whom we have to do. He judges sin, but He saves the sinner. Faith sees sin reduced to ashes at the brazen altar; it sees all uncleanness washed away at the brazen laver: and, finally, is enjoys Christ, as He is unfolded, in the secret of the divine presence, by the light and power of the Holy Ghost. It finds Him at the golden altar, in all the value of His intercession. It feeds on Him at the pure table. It recognises Him in the ark and mercy-seat as the One who answers all the claims of justice, and, at the same time, meets all human need. It beholds Him in the vail, with all its mystic figures. It reads His precious name on everything. Oh! for a heart to prize and praise this matchless, glorious Christ!

Nothing can be of more vital importance than a clear understanding of the doctrine of the brazen altar; that is to say, of the doctrine taught there. It is from the want of clearness as to this, that so many souls go mourning all their days. They have never had a clean, thorough settlement of the whole matter of their guilt at the brazen altar. They have never really beheld, by faith, God Himself settling on the cross, the entire question of their sins. They are seeking peace for their uneasy consciences in regeneration and its evidences, – the fruits of the Spirit, frames, feelings, experiences, – things quite right and most valuable in themselves, but they are not the ground of peace. What fills the soul with perfect peace is the knowledge of what God hath wrought at the brazen altar. The ashes in yonder pan tell me the peace-giving story that ALL IS DONE. The believer's sins were all put away by God's own hand of redeeming love. "He hath made Christ to be sin for us, who knew no sin, that we might be made the righteousness of God in him" (2 Cor. 5). All sin must be judged: but the believer's sins have been already judged in the cross; hence, he is perfectly justified. To suppose that there could be anything against the very feeblest believer, is to deny the entire work of the cross. His sins and iniquities have been *all* put away by God Himself, and therefore they must needs be perfectly put away. They all went with the outpoured life of the Lamb of God.

Dear Christian reader, see that your heart is thoroughly established in the peace which Jesus has made "by the blood of His cross."

Chapters 28 & 29

THE PRIESTHOOD

These chapters unfold to us the Priesthood, in all its value and efficacy. They are full of deep interest. The very word "Priesthood" awakens in the heart, feelings of the most profound thankfulness for the grace which has not only provided a way for us to get into the divine presence, but also the means of keeping us there, according to the character and claims of that high and holy position.

The Aaronic priesthood was God's provision for a people who were, in themselves, at a distance, and needed one to appear in His presence continually. We are taught in Hebrews 7, that this order of priesthood belonged to the law – that it was made "after the law of carnal commandment" – that it "could not continue by reason of death" – that the priests belonging to it had infirmity. It could not, therefore, impart perfection, and hence we have to bless God that it was instituted "without an oath." The oath of God could only stand connected with that which was to endure for ever, even the perfect, immortal, untransferrable priesthood of our great and glorious Melchisedec, who imparts, both to His sacrifice and His priesthood, all the value, the dignity, and the glory of His own peerless Person. The thought of having such a sacrifice and such a Priest as He causes the bosom to heave with emotions of the liveliest gratitude.

But we must proceed to the examination of the chapters which lie before us.

Aaron's robes

In chapter 28 we have the robes, and in chapter 29 we have

the sacrifices. The former have more especial reference to the need of the people; the latter, on the other hand, to the claims of God. The robes express the varied functions and qualities of the priestly office. "The ephod" was the great priestly robe. It was inseparably connected with the shoulder-pieces and the breastplate, teaching us, very distinctly, that the *strength* of the priest's shoulder, and the *affection* of the priest's heart, were wholly devoted to those whom he represented, and on whose behalf he wore the ephod – that special priestly robe. This, which was typified in Aaron, is actualized in Christ. His omnipotent strength and infinite love are ours – ours eternally – ours unquestionably. The shoulder which sustains the universe, upholds the feeblest and most obscure member of the blood-bought congregation. The heart of Jesus beats with an undying affection, with an everlasting and an all-enduring love for the most neglected member of the redeemed assembly.

The names of the twelve tribes engraven on precious stones, were borne both on the shoulders and on the breast of the high priest (see ver. 9-12, 15-29). The peculiar excellence of a precious stone is seen in this, that the more intense the light that is brought to bear upon it, the more brightly it shines. Light can never make a precious stone look dim; it only increases and develops its lustre. The twelve tribes, one as well another, the smallest as well as the greatest, were borne continually upon the breast and shoulders of Aaron before the Lord. They were, each and every one, maintained, in the divine presence, in all that undimmed lustre and unalterable beauty which belonged to the position in which the perfect grace of the God of Israel had set them. The people were represented before God by the high priest. Whatever might be their infirmities, their errors, or their failures, yet their names glittered on the breastplate with unfading brilliancy. Jehovah had set them there, and who could pluck them thence? Jehovah had put them thus, and who could put them otherwise? Who could penetrate into the holy place to snatch from Aaron's breast the name of one of Israel's tribes?

Who could sully the lustre which gathered round those names, in the position which Jehovah had placed them? Not one. They lay beyond the reach of every enemy – beyond the influence of every evil.

How encouraging and consolatory it is for the tried, tempted, buffeted, and self-abased children of God to remember that God only sees them on the heart of Jesus! In His view, they ever shine in all the effulgence of Christ; they are arrayed in divine comeliness. The world cannot see them thus; but God does, and this makes all the difference. Men, in looking at the people of God, see only their blots and blemishes. They have no ability whatever to see further, and as a consequence, their judgment is always wrong – always one-sided. They cannot see the sparkling jewels, bearing the names of God's redeemed, engraven by the hand of changeless love. True it is that Christians should be most careful not to furnish the men of the world with any just occasion to speak reproachfully. They should seek "by patient continuance in well doing, to put to silence the ignorance of foolish men." If only they entered, by the power of the Holy Ghost, into the comeliness in which they ever shine, in God's vision, it would assuredly lead to a walk of practical holiness, moral purity, and elevation, before the eyes of men. The more clearly we enter, by faith, into objective truth, or what is true of us in Christ, the deeper, more experimental, and practical will be the subjective work in us; and the more complete will be the exhibition of the moral effect in our life and character.

But, thank God, our judgment is not with men, but with Himself: and He graciously shows us our great high priest, "bearing our judgment on His heart, before the Lord continually." This imparts deep and settled peace – a peace which nothing can shake. We may have to confess and mourn over our constant failures and short-comings; the eye may, at times, be so dimmed with the tears of a genuine contrition as to be but little able to catch the lustre of the precious stones on which our names are graven, yet there they are all the while. God sees them, and that is enough. He is glorified by their brightness – a brightness not of our attaining, but of His imparting. We had nought save darkness, dullness, and deformity. He has imparted brightness, lustre, and beauty. To Him be all the praise, throughout the everlasting ages!

"The girdle" is the well-known symbol of service; and Christ is the perfect Servant – the Servant of the divine counsels and affections, and of the deep and manifold need of His people. With an earnest spirit of devotedness, which nothing could damp, He girded Himself for His work; and when faith sees the Son of God thus girded, it judges, assuredly, that no occasion can be too great for Him. We find, from the type before us, that all the virtues, the dignities, and the glories of Christ, in His divine and human nature, enter fully into His servant character. "The curious girdle of the ephod, which is upon it, shall be of the same, according to the work thereof, even of gold, of blue, and purple, and scarlet, and fine twined linen" (verse 8). The faith of this must meet every necessity of the soul, and satisfy the most ardent longings of the heart. We not only see Christ as the slain victim at the brazen altar, but also as the girded High Priest over the house of God. Well, therefore, may the inspired apostle say, *"Let us draw near"* – *"let us hold fast"* – *"let us consider one another"* (Heb. 10:19-24).

"And thou shalt put in the breastplate of judgment the Urim and the Thummim ("lights and perfections") and they shall be upon Aaron's heart, when he goeth in before the Lord: and Aaron shall bear the judgment of the children of Israel before the Lord continually." We learn from various passages of the Word, that the "Urim" stood connected with the communication of the mind of God, in reference to the various questions which arose in the details of Israel's history. Thus, for example, in the appointment of Joshua, we read, "And he shall stand before Eleazar the priest, who shall ask counsel for him, *after the judgment of Urim before the Lord"*(Numb. 27:21). "And of Levi he said. Let thy Thummim and thy Urim (the perfections and they lights) be with thy holy one . . . they shall teach Jacob thy judgments, and Israel thy law" (Deut. 33:8-10). "And when Saul enquired of the Lord, the Lord answered him not, neither by dreams, *nor by Urim,* nor by prophets" (1 Sam. 28:6). "And the Tirshatha said unto them that they should not eat of the most holy things, till there stood up a priest with Urim and Thummim" (Ezra 2:63). Thus we learn that the high priest not only bore the judgment of the congregation before the Lord, but also communicated the judgment of the Lord to the congregation – solemn, weighty and most precious functions! All this we have, in divine perfectness, in our "great High Priest who has passed through the heavens." He bears the judgment of His people on His heart continually; and He, by the Holy Ghost, communicates to us the counsel of God, in reference to the most minute circumstances of our daily course. We do not want dreams or visions; if only we walk in the Spirit, we shall enjoy all the certainty which the perfect "Urim" on the breast of our High Priest, can afford.

"And thou shalt make the robe of the ephod all of blue . . . and, beneath, upon the hem of it, thou shalt make pomegranates of blue, and of purple, and of scarlet, round about the hem thereof; and bells of gold between them round about: a golden bell and a pomegranate, a golden bell and a pomegranate, upon the hem of the robe round about. And it shall be upon Aaron to minister; and his sound shall be heard when he goeth in unto the holy place before the Lord, and when he cometh out, that he die not" (ver. 31-35). The blue robe is expressive of the entirely heavenly character of our High Priest. He is gone into heaven; He is beyond the range of mortal vision; but, by the power of the Holy Ghost, there is divine testimony to the truth of His being alive, in the presence of God; and not only testimony, but fruit likewise. "A golden bell and a pomegranate, a golden bell and a pomegranate." Such is the beauteous order. True testimony to the great truth that Jesus ever liveth to make intercession for us will be inseparably connected with fruitfulness in His service. Oh! for a deeper understanding of these precious and holy mysteries![12]

"And thou shalt make a plate of pure gold, and engrave upon it like the engravings of a signet, HOLINESS TO THE LORD. And thou shalt put it on a blue lace, that it may be upon the mitre, upon the forefront of the mitre it shall be. And it shall be upon Aaron's forehead, that Aaron may bear the iniquity of the holy things, which the children of Israel shall hallow in all their holy gifts; and it shall be always upon *his* forehead, that *they* may be accepted before the Lord" (ver. 36-38). Here is a weighty truth for the soul. The golden plate on Aaron's forehead was the type of the essential holiness of the Lord Jesus Christ. "It shall be ALWAYS upon HIS forehead, that THEY may be accepted before the Lord." What rest for the heart amid all the fluctuations of one's experience! Our High Priest is "always" in the presence of God for us. We are represented by, and accepted in, Him. His holiness is ours. The more deeply we become acquainted with our own personal vileness and infirmity, the more we enter into the humiliating truth that in us dwelleth no good thing, the more fervently shall we bless the God of all grace for the soul-sustaining truth contained in these words, "it shall be always upon *his* forehead, that *they* may be accepted before the Lord."

If my reader should happen to be one who is frequently tempted and harassed with doubts and fears, ups and downs in his spiritual condition, with a constant tendency to look inward upon his poor, cold, wandering, wayward heart; if he be tried with an excessive vagueness and want of holy reality – oh! let him stay his whole soul upon the precious truth that this great High Priest represents him before the throne of God. Let him fix his eye upon the golden plate and read, in the inscription thereon, the measure of his eternal acceptance with God. May the Holy Spirit enable him to taste the peculiar sweetness and sustaining power of this divine and heavenly doctrine!

The robes of the sons of Aaron

"And for Aaron's sons thou shalt make coats, and thou

shalt make for them girdles, and bonnets shalt thou make for them, for glory and for beauty . . . and thou shalt make them linen breeches to cover their nakedness . . . And they shall be upon Aaron, and upon his sons, when they come in unto the tabernacle of the congregation, or when they come near unto the altar to minister in the holy place; that they bear not iniquity and die." Here we have Aaron and his sons, typifying Christ and the Church, standing in the power of one divine and everlasting righteousness. Aaron's priestly robes express those inherent, essential, personal, and eternal qualities in Christ; while the "coats" and "bonnets" of Aaron's sons represent those graces with which the Church is endowed, in virtue of its association with the great head of the priestly family.

Thus, in all that has passed before us in this chapter, we may see with what gracious care Jehovah made provision for the need of His people in that He allowed them to see the one who was about to act on their behalf, and to represent them in His presence, clothed with all those robes which directly met their actual condition, as known to Him. Nothing was left out which the heart could possibly need or desire. They might survey him from head to foot and see that all was complete. From the holy mitre that wreathed his brow, to the bells and pomegranates on the hem of his garment, all was as it should be, because all was according to the pattern shown in the mount – all was according to Jehovah's estimate of the people's need and of His own requirements.

The divinity and humanity of Christ

But there is yet one point connected with Aaron's robes which demands the reader's special attention, and that is the mode on which the gold was introduced in the making of them. This is presented to us in chapter 39, but the interpretation comes in suitably enough in this place. "And they did beat the gold into thin plates, and cut it into wires, to work it in the blue, and in the purple, and in the scarlet, and in the fine linen with cunning work" (ver. 3). We have already remarked that "the blue, the purple, the scarlet and fine twined linen" exhibit the various phases of Christ's manhood, and the gold represents His divine nature. The wire of gold was curiously insinuated into all the other materials, so as to be inseparably connected with, and yet perfectly distinct from, them.

The application of this striking figure to the character of the Lord Jesus is full of interest. In various scenes, throughout the gospel narrative, we can easily discern this rare and beauteous union of Manhood and Godhead, and, at the same time, their mysterious distinctness.

Look, for example, at Christ on the sea of Galilee. In the midst of the storm "he was asleep on a pillow" – precious exhibition of His perfect manhood! But, in a moment, He rises from the attitude of real humanity into all the dignity and majesty of Godhead, and, as the supreme Governor of the universe, He hushes the storm, and calms the sea. There is no effort, no haste, no girding Himself up for an occasion. With perfect ease, He rises from the condition of positive humanity into the sphere of essential Deity. The repose of the former is not more natural than the activity of the latter. He is as perfectly at home in the one as in the other.

Again, see Him in the case of the collection of tribute; at the close of Matthew 17. As the "Most High God, possessor of heaven and earth," He lays His hand upon the treasures of the ocean, and says, "they are mine;" and having declared that "the sea is his and he made it," He turns round and, in the exhibition of perfect humanity, He links Himself with His poor servant, by those touching words, "that take and give unto them *for me and for thee."* Gracious words! peculiarly gracious, when taken in connexion with the miracle so entirely expressive of the Godhead of the One who was thus linking Himself, in infinite condescension, with a poor feeble worm.

Once more, see Him at the grave of Lazarus (John 11). He groans and weeps, and those groans and tears issue from the profound depths of a perfect manhood – from that perfect human heart which felt, as no other heart could feel, what it was to stand in the midst of scene in which sin had produced such terrible fruits. But then, as the Resurrection and the Life, as the One who held in His omnipotent grasp "the keys of hell and of death," He cries, "Lazarus, come forth;" and death and the grave, responsive to His authoritative voice, throw open their massy doors and let go their captive.

My reader's mind will easily recur to other scenes in the gospels illustrative of the beautiful combination of the wire of gold with "the blue, the purple, the scarlet, and the fine twined linen;" that is to say, the union of the Godhead with the manhood, in the mysterious Person of the Son of God. There is nothing new in the thought. It has often been noticed by those who have studied, with any amount of care, the Scriptures of the Old Testament.

It is, however, always edifying to have the blessed Lord Jesus introduced to our thoughts as "very God and very man." The Holy Ghost has, with "cunning workmanship," wrought the two together and presented them to the renewed mind of the believer to be enjoyed and admired. May we have hearts to appreciate such teaching!

The consecration of Aaron and his sons

Let us now, ere we close this section, look for a moment at chapter 29.

It has already been remarked that Aaron and his sons represent Christ and the Church, but in the opening verses of this chapter, Aaron gets the precedency. "And Aaron and his sons thou shalt bring unto the door of the tabernacle of the congregation, and thou shalt wash them with water." The washing of water rendered Aaron, typically, what Christ is, intrinsically, holy. The Church is holy in virtue of her being linked with Christ in resurrection life. He is the perfect definition of what she is before God. The ceremonial act of washing with water expresses the action of the Word of

God (see Eph. 5:26). "For their sakes," says Christ, "I sanctify myself, that they also might be sanctified through the truth" (John 17:19). He separated Himself to God in the power of a perfect obedience, being governed in all things, as man, by the Word, through the eternal Spirit, in order that all those who belong to Him might be thoroughly separated by the moral power of the truth.

"Then shalt thou take the anointing oil and pour it upon *his* head and anoint *him*" (ver 7). Here we have the Spirit; but let it be noted that Aaron was anointed *before the blood was shed*, because he stands before us as the type of Christ, who, in virtue of what He was, in His own Person, was anointed with the Holy Ghost, long before the work of the cross was accomplished. The sons of Aaron, on the other hand, were not anointed until after the blood was shed. "Then shalt thou kill the ram, and take of his blood, and put it upon the tip of the right ear of Aaron, and upon the tip of the right ear of his sons, and upon the thumb of their right hand, and upon the great toe of their right foot, and sprinkle the blood on the altar round about.[13] And thou shalt take of the blood that is upon the altar, and of *the anointing oil*, and sprinkle it upon Aaron, and upon his garments, and upon his sons, and upon the garments of his sons with him" (ver. 20, 21). As regards the Church, the blood of the cross lies at the foundation of everything. She could not be anointed with the Holy Ghost until Her risen Head had gone into heaven, and laid upon the throne of the divine Majesty the record of His accomplished sacrifice. "This Jesus hath God raised up, whereof we are all witnesses. Therefore being by the right hand of God exalted, and having received of the Father the promise of the Holy Ghost, he hath shed forth this which ye now see and hear" (Acts 2:32, 33. Comp. also John 7:39; Acts 19:1-6). From the days of Abel downward, souls had been regenerated, influenced, acted upon, and qualified for office by the Holy Ghost; but the Church could not be anointed with the Holy Ghost until her victorious Lord had entered heaven and received on her behalf the promise of the Father. The truth of this doctrine is taught, in the most direct and absolute manner, throughout the New Testament; and its strict integrity is maintained, in the type before us, by the obvious fact that, though Aaron was anointed before the blood was shed (ver. 7), yet his sons were not, and could not be, anointed till after (ver 21).

But we learn more from the order of the anointing in our chapter, than the important truth with respect to the work of the Spirit, and the position of the Church. We have also set before us the personal pre-eminence of the Son. "Thou hast loved righteousness, and hated iniquity; therefore God, even thy God, hath anointed thee with the oil of gladness *above* thy fellows" (Ps. 45:7; Heb 1:9). This must ever be held fast in the convictions and experience of the people of God. True, the infinite grace of God is set forth in the marvellous fact that guilty, hell-deserving sinners should ever be spoken of in such terms – should ever be styled the *"fellows"* of the Son of God; but let us never, for a moment, forget the word *"above."* No matter how close the union – and it as close as God's eternal counsels of redeeming love could make it – yet, "in all things" Christ must "have the pre-eminence." It could not be otherwise. He is Head over all – Head of the Church – Head of creation – Head of angels – Lord of the universe. There is not a single orb that rolls along the heavens that does not belong to Him and move under His control. There is not a single worm that crawls along the earth which is not under His sleepless eye. He is "high over all," "the first-begotten from the dead," and "of the whole creation," "the beginning of the creation of God." "Every family in heaven and earth" must range itself, in the divine category, under Christ. All this will ever be thankfully owned by every spiritual mind; yea, the very enunciation of it sends a thrill through the Christian's heart. All who are led of the Spirit will rejoice in every unfolding of the personal glories of the Son; nor can they tolerate, for a single instant, anything derogatory thereto. Let the Church be raised to the loftiest heights of glory, it will be her joy to bow at the feet of Him who stooped to raise her, by virtue of His completed sacrifice, into union with Himself; who, having satisfied, in the fullest manner, all the claims of divine justice, can gratify all the divine affections by making her inseparably one with Himself, in all His infinite acceptableness with the Father, and in His eternal glory. "He is not *ashamed* to call them brethren."

NOTE. I purposely forbear from entering upon the subject of the offerings in chap. 29, inasmuch as we shall have the various classes of offerings, in all their minute detail, fully before us in the Book of Leviticus, if the Lord will.

---

[12] It is needless to remark that there is divine appropriateness as well as significancy, in all the figures presented to us in the Word. Thus, the "pomegranate," when opened, is found to consist of a number of seeds, contained in a *red* fluid. Surely this has a voice. Let spirituality, not imagination, judge.

[13] The ear, the hand, and the foot are all consecrated to God in the power of accomplished atonement, and by the energy of the Holy Ghost.

THE WORSHIP

The golden altar

The priesthood being instituted, as in the two preceding chapters, we are here introduced to the position of true priestly worship and communion. The order is marked and instructive; and, moreover, precisely corresponds with the order of the believer's experience. At the brazen altar, he sees the ashes of his sins; he then sees himself linked with One who, though personally pure and spotless, so that He could be anointed without blood, has, nevertheless, associated us with Himself in life, righteousness, and favour; and, finally, he beholds, in the golden altar, the preciousness of Christ, as the material on which the divine affections feed.

Thus it is ever; there must be a brazen altar and a priest before there can be a golden altar and incense. Very many of the children of God have never passed the brazen altar. They have never yet, in spirit, entered into the power and reality of true priestly worship. They do not rejoice in a full, clear, divine sense of pardon and righteousness; they have never reached the golden altar. They hope to reach it when they die; but it is their privilege to be at it *now*. The work of the cross has removed out of the way everything which could act as a barrier to their free and intelligent worship. The present position of all true believers is at the golden altar of incense.

This altar typifies a position of wondrous blessedness. There we enjoy the reality and efficacy of Christ's intercession. For ever done with self and all pertaining thereto, so far as any expectation of good is concerned, we are to be occupied with what He is before God. We shall find nothing in self but defilement. Every exhibition of it is defiling; it has been condemned and set aside in the judgment of God, and not a shred or particle thereof is to be found in the pure incense and pure fire, on the altar of pure gold: it could not be. We have been introduced, "by the blood of Jesus," into the sanctuary – a sanctuary of priestly service and worship, in which there is not so much as a trace of sin. We see the pure table, the pure candlestick, and the pure altar; but there is nothing to remind us of self and its wretchedness. Were it possible for anything of that to meet our view, it could but prove the death knell of our worship, mar our priestly food, and dim our light. Nature can have no place in the sanctuary of God. It, together with all its belongings, has been consumed to ashes; and we are now to have before our souls the fragrant odour of Christ, ascending in grateful incense to God: this is what God delights in. Everything that presents Christ in His own proper excellence, is sweet and acceptable to God. Even the feeblest expression or exhibition of Him, in the life or worship of a saint, is an odour of a sweet smell, in which God is well pleased.

Too often, alas! we have to be occupied with our failures and infirmities. If ever the workings of indwelling sin be suffered to rise to the surface, we must deal with our God about them, for He cannot go on with sin. He can forgive it, and cleanse us from it; He can restore our souls by the gracious ministry of our great High Priest; but He cannot go on in company with a single sinful thought. A light or foolish thought as well as an unclean or covetous one, is amply sufficient to mar a Christian's communion, and interrupt his worship. Should any such thought spring up, it must be judged and confessed, ere the elevated joys of the sanctuary can be known afresh. A heart in which lust is working, is not enjoying the proper occupations of the sanctuary. When we are in our proper priestly condition, nature is as though it had no existence; then we can feed upon Christ. We can taste the divine luxury of being wholly at leisure from ourselves, and wholly engrossed with Christ.

All this can only be produced by the power of the Spirit. There is no need of seeking to work up nature's devotional feelings, by the various appliances of systematic religion. There must be pure fire as well as pure incense (compare Lev. 10:1, with Lev. 16:12). All efforts at worshipping God, by the unhallowed powers of nature, come under the head of "strange fire." God is the object of worship; Christ the ground and the material of worship; and the Holy Ghost the power of worship.

Properly speaking, then, as in the brazen altar, we have Christ in the value of His sacrifice, so in the golden altar, we have Christ in the value of His intercession. This will furnish my reader with a still clearer sense of the reason why the priestly office is introduced between the two altars. There is, as might be expected, an intimate connexion between the two, for Christ's intercession is founded upon His sacrifice. "And Aaron shall make an atonement upon the horns of it, once in a year, with the blood of the sin-offering of atonements: once in the year shall he make atonement upon it throughout your generations: it is most holy unto the Lord." All rests upon the immovable foundation of SHED BLOOD. "Almost all things are by the law purged with blood; and without shedding of blood is no remission. It was therefore necessary that the pattern of things in the heavens should be purified with these; but the heavenly things themselves with better sacrifices than these. For Christ is not entered into the holy places made with hands, which are the figures of the true; but into heaven itself, now to appear in the presence of God for us" (Heb. 9:22-24).

The atonement half-shekel

From verse 11-16 we have the atonement money for the congregation. All were to pay alike. "The rich shall not give more, and the poor shall not give less than half a shekel, when they give an offering unto the Lord, to make an atonement for your souls." In the matter of atonement, all must stand on one common platform. There may be a vast difference in knowledge, in experience, in capacity, in attainment, in zeal, in devotedness, but the ground of atonement is alike to all. The great apostle of the Gentiles, and the feeblest lamb in all the flock of Christ, stand on the same level, as regards atonement. This is a very simple and a very blessed truth. All may not be alike devoted and fruitful; but "the precious blood of Christ," and not devotedness or fruitfulness, is the solid and everlasting ground of the believer's rest. The more we enter into the truth and power of this, the more fruitful shall we be.

In the last chapter of Leviticus, we find another kind of valuation. When any one made "a singular vow," Moses valued him according to his age. In other words, when any one ventured to assume the ground of capacity, Moses, as the representative of *the claims* of God, estimated him "after the shekel of the sanctuary" If he were "poorer" than Moses' estimation, then he was to "present himself before the priest," the representative of *the grace* of God, who was to value him "according to his ability that vowed."

Blessed be God, we know that all His claims have been answered, and all our vows discharged by One who was at once the Representative of His claims and the Exponent of His grace, who finished the work of atonement upon the cross, and is now at the right hand of God. Here is sweet rest for the heart and conscience. Atonement is the first thing we get hold of, and we shall never lose sight of it. Let our range of intelligence be ever so wide, our fund of experience ever so rich, our tone of devotion ever so elevated, we shall always have to fall back upon the one simple, divine, unalterable, soul-sustaining doctrine of THE BLOOD. Thus it has ever been in the history of God's people, thus it is, and thus it ever will be. The most deeply-taught and gifted servants of Christ have always rejoiced to come back to "that one well-spring of delight," at which their thirsty spirits drank when first they knew the Lord; and the eternal song of the Church in glory will be, "Unto Him that loved us and washed us from our sins in His own blood." The courts of heaven will for ever resound with the glorious doctrine of the blood.

The brazen laver

From ver. 17-21 we are presented with "the brazen laver and its foot" – the vessel of washing and the basis thereof. These two are always presented together (see chap. 30:28; 38:8; 40:11). In this laver the priests washed their hands and feet, and thus maintained that purity which was essential to the proper discharge of their priestly functions. It was not, by any means, a question of a fresh presentation of blood; but simply that action by which they were preserved in fitness for priestly service and worship. "When they go into the tabernacle of the congregation, they shall wash with water that they die not; or when they come near to the altar to minister, to burn offering made by fire unto the Lord: so they shall wash their hands and their feet that they die not."

There can be no true communion with God, save as personal holiness is diligently maintained. "If we say that we have fellowship with Him and walk in darkness, we lie, and do not the truth" (1 John 1:6). This personal holiness can only flow from the action of the word of God on our works and ways. "By the words of thy lips I have kept me from the paths of the destroyer." Our constant failure in priestly ministry may be accounted for by our neglecting the due use of the laver. If our ways are not submitted to the purgative action of the word – if we continue in the pursuit or practice of that which, according to the testimony of our own consciences, the word distinctly condemns, the energy of our priestly character will, assuredly, be lacking. Deliberate continuance in evil and true priestly worship are wholly incompatible. "Sanctify them through thy truth, thy word is truth." If we have any uncleanness upon us, we cannot enjoy the presence of God. The effect of His presence would then be to convict us by its holy light. But when we are enabled, through grace, to cleanse our way, by taking heed thereto according to God's word, we are then morally capacitated for the enjoyment of His presence.

My reader will at once perceive what a vast field of practical truth is here laid open to him, and also how largely the doctrine of the brazen laver is brought out in the New Testament. Oh! that all those who are privileged to tread the courts of the sanctuary, in priestly robes, and to approach the altar of God, in priestly worship, may keep their hands and feet clean by the use of the true laver.

It may be interesting to note that the laver, with its foot, was made "of the looking-glasses of the women assembling, which assembled at the door of the tabernacle of the congregation" (see chap. 38:8). This fact is full of meaning. We are ever prone to be "like a man beholding his natural face in a glass; for he beholdeth himself and goeth away, and straightway forgetteth what manner of man he was." Nature's looking-glass can never furnish a clear and permanent view of our true condition. "But whoso looketh into the perfect law of liberty, and continueth therein, he being not a forgetful hearer but a doer of the word, this man shall be blessed in his deed" (James 1:23-25). The man who has constant recourse to the word of God, and who allows that word to tell upon his heart and conscience, will be maintained in the holy activities of the divine life.

Intimately connected with the searching and cleansing action of the word is the efficacy of the priestly ministry of Christ. "For the word of God is quick and powerful, (i.e., *living* and *energetic*,) and sharper than any two-edged sword, piercing even to the dividing asunder of soul and spirit, and of the joints and marrow, and is a discerner of the thoughts and intents of the heart; neither is there any creature that is not manifest in his sight; but all things are naked and open to the eyes of him with whom we have to do." Then the inspired apostle immediately adds, "Seeing then that we have a great High Priest, that is passed through the heavens, Jesus the Son of God, let us hold fast our profession. For we have not an high priest which cannot be touched with a feeling of our infirmities; but was in all points tempted like as we are, yet without sin. Let us therefore come boldly unto the throne of grace, that we may obtain mercy and find grace to help in time of need" (Heb. 4:12-16).

The more keenly we feel the edge of the word, the more we shall prize the merciful and gracious ministry of our High Priest. The two things go together. They are the inseparable companions of the Christian's path. The High Priest sympathises with the infirmities which the word detects and exposes. He is "a faithful" as well as "a merciful High Priest." Hence, it is only as I am making use of the laver that I can approach the altar. Worship must ever be presented in the power of holiness. We must lose sight of nature, as reflected in a looking-glass, and be wholly occupied with Christ, as presented in the word. In this way only shall the "hands and feet," the works and ways be cleansed, according to the purification of the sanctuary.

The holy anointing oil

From ver. 22 – 23 we have the "holy anointing oil," with which the priests, together with all the furniture of the tabernacle, were anointed. In this we discern a type of the varied graces of the Holy Ghost, which were found, in all their divine fullness, in Christ. "All thy garments smell of myrrh, and aloes, and cassia, out of the ivory palaces, whereby they have made thee glad" (Ps. 45:8). "God anointed Jesus of Nazareth with the Holy Ghost and with power." (Acts 10:38). All the graces of the Spirit, in their perfect fragrance, centred in Christ; and it is from Him alone they can flow. He, as to His humanity, was conceived of the Holy Ghost; and, ere He entered upon His public ministry, He was anointed with the Holy Ghost; and, finally, when He had taken His seat on high, in token of an accomplished redemption, He shed forth upon His body, the Church, the precious gift of the Holy Ghost (see Matt. 1:20; 3:16, 17; Luke 4:18, 19; Acts 2:33; 10:45, 46; Eph. 4:8-13).

It is as those who are associated with this ever blessed and highly-exalted Christ that believers are partakers of the gifts and graces of the Holy Ghost; and, moreover, it is as they walk in habitual nearness to Him, that they either enjoy or emit the fragrance thereof. The unrenewed man knows nothing of this. "Upon man's flesh it shall not be poured." The graces of the Spirit can never be connected with man's flesh, for the Holy Ghost cannot own nature. Not one of the fruits of the Spirit was ever yet produced "in nature's barren soil." "We must be born again." It is only as connected with the new man, as being part of "the new creation," that we can know anything of the fruits of the Holy Ghost. It is of no possible value to seek to imitate those fruits and graces. The fairest fruits that ever grew in nature's fields, in their highest state of cultivation – the most amiable traits which nature can exhibit, must be utterly disowned in the sanctuary of God. "Upon man's flesh shall it not be poured; neither shall ye make any other like it, after the composition of it: it is holy, and it shall be holy unto you. Whosoever compoundeth any like it, or whosoever putteth any of it upon a stranger, shall even be cut off from his people." There must be no counterfeit of the Spirit's work; all must be of the Spirit – wholly, really of the Spirit. Moreover, that which is of the Spirit must not be attributed to man. "The natural man receiveth not the things of the Spirit of God; for they are foolishness unto him: neither can he know them, because they are spiritually discerned" (1 Cor. 2:14).

There is a very beautiful allusion to this "holy anointing oil" in one of the "songs of degrees." "Behold," says the Psalmist, "how good and how pleasant it is for brethren to dwell together in unity! It is like the precious ointment upon the head, that ran down upon the beard, even Aaron's beard; that went down to the skirts of his garments" (Ps. 133:1, 2). The head of the priestly house being anointed with the holy oil, the very "skirts of his garments" must exhibit the precious effects. May my reader experience the power of this anointing! May he know the value of having "an unction from the Holy

One," and of being " sealed with that Holy Spirit of promise!" Nothing is of any value, in the divine estimation, save that which connects itself immediately with Christ, and whatever is so connected can receive the holy anointing.

The incense

In the concluding paragraph of this most comprehensive chapter, we have the "sweet spices tempered together, pure and holy." This surpassingly precious perfume presents to us the unmeasured and unmeasurable perfections of Christ. There was no special quantity of each ingredient prescribed, because the graces that dwell in Christ, the beauties and excellencies that are concentrated in His adorable Person, are without limit. Nought save the infinite mind of Deity could scan the infinite perfections of Him in whom all the fullness of Deity dwelleth; and as eternity rolls along its course of everlasting ages, those glorious perfections will ever be unfolding themselves in the view of worshipping saints and angels. Ever and anon, as some fresh beams of light shall burst forth from that central Sun of divine glory, the courts of heaven above, and the wide fields of creation beneath, shall resound with thrilling Alleluias to Him who was, who is, and who ever shall be the object of praise to all the ranks of created intelligence.

But not only was there no prescribed quantity of the ingredients; we also read, "of each there shall be a like weight." Every feature of moral excellence found its due place and proper proportion in Christ. No one quality ever displaced or interfered with another; all was "tempered together, pure and holy," and emitted an odour so fragrant that none but God could appreciate it.

"And thou shalt beat some of it *very small*, and put of it before the testimony in the tabernacle of the congregation, where I will meet with thee: it shall be unto you most holy." There is uncommon depth and power in the expression "very small." It teaches us that every little movement in the life of

Christ, every minute circumstance, every act, every word, every look, every feature, every trait, every lineament, emits an odour produced by an equal proportion – "a like weight" of all the divine graces that compose His character. The smaller the perfume was beaten, the more its rare and exquisite temper was manifested.

"And as for the perfume which thou shalt make, ye shall not make to yourselves according to the composition thereof: it shall be unto thee holy for the Lord. Whosoever shall make like unto that, to smell thereto, shall even be cut off from his people." This fragrant perfume was designed, exclusively, for Jehovah. Its place was "before the testimony." There is that in Jesus which only God could appreciate. True, every believing heart can draw nigh to His matchless Person, and more than satisfy its deepest and most intense longings; still, after all God's redeemed have drunk, to the utmost of their capacity; after angels have gazed on the peerless glories of the man Christ Jesus, as earnestly as their vision is capable of; after all, there will be that in Him which God alone can fathom and enjoy. No human or angelic eye could duly trace the exquisitely minute parts of that holy perfume "beaten very small." Nor could earth afford a proper sphere in which to emit its divine and heavenly odour.

Thus, then, we have, in our rapid sketch, reached the close of a clearly marked division of our book. We began at "the ark of the covenant," and travelled out to "the altar of brass;" we returned from "the altar of brass," and have come to the "holy perfume;" and, oh! what a journey is this, if only it be travelled, not in company with the false and flickering light of human imagination, but by the infallible lamp of the Holy Ghost! What a journey if only it be travelled, not amid the shadows of a bygone dispensation, but amid the personal glories and powerful attractions of the Son, which are there portrayed! If my reader has so travelled it, he will find his affections more drawn to Christ than ever; he will have a loftier conception of His glory, His beauty, His preciousness, His excellency, His ability to heal a wounded conscience, and satisfy a longing heart; he will have his eyes more thoroughly closed to all earth's attractions, and his ears closed to all earth's pretensions and promises. In one word, he will be prepared to utter a deeper and more fervent amen to the words of the inspired apostle, when he says, "IF ANY MAN LOVE NOT THE LORD JESUS CHRIST, LET HIM BE ANATHEMA MARANATHA"[14] (1 Cor. 16:22).

---

[14] It is interesting to note the position of this most solemn and startling denunciation. It occurs at the close of a long epistle, in the progress of which the apostle had to rebuke some of the grossest practical evils and doctrinal errors. How solemn, therefore, how full of meaning the fact, that when he comes to pronounce his anathema, it is not hurled at those who had introduced those errors and evils, but at the man who loves not the Lord Jesus Christ. Why is this? Is it because the Spirit of God makes little of errors and evils? Surely not; the entire epistle unfolds His thoughts as to these. But the truth is, when the heart is filled with love to the Lord Jesus Christ, there is an effectual safeguard against all manner of false doctrine and malpractice. If a man does not love Christ, there is no accounting for the notions he may adopt, or the course he may pursue. Hence the form and the position of the apostolic anathema.

Chapter 31

THE WORK OF SERVICE

Bezaleel and Oholiab

The opening of this brief chapter records the divine call and the divine qualification of "Bezaleel and Aholiab" to do the work of the tabernacle of the congregation. "And the Lord spake unto Moses, saying, See, *I have called* by name Bezaleel the son of Uri, the son of Hur, of the tribe of Judah: and *I have filled* him with the Spirit of God, in wisdom, and in understanding, and in knowledge, and in all manner of workmanship ... And I, behold, *I have given* with him Aholiab the son of Ahisamach, of the tribe of Dan: and in the hearts of all that are wise-hearted *I have put* wisdom, that they may make all that *I have commanded*." Whether for "the work of the tabernacle" of old, or "the work of the ministry" now, there should be the divine selection, the divine call, the divine qualification, the divine appointment; and all must be done according to the divine commandment. Man could not select, call, qualify, or appoint to do the work of the tabernacle; neither can he, to do the work of the ministry. Furthermore, no man could presume to appoint himself to do the work of the tabernacle; neither can he to do the work of the ministry. It was, it is, it must be, wholly and absolutely divine. Men may run as sent of their fellow, or men may run of themselves; but let it be remembered that all who run, without being sent of God, shall, one day or other, be covered with shame and confusion of face. Such is the plain and wholesome doctrine suggested by the words, "I have called" "I have filled," "I have given," "I have put," "I have commanded." The words of the Baptist must ever hold good, "a man can receive nothing except it be given him from heaven" (John 3:27). He can, therefore, have but little room to boast of himself; and just as little to be jealous of his fellow.

There is a profitable lesson to be learnt from a comparison of this chapter with Genesis 6. "Tubal-cain was an instructor of every artificer in brass and iron." The descendants of Cain were endowed with unhallowed skill to make a cursed and groaning earth a delectable spot, without the presence of God. "Bezaleel and Aholiab," on the contrary, were endowed with divine skill to beautify a sanctuary which was to be hallowed and blessed by the presence and glory of the God of Israel.

Reader, let me ask you just to pause and put this solemn question to your conscience, "Whether am I devoting whatever of skill or energy I possess to the interests of the Church, which is God's dwelling place, or to beautify an ungodly, Christless world?" Say not, in thine heart, "I am not divinely called or divinely qualified for the work of the ministry." Remember that though all Israel were not Bezaleels or Aholiabs, yet all could serve the interests of the sanctuary. There was an open door for all to communicate. Thus it is now. Each one has *a* place to occupy, a ministry to fulfil, a responsibility to discharge; and you and I are, at this moment, either promoting the interests of the house of God – the body of Christ – the Church, or helping on the godless schemes of a world, yet stained with the blood of Christ and the blood of all His martyred saints. Oh! let us deeply ponder this, as in the presence of the great Searcher of hearts, whom none can deceive – to whom all are known.

The Sabbath and the Day of the Lord

Our chapter closes with a special reference to the institution of the Sabbath. It was referred to in chapter 16 in connexion with the manna; it was distinctly enjoined in chapter 20, when the people were formally put under law; and here we have it again in connexion with the setting up of the tabernacle. Whenever the nation of Israel is presented in some special position, or recognised as a people in special responsibility, then the Sabbath is introduced. And let my reader carefully note both the day and the mode in which it was to be observed, and also the object for which it was instituted in Israel. "Ye shall keep the Sabbath, therefore, for it is holy unto you: *every one that defileth it shall surely be put to death:* for whosoever doeth *any work* therein, that soul shall be *cut off* from among his people. Six days may work be done; but *in the seventh* is the Sabbath of rest, holy to the Lord: whosoever doeth any work in the Sabbath day, *he shall surely be put to death."* This is as explicit and absolute as anything can be. It fixes "the seventh day" and none other; and it positively forbids, on pain of death, all manner of work. There can be no avoiding the plain sense of this. And, be it remembered, that there is not so much as a single line of Scripture to prove that the Sabbath has been changed, or the strict principles of its observance, in the smallest degree, relaxed. If there be any Scripture proof, let my reader look it out for his own satisfaction.

Now, let us inquire if indeed professing Christians do keep God's Sabbath on the day and after the manner which He commanded. It were idle to lose time in proving that they do not. Well, what are the consequences of a single breach of the Sabbath? *"Cut off" – "put to death."*

But, it will be said, "we are not under law, but under grace." Blessed be God for the sweet assurance! Were we under law, there is not one throughout the wide range of Christendom who should not, long since, have fallen beneath the stone of judgment, even upon the one solitary point of the Sabbath. But, if we are under grace, what is the day which belongs to us? Assuredly, "the first day of the week," "the Lord's day." This is the Church's day, the resurrection day of Jesus, who, having spent the Sabbath in the tomb, rose triumphant over all the powers of darkness, thus leading His people out of the old creation, and all that pertains thereto, into the new creation, of which He is the Head, and of which the first day of the week is the apt expression.

This distinction is worthy of the serious attention of the reader. Let him examine it prayerfully in the light of Scripture. There may be nothing and there may be a great deal in a mere name. In the present instance, there is a great deal more involved in the distinction between "the Sabbath" and "the Lord's day" than many Christians seem to be aware of. It is very evident that the first day of the week gets a place, in the Word of God, which no other day gets. No other day is ever called by that majestic and elevated title, "the Lord's day." Some, I am aware, deny that Rev. 1:10 refers to the first day of the week; but I feel most fully assured that sound criticism and sound exegesis do both warrant, yea, demand the application of that passage, not to the day of Christ's advent in glory, but to the day of his resurrection from the dead.

But, most assuredly, the Lord's day is never once called the Sabbath. So far from this, the two days are, again and again, spoken of in their proper distinctness. Hence, therefore, my reader will have to keep clear of two extremes. In the first place, he will have to avoid the legalism which one finds so much linked with the term "sabbath;" and, in the second place, he will need to bear a very decided testimony against every attempt to dishonour the Lord's day, or lower it to the level of an ordinary day. The believer is delivered, most completely, from the observance of "days and months, and times and years." Association with a risen Christ has taken him clean out of all such superstitious observances. But, while this is most blessedly true, we see that "the first day of the week." has a place assigned to it in the New Testament which no other has. Let the Christian give it that place. It is a sweet and happy privilege, not a grievous yoke.

Space forbids my further entrance upon this interesting subject. It has been gone into, elsewhere, as already intimated, in the earlier pages of this volume. I shall close these remarks by pointing out, in one or two particulars, the contrast between "the Sabbath" and "the Lord's day."

1. The Sabbath was the *seventh* day; the Lord's day is the *first*.

2. The Sabbath was a *test* of Israel's condition; the Lord's day is the *proof* of the Church's acceptance, on wholly unconditional grounds.

3. The Sabbath belonged to the old creation; the Lord's day belongs to the new.

4. The Sabbath was a day of *bodily* rest for the Jew; the Lord's day is a day of *spiritual* rest for the Christian.

5. If the Jew worked on the Sabbath, he was to be put to *death*: if the Christian does not work on the Lord's day, he gives little proof of *life*. That is to say, if he does not work for the benefit of the souls of men, the extension of Christ's glory, and the spread of His truth. In point of fact, the devoted Christian, who possesses any gift, is generally more fatigued on the evening of the Lord's day than on any other in the week, for how can he *rest* while souls are perishing around him?

6. The Jew was *commanded* by the *law* to abide in his tent; the Christian is *led* by the spirit of the *gospel* to go forth, whether it be to attend the public assembly, or to minister to the souls of perishing sinners.

The Lord enable us, beloved reader, to rest more artlessly *in*, and labour more vigorously *for*, the name of the Lord Jesus Christ! We should *rest* in the spirit of a *child*; and *labour* with the energy of a *man*.

THE GOLDEN CALF

Make us a god which shall go before us

We have now to contemplate something very different from that which has hitherto engaged our attention. "The pattern of things in the heavens," has been before us – Christ in His glorious Person, gracious offices, and perfect work, as set forth in the tabernacle and all its mystic furniture. We have been, in spirit, on the mount, hearkening to God's own words – the sweet utterances of Heaven's thoughts, affections, and counsels, of which Jesus is "the Alpha and Omega, the beginning and the ending, the first and the last."

Now, however, we are called down to earth, to behold the melancholy wreck which man makes of everything to which he puts his hand. "And when the people saw that Moses delayed to come down out of the mount, the people gathered themselves together unto Aaron and said unto him, Up, make us gods which shall go before us; for as for this Moses, the man that brought us up out of the land of Egypt, we wot not what is become of him." What degradation is here! *Make us gods!* They were abandoning Jehovah, and placing themselves under the conduct of manufactured gods – gods of man's making. Dark clouds and heavy mists had gathered round the mount. They grew weary of waiting for the absent one, and of hanging on an unseen but real arm. They imagined that a god formed by "graving tool" was better than Jehovah; that a calf which they could *see* was better than the invisible, yet everywhere present, God; a visible counterfeit, than an invisible reality.

Alas! alas! it has ever been thus in man's history. The

human heart loves something that can be seen; it loves that which meets and gratifies the senses. It is only faith that can "endure, as seeing him who is invisible." Hence, in every age, men have been forward to set up and lean upon human imitations of divine realities. Thus it is we see the counterfeits of corrupt religion multiplied before our eyes. Those things which we know, upon the authority of God's Word, to be divine and heavenly realities, the professing Church has transformed into human and earthly imitations. Having become weary of hanging upon an invisible arm, of trusting in an invisible sacrifice, of having recourse to an invisible priest, of committing herself to the guidance of an invisible head, she has set about "making" these things; and thus, from age to age, she has been busily at work, with "graving tool" in hand, graving and fashioning one thing after another, until we can, at length, recognise as little similarity between much that we see around us, and what we read in the word, as between "a molten calf" and the God of Israel.

"Make us gods!" What a thought! Man called upon to make gods, and people willing to put their trust in such! My reader, let us look within, and look around, and see if we cannot detect something of all this. We read, in 1 Cor. 10, in reference to Israel's history, that "all these things happened unto them for ensamples, (or types,) and they are written *for our admonition,* upon whom the ends of the world are come" (ver. 11). Let us, then, seek to profit by the "admonition." Let us remember that, although we may not just form and bow down before a "molten calf" yet, that Israel's sin is a "type" of something into which we are in danger of falling. Whenever we turn away in heart from leaning exclusively upon God Himself, whether in the matter of salvation or the necessities of the path, we are, in principle, saying, "up, make us gods." It is needless to say we are not, in ourselves, a whit better than Aaron or the children of Israel; and if they acknowledge a calf instead of Jehovah, we are in danger of acting on the same principle, and manifesting the same spirit. Our only safeguard is to be much in the presence of God. Moses knew

that the "molten calf" was not Jehovah, and therefore he did not acknowledge it. But when we get out of the divine presence, there is no accounting for the gross errors and evils into which we may be betrayed.

We are called to live by faith; we can see nothing with the eye of sense. Jesus is gone up on high, and we are told to wait patiently for His appearing. God's word carried home to the heart, in the energy of the Holy Ghost, is the ground of confidence in all things, temporal and spiritual, present and future. He tells us of Christ's completed sacrifice; we, by grace, believe, and commit our souls to the efficacy thereof, and know we shall never be confounded. He tells us of a great High Priest, passed into the heavens, Jesus, the Son of God, whose intercession is all-prevailing; we, by grace, believe, and lean confidingly upon His ability, and know we shall be saved to the uttermost. He tells us of the living Head to whom we are linked, in the power of the Holy Ghost, and from whom we can never be severed by any influence, angelic, human, or diabolical; we, by grace, believe, and cling to that blessed Head, in simple faith, and know we shall never perish. He tells us of the glorious appearing of the Son from heaven; we, through grace, believe, and seek to prove the purifying and elevating power of "that blessed hope," and know we shall not be disappointed. He tells us of "an inheritance, incorruptible, undefiled, and that fadeth not away, reserved in heaven for us, who are kept by the power of God," for entrance thereinto in due time; we, through grace, believe and know we shall never be confounded. He tells us the hairs of our head are all numbered, and that we shall never want any good thing; we, through grace, believe, and enjoy a sweetly tranquillised heart.

Thus it is, or, at least, thus our God would have it. But then the enemy is ever active in seeking to make us cast away these divine realities, take up the "graving tool" of unbelief, and "make gods" for ourselves. Let us watch against him, pray against him, believe against him, testify against him, act against him: thus he shall be confounded, God glorified, and we ourselves abundantly blessed.

As to Israel, in the chapter before us, their rejection of God was most complete. "And Aaron said unto them, Break off the golden earrings, which are in the ears of your wives, of your sons, and of your daughters, and bring them unto me . . . And he received them at their hand, and fashioned it with a graving tool, after he had made it a molten calf: and they said, *These be thy gods*, O Israel, which brought thee up out of the land of Egypt. And when Aaron saw it, he built an altar before it; and Aaron made proclamation, and said, Tomorrow is *a feast unto the Lord.*" This was entirely setting aside God, and putting a calf in His stead. When they could say that a calf had brought them up out of Egypt, they had, evidently, abandoned all idea of the presence and character of the true God. How "*quickly*" they must "have turned aside out of the way," to have made such a gross and terrible mistake! And Aaron, the brother and yoke-fellow of Moses, led them on in this; and, with a calf before him, he could say, "Tomorrow is a feast unto Jehovah!" How sad! how deeply humbling! God was displaced by an idol. A thing, "graven by art and man's device," was set in the place of "the Lord of all the earth."

Moses' intercession

All this involved, on Israel's part, a deliberate abandonment of their connexion with Jehovah. They had given Him up; and, accordingly, we find Him, as it were, taking them on their own ground. "And the Lord said unto Moses, Go, get thee down; for thy people, which thou broughtest out of the land of Egypt, have corrupted themselves; they have turned aside quickly out of the way which I commanded them . . .
I have seen this people, it is a stiff-necked people: now therefore let me alone, that my wrath may wax hot against them, and that I may consume them; and I will make of thee a greater nation." Here was an open door for Moses; and here he displays uncommon grace and similarity of spirit to that Prophet whom the Lord was to raise up like unto him. He

refuses to be or to have anything without the people. He pleads with God on the ground of His own glory, and puts the people back upon Him in these touching words, "Lord, why doth thy wrath wax hot against *thy people* which *thou* hast brought up out of the land of Egypt with great power and a mighty hand? Wherefore should the Egyptians speak and say, For mischief did he bring them out, to slay them in the mountains, and to consume them from the face of the earth. Turn from thy fierce wrath and repent of this evil against *thy* people. Remember Abraham, Isaac, and Israel, thy servants, to whom thou swearest by thine own self, and saidst unto them, I will multiply your seed as the stars of heaven; and all this land that I have spoken of will I give unto your seed, and they shall inherit it for ever." This was powerful pleading. The glory of God, the vindication of His holy name, the accomplishment of His oath. These are the grounds on which Moses entreats the Lord to turn from His fierce wrath. He could not find, in Israel's conduct or character, any plea or ground to go upon. He found it all in God Himself.

The Lord had said unto Moses, "*Thy* people which *thou* broughtest up;" but Moses replies to the Lord, "*Thy* people which *thou* hast brought up." They were the Lord's people notwithstanding all; and His name, His glory, His oath were all involved in their destiny. The moment the Lord links Himself with a people, His character is involved, and faith will ever look at Him upon this solid ground. Moses loses sight of himself entirely. His whole soul is engrossed with thoughts of the Lord's glory and the Lord's people. Blessed servant! How few like him! And yet when we contemplate him in all this scene, we perceive how infinitely he is below the blessed Master. He came down from the mount, and when he saw the calf and the dancing, "his anger waxed hot, and he cast the tables out of his hands and brake them beneath the mount." The covenant was broken and the memorials thereof shattered to pieces; and then, having executed judgment in righteous indignation, "he said unto the people, Ye have sinned a great sin: and now I will go up unto the Lord;

peradventure I shall make an atonement for your sin."

How different is this from what we see in Christ! He came down from the bosom of the Father, not with the tables in His hands, but with the law in his heart. He came down, not to be made acquainted with the condition of the people, but with a perfect knowledge of what that condition was. Moreover, instead of destroying the memorials of the covenant and executing judgment, He magnified the law and made it honourable, and bore the judgment of His people, in His own blessed Person, on the cross; and, having done all, He went back to heaven, not with a *"peradventure* I shall make an atonement for your sin," but to lay upon the throne of the Majesty in the highest, the imperishable memorials of an atonement already accomplished. This makes a vast and truly glorious difference. Thank God, we need not anxiously gaze after our Mediator to know if haply He shall accomplish redemption for us, and reconcile offended Justice. No, He has done it all. His presence on high declares that the whole work is finished. He could stand upon the confines of this world, ready to take His departure, and, in all the calmness of a conscious victor – though He had yet to encounter the darkest scene of all – say, "I have glorified thee on earth: I have finished the work which thou gavest me to do" (John 17). Blessed Saviour! we may well adore thee, and well exult in the place of dignity and glory in which eternal justice has set thee. The highest place in heaven belongs to thee; and thy saints only wait for the time when "every knee shall bow and every tongue confess that Jesus Christ is Lord, to the glory of God the Father." May that time speedily arrive!

At the close of this chapter Jehovah asserts His rights, in moral government, in the following words: "Whosoever hath sinned against me, him will I blot out of my book. Therefore, now go, lead the people unto the place of which I have spoken unto thee: behold, mine angel shall go before thee: nevertheless, in the day when I visit I will visit their sin upon them." This is God *in government,* not God in *the gospel.* Here He speaks of blotting out the *sinner;* in the gospel He is seen blotting out *sin*. A wide difference!

   The people are to be sent forward, under the mediatorship of Moses, by the hand of an angel. This was very unlike the condition of things which obtained from Egypt to Sinai. They had forfeited all claim on the ground of law, and hence it only remained for God to fall back upon His own sovereignty and say, "I will be gracious to whom I will be gracious, and will show mercy on whom I will show mercy."

MEDIATION AND RESTORATION

The tabernacle of the congregation

Jehovah refuses to accompany Israel to the land of promise. "I will not go up in the midst of thee; for thou art a stiff-necked people; lest I consume thee in the way." At the opening of this book, when the people were in the furnace of Egypt, the Lord could say, "I have surely seen the affliction of my people which are in Egypt, and have heard their cry by reason of their taskmasters; for I know their sorrows." But now He has to say, "I have seen this people, and, behold, it is a stiff-necked people." An afflicted people is an object of grace; but a stiff-necked people must be humbled. The cry of oppressed Israel had been answered by the exhibition of grace; but the song of idolatrous Israel must be answered by the voice of stern rebuke.

"Ye are a stiff-necked people: I will come up into the midst of thee in a moment and consume thee: therefore now put off thy ornaments from thee that I may know what to do unto thee," It is only when we are really stripped of all nature's ornaments that God can deal with us. A naked sinner can be clothed; but a sinner decked in ornaments must be stripped. This is always true. We must be stripped of all that pertains to self, ere we can be clothed with that which pertains to God.

"And the children of Israel stripped themselves of their ornaments by the mount Horeb." There they stood beneath that memorable mount, their feasting and singing changed into bitter lamentations, their ornaments gone, the tables of testimony in fragments. Such was their condition, and Moses at once proceeds to act according to it. He could no longer own the people in their corporate character. The assembly had become entirely defiled, having set up an idol of their own making, in the place of God – a calf instead of Jehovah. "And Moses took the tabernacle and pitched it *without the camp,* afar off from the camp, and called it the tabernacle of the congregation." Thus the camp was disowned as the place of the divine presence. God was not – could not – be there. He had been displaced by a human invention. A new gathering point was, therefore, set up. "And it came to pass that every one which sought the Lord went out unto the tabernacle of the congregation, which was without the camp."

There is here a fine principle of truth, which the spiritual mind will readily apprehend. The place which Christ now occupies is "without the camp," and we are called upon to "go forth unto him." It demands much subjection to the word to be able, with accuracy, to know what "the camp" really is, and much spiritual power to be able to go forth from it; and still more to be able, while "far off from it," to act towards those in it, in the combined power of holiness and grace – holiness, which separates from the defilement of the camp; grace, which enables us to act toward those who are involved therein.

"And the Lord spake unto Moses face to face, as a man speaketh unto his friend. And he turned again into the camp: but his servant Joshua, the son of Nun, a young man, departed not out of the tabernacle." Moses exhibits a higher degree of spiritual energy than his servant Joshua. It is much easier to assume a position of separation from the camp, than to act aright towards those within.

"And Moses said unto the Lord, See, thou sayest unto me, Bring up this people: and thou hast not let me know whom thou wilt send with me: yet thou hast said, I know thee by name, and thou hast also found grace in my sight." Moses entreats the accompanying presence of Jehovah as a proof of their having found *grace* in His sight. Were it a question of mere *justice,* He could only consume them by coming in their midst, because they were "a stiff-necked people." But directly He speaks of grace, in connexion with the mediator, the very stiff-neckedness of the people is made a plea for demanding His presence. "If now I have found grace in thy sight, O Lord, let my Lord, I pray thee, go among us; *for it is a stiff-necked people;* and pardon our iniquity and our sin, and take us for thine inheritance." This is touchingly beautiful. A "stiff-necked people" demanded the boundless grace and exhaustless patience of God. None but He could bear with them.

My presence shall go with thee

"And He said, My presence shall go with thee, and I will give thee rest." Precious portion! Precious hope! The presence of God with us, all the desert through, and everlasting rest at the end! Grace to meet our present need, and glory as our future portion! Well may our satisfied hearts exclaim, "It is enough, my precious Lord."

In chapter 34 the second set of tables is given, not to be broken, like the first, but to be hidden in the ark, above which, as already noticed, Jehovah was to take His place, as the Lord of all the earth, in moral government. "And he hewed two tables of stone, like unto the first: and Moses rose up early in the morning and went up unto mount Sinai, as the Lord had commanded him, and took in his hand the two tables of stone. And the Lord descended in the cloud, and stood with them there, and proclaimed the name of the Lord. And the Lord passed by before him, and proclaimed the Lord, the Lord God, merciful and gracious, long-suffering, and abundant in goodness and truth, keeping mercy for thousands, forgiving iniquity, and transgression, and sin, and that will by no means clear the guilty; visiting the iniquity of the fathers upon the children, and upon the children's children, unto the third, and to the fourth generation." This, be it remembered, is God, as seen in His moral government of the world, and not as He is seen in the cross – not as He shines in the face of Jesus

Christ – not as He is proclaimed in the gospel of His grace. The following is an exhibition of God in the gospel: "And all things are of God, *who hath reconciled us to himself, by Jesus Christ,* and hath given to us the ministry of reconciliation; to wit, that God was in Christ, *reconciling the world unto himself;* NOT IMPUTING their trespasses unto them, and hath committed unto us the *word of reconciliation."* (2 Cor. 5:18,19). "Not clearing" and "not imputing" present two totally different ideas of God. "Visiting iniquities" and cancelling them are not the same thing. The former is God in government, the latter is God in the gospel. In 2 Cor. 3 the apostle contrasts the "ministration" recorded in Exodus 34 with "the ministration" of the gospel. My reader would do well to study that chapter with care. From it he will learn that any one who regards the view of God's character given to Moses, on Mount Horeb, as unfolding the gospel, must have a very defective apprehension, indeed, of what the gospel is. Neither in creation, nor yet in moral government, do I, or can I, read the deep secrets of the Father's bosom. Could the prodigal have found his place in the arms of the One revealed on Mount Sinai? Could John have leaned his head on the bosom of that One? Surely not. But God has revealed Himself in the face of Jesus Christ. He has told out, in divine harmony, all His attributes in the work of the cross. There "mercy and truth have met together, righteousness and peace have kissed each other." Sin is perfectly put away, and the believing sinner perfectly justified "BY THE BLOOD OF THE CROSS." When we get a view of God, as thus unfolded, we have only, like Moses, "to bow our head toward the earth and worship," – suited attitude for a pardoned and accepted sinner in the presence of God!

Chapters 35-40

THE CONSTRUCTION OF THE TABERNACLE

These chapters contain a recapitulation of the various parts of the tabernacle and its furniture; and inasmuch as I have already given what I believe to be the import of the more prominent parts, it were needless to add more. There are, however, two things in this section from which we may deduce most profitable instruction, and these are, first, the *voluntary devotedness*; and, secondly, the *implicit obedience* of the people with respect to the work of the tabernacle of the congregation.

And first, as to their voluntary devotedness, we read, "And all the congregation of the children of Israel departed from the presence of Moses. And they came, every one *whose heart stirred him up,* and every one whom *his spirit made willing,* and they brought *the Lord's offering* to the work of the tabernacle of the congregation, and for all his service, and for the holy garments. And they came, both men and women, *as many as were willing-hearted,* and brought bracelets and earrings, and rings, and tablets, all jewels of gold: and every man that offered an offering of gold unto the Lord. And every man with whom was found blue, and purple, and scarlet, and fine linen, and goats' hair, and red skins of rams, and badgers' skins, brought them. Every one that did offer an offering of silver and brass, brought the Lord's offering: and every man with whom was found shittim wood for any work of the service, brought it. And all the women that were wise-hearted did spin with their hands, and brought that which they had spun, both of blue, and of purple, and of scarlet, and of fine linen. And all the women *whose heart stirred them up* in wisdom spun goats' hair. And the rulers brought onyx stones, and stones to be set for the ephod, and for the breastplate: and spice and oil for the light, and for the anointing oil, and for the sweet incense. The children of Israel brought *a willing offering* unto *the Lord* every man and woman, *whose heart made them willing* to bring, for all manner of work which the Lord had commanded to be made by the hand of Moses" (chap. 35:20-29). And, again, we read, "And all the wise men that wrought all the work of the sanctuary, came every man from his work which they made; and they spake unto Moses, saying, The people bring *much more than enough* for the service of the work, which the Lord commanded to make, . . . for the stuff they had was sufficient for all the work to make it, and too much" (ver. 4-7).

A lovely picture this of devotedness to the work of the sanctuary! It needed no effort to move the hearts of the people to give, no earnest appeals, no impressive arguments. Oh! no; their *"hearts* stirred them up." This was the true way. The streams of voluntary devotedness flowed from within. "Rulers," "men," "women" – all felt it to be their sweet privilege to give to the Lord, not with a narrow heart or niggard hand, but after such a princely fashion that they had *"enough and too much."*

Then, as to their *implicit obedience,* we read, *"according to all that the Lord commanded Moses,* so the children of Israel made all the work. And Moses did look upon all the work, and, behold, *they had done it as the Lord had commanded, even so had they done it:* and Moses blessed them" (chap. 39:42, 43). The Lord had given the most minute instructions concerning the entire work of the tabernacle. Every pin, every socket, every loop, every tach, was accurately set forth. There was no room left for man's expediency, his reason, or his common sense. Jehovah did not give a great outline and leave man to fill it up. He left no margin whatever in which man might enter his regulations. By no means. "See, saith he, that thou make *all things according to the pattern showed to thee in the mount"* (Exod. 25:40; 26:30; Heb. 8:5). This left no room for human device. If man had been allowed to make a single pin, that pin would, most assuredly, have been out of place in the judgment of God. We can see what man's "graving tool" produces in chapter 32. Thank God, it had no place in the tabernacle. They did, in this matter, just what they were told – nothing more – nothing less. Salutary lesson this for the professing church! There are many things in the history of Israel which we should earnestly seek to avoid – their impatient murmurings, their legal vows, and their idolatry; but in those two things may we imitate them. May our devotedness be more whole hearted, and our obedience more implicit. We may safely assert, that if all had not been done "according to the pattern showed in the mount," we should not have to read, "then a cloud covered the tent of the congregation, and the glory of the Lord filled the tabernacle. And Moses was not able to enter into the tent of the congregation, because the cloud abode thereon, and the glory of the Lord filled the tabernacle" (chap. 40:34, 35). The tabernacle was, in all respects, according to the *divine pattern*, and, therefore, it could be filled with the *divine glory*.

There is a volume of instruction in this. We are too prone to regard the Word of God as insufficient for the most minute details connected with His worship, and service. This is a great mistake, a mistake which has proved the fruitful source of evils and errors, in the professing Church. The word of God is amply sufficient for everything, whether as regards personal salvation and walk, or the order and rule of the assembly. "All scripture is given by inspiration of God, and is profitable for doctrine, for reproof, for correction, for instruction in righteousness, that the man of God may be *perfect, thoroughly furnished* unto *all good works"* (2 Tim. 3:16, 17). This settles the question. If the Word of God furnishes a man *thoroughly* unto "*all* good works," it follows, as a, necessary consequence, that whatever I find not in its pages, cannot possibly be a good work. And, further, be it remembered, that the divine glory cannot connect itself with anything that is not according to the divine pattern.

— — — — — — —

Beloved reader, we have now travelled together through this most precious book. We have, I fondly hope, reaped some profit from our study. I trust we have gathered up some refreshing thoughts of Jesus and His sacrifice as we passed along. Feeble, indeed, must be our most vigorous thoughts, and shallow our deepest apprehensions, as to the mind of God in all that this book contains. It is happy to remember that through grace, we are on our way to that glory where we shall know, even as we are known; and where we shall bask in the sunshine of His countenance who is the beginning and ending of all the ways of God, whether in creation, in providence, or redemption. To Him I do most affectionately commend you, in body, soul, and spirit. May you know the deep blessedness of having your portion in Christ, and be kept in patient waiting for His glorious advent. Amen.

C. H. M.

CONTENTS

Preface	5
Preface to the third edition	11

Chapter 1
The ways of God towards Israel	13
Why was Israel in Egypt?	13
How God accomplishes His purposes	14
The efforts of Pharaoh to crush Israel	15

Chapter 2
The Birth of Moses	20
The activity of that which had the power of death	20
Faith triumphant over death	21
God's providential intervention	24
Moses when forty	26
Preparation for service	26
The fear of man	27
The way of faith	30
The typical character of Moses	35

Chapter 3
The call of Moses	38
The school of God	38
The burning bush	42
The holiness of God	43
The grace of God towards His people	45
The secret of effective service	47
The sending of Moses	49
"I AM THAT I AM"	50

Chapter 4
Moses' objections 56
   The first objection: they will not believe me 56
   The second objection: I am not an eloquent man 59
   Moses refuses his commission 60
   A companion in service 62
Moses' return to Egypt 64
   Circumcision 64
   The Christian position 65
   Moses and Aaron 67

Chapters 5 & 6
Israel's slavery becomes even harder 72
   Moses' and Aaron's first visit to Pharaoh 72
   The sinner delivered from Satan's slavery 73
   The purpose of Israel's deliverance 77
   Pharaoh's thoughts 77
   Moses misunderstood by his brethren 80
   Encouragement for Moses 81
   God reveals His name as Jehovah 82
   God loves us as we are 83
   Record of the families of Israel 84

Chapters 7-11
The ten plagues of Egypt 86
   The judgments of the Lord on the oppressors 86
   The opposition of the magicians 89
Pharaoh's objections to Israel's leaving 94
   The first objection 94
   The three days' journey and the true position of the
   believer outside the world 98
   The second objection 103
   The third objection 105
   The fourth objection 106

Chapter 12
The Passover and the last plague 109
   The hardening of Pharaoh 109
   The destruction of the firstborn 111
   The beginning of months 113
   The Passover Lamb 114
   The blood of the Lamb 117
   The work of Christ for us 119
   The work of the Holy Spirit in us 121
   The death of Christ, the sole ground of our salvation 123
   A centre of gathering for Israel 125
   The ordinance of the Passover 126
   The unleavened bread 128
   The bitter herbs 131
   Nothing remaining 132
   The loins girded and shoes on the feet 133
   And if a stranger will keep the Passover 134
   You shall not break a bone of it 135

Chapter 13
The consecration of the firstborn 137
The flight from Egypt 141

Chapter 14
Crossing the Red Sea 145
   An impasse 145
   The purpose of God 146
   The unbelief of the Israelites 147
   See the salvation of the LORD 149
   Stand still 150
   *The L*ORD *shall fight for you* 152
   Speak unto the children of Israel that they go forward .. 153
   God makes a path for faith 154
   *The L*ORD *between the Egyptians and Israel* 155
   Pharaoh' armies are drowned 157
   The typical meaning 157

Chapter 15
The song of deliverance 160
  I will sing unto the Lord 160
  God glorified 162
  The habitation of God is with men 165
Departure for the wilderness 166
  Mara – the bitter waters 167
  Elim – the wells and the palms 169

Chapter 16
The manna 171
  The people's murmurings 171
  The bread from heaven 174
  Christ, the bread of life which came down from heaven .. 174
  The glory of the Lord in the cloud 176
  The Christian's nourishment 177
  The omer of manna as a witness 179
  Assimilating the truth and putting the Word into practice 180
  The Sabbath 182

Chapter 17
Rephidim 185
  The struck rock 185
  The battle against Amalek 189
  The Christian's struggle with the flesh 192
  Christ, our intercessor 194

Chapter 18
The visit of Jethro 195
  Israel, the Gentiles and the Church 195
  The rulers who assisted Moses 198

Chapter 19
Israel at the foot of Mount Sinai 202
  The covenant of grace 202
  A presumptuous commitment 204

Chapter 20
The law 208
   Law and grace 208
   The purpose of the law 210
   The curse of the law 212
   A yoke impossible to carry 213
   The law and the gospel 215
   The two great commandments 218
   Thou shalt make me an altar of earth 219

Chapters 21-23
The ordinances 222
   The justice of God and the corruption of man 222
   The Hebrew servant 224

Chapter 24
The blood of the covenant 228

Chapter 25
The tabernacle 231
   Introduction 231
   The ark and its contents 234
   The mercy-seat 237
   The table of showbread 239
   The candlestick of pure gold 239

Chapter 26
The curtains, coverings and boards 242
   The materials of the first covering 242
   The fine twined linen 242
   The blue, purple and scarlet 245
   The curtain of goats' hair 249
   The rams' skins dyed red 250
   The badgers' skins 251
   The boards 252
   Christ the door 252

Chapter 27
The brazen altar 254
   The order of divine communications 254
   The altar 255
   The gold and the brass 256

Chapters 28 & 29
The priesthood 259
   Aaron's robes 259
   The robes of the sons of Aaron 264
   The divinity and humanity of Christ 265
   The consecration of Aaron and his sons 267

Chapter 30
The worship 271
   The golden altar 271
   The atonement half-shekel 273
   The brazen laver 275
   The holy anointing oil 277
   The incense 279

Chapter 31
The work of service 282
   Bezaleel and Oholiab 282
   The Sabbath and the Day of the Lord 283

Chapter 32
The golden calf 287
   Make us a god which shall go before us 287
   Moses' intercession 290

Chapters 33 & 34
Mediation and restoration 294
   The tabernacle of the congregation 294
   My presence shall go with thee 296

Chapters 35-40
The construction of the tabernacle 298